IMAGES
of America

ROCK COUNTY

On the Cover: This photograph of an early threshing machine emphasizes the importance of agriculture in Rock County's history. The steam engine was hired out to operate the threshing machines in the area. (Courtesy of the Rock County Historical Society.)

IMAGES
of America

ROCK COUNTY

Rock County Historical Society

ARCADIA
PUBLISHING

ISBN 978-1-4671-1138-6

Published by Arcadia Publishing
Charleston, South Carolina

Printed in the United States of America

Library of Congress Control Number: 2013949415

For all general information, please contact Arcadia Publishing:
Telephone 843-853-2070
Fax 843-853-0044
E-mail sales@arcadiapublishing.com
For customer service and orders:
Toll-Free 1-888-313-2665

Visit us on the Internet at www.arcadiapublishing.com

To Betty Mann, whose inspired preservation of Rock County history has made the difference

Contents

Acknowledgments

From its founding in 1974, the Rock County Historical Society has been made up of hundreds of volunteers who have contributed thousands of hours to preserve the history of Rock County. It is impossible to thank all those volunteers individually, but without their hard work and love of local history, this book would not have been possible. The Rock County Historical Society's research library, archives, and photograph collections have offered a great deal of information, which, along with others in Rock County who provided historical photographs, make up this treasure of fascinating stories and information about the county's history.

We would also like to thank the historical society's board of directors for its leadership, support, and time put into this book. All images in this book have been graciously provided by the Rock County Historical Society.

INTRODUCTION

The first settlers to Rock County saw nothing but prairie grass when they arrived in the early to mid-1860s. Trees lined the rivers and streams, and Native Americans roamed the land. Occasionally, one would see hunters and trappers looking for the abundant wildlife.

In 1838, Joseph Nicolas Nicollet was the first white man of record to visit the county. His party gave names to many of the streams, rivers, and other physical features of the land as he created the first map of the area.

Rock County was named for the abundant natural feature of Sioux Quartzite outcroppings, readily seen in the north half of Rock County. The county is located in the southwest corner of Minnesota and was platted 20 miles east to west and 24 miles north to south. It is divided into 12 townships.

Although the county has no natural lake, it has one of the most perfect drainage systems in the West. Each township has a river or creek of significance that runs within its borders. The streams and rivers drain into the Missouri River, and Rock County is the only county in the state where all its waterways run into the Missouri tributary. The principal waterways are Rock River, Kanaranzi Creek, Champepadan Creek, Split Rock River, and Beaver Creek.

As the county was settled, communities developed, approximately every 7 to 10 miles apart, to support the needs of the rural residents. The communities include Luverne, Beaver Creek, Hills, Steen, Ash Creek, Kanaranzi, Magnolia, Kenneth, Hardwick, Manley, Bruce, Warner, and Jasper.

Philo Hawes has been credited as settling the first city in the county in 1867. Having secured the contract for carrying the mail from Jackson to Yankton, Hawes traveled the route and set up camps or water stops. Hawes was so favorably impressed with the area that he built a dugout on the embankment of the Rock River. He also built a stable for the mail horses. Hawes named the settlement Luverne, after his daughter Eva LuVerne.

At the end of the Civil War in 1865, soldiers returned to their homes in the North. Many of them found that their farms, businesses, and families continued without them. The solution for many of these adventure-seekers was to head west. With the federal government's Homestead Act, these men saw opportunities for personal success. If they could live on the land for five years, the land would be theirs, and if they served in the military, their time in military service could be deducted from those five years.

Veterans and their families were very patriotic. They understood how wonderful it was to "live in the land of the free and the home of the brave." That tradition of sacrifice and service has continued throughout the county's existence. Rock County has one of the largest per-capita records of military service in the state of Minnesota.

Early pioneers witnessed hard times with blizzards, drought, prairie fires, epidemics, hail, wind, and plagues. In 1873, the grasshopper plague began that engulfed Rock County for almost four years. During that time, farmers had no money to spend in the towns. Businesses failed, and people moved away. Settlers faced those hardships with determination and grit.

Each of the county's four seasons brought its own challenges. Blizzards were very difficult for people before machinery. In the early days, the only way to get through the snow was to shovel it by hand. When snowplows and blowers became common, even the worst winter storm would only close business for a short period of time.

During these early years, it was also a challenge to travel anywhere. In general, with a team of horses a round trip of 10 miles took a full day to accomplish. Organizations, schools, and religious institutions developed within that boundary to accommodate the growing population. Rock County has a long tradition of these organizations. They created social opportunities for children as well as adults.

Rock County was organized in 1870, and the governor of Minnesota appointed three commissioners to manage its affairs. The citizens of the county elected an auditor, treasurer, clerk of court, registrar of deeds, superintendent of schools, and sheriff. Luverne became the county seat, due in part to its location in the center of the county. After utilizing a small wooden building during its first years of organization, residents constructed a three-story Sioux Quartzite courthouse on the northeastern block of Luverne and Cedar Streets in 1888. The courthouse is still in use today.

Education has always been a priority of Rock County citizens. Country schools that educated students through eighth grade dotted the county. High schools were built in Luverne, Beaver Creek, Hills, and Magnolia.

Churches were always very important to the people of the community. Neighbors, families, social, and ethnic groups founded churches. Some ministers traveled from village to village to preach and minister to congregations.

Railroads came to the area and opened up Rock County. New business, social, educational, and agricultural opportunities spurred growth when trains brought goods, services, and people to the communities. As the road system developed from dirt to gravel to paved roads, local transportation inside and outside the county became more common. With the introduction of the personal automobile, there was no stopping where people could travel.

Rock County has a strong work ethic, but it also knows how to have fun. Every community had celebrations, parades, and local entertainment. Competitive sports have always played a major recreational role in the county. Baseball, kittenball, football, basketball, skating, swimming, golf, and hockey are just a few of the sports regularly played. Local talent shows, traveling circuses, and Chautauquas were yearly events during the first half of the 20th century. Dance halls throughout the county offered regularly scheduled live bands.

The photographs in this book illustrate the daily lives of the people of Rock County. They give us a glimpse of life as it was in the past. We are proud of those who lived before us. We cannot live in the past, but by studying the past, we can learn from it.

One

Agricultural Roots

Rock County has always been primarily agricultural in nature. Early settlers moving from the East were looking for fertile soil to plant their crops, raise their livestock, and raise a family. Many early residents were emigrants from Germany and Scandinavian countries and often would encourage other family members to immigrate to this area and help them start farms. From 1870 to 1873, the population of settlers grew from 138 to 2,119. After erecting a shanty or dwelling, farmers began to till, plant, and harvest by hand or with oxen. The center of the county was Luverne, but the other communities in Rock County provided goods and services for its area farmers. Within a few years, horses became more prevalent, and with the advent of the railroads, wood and iron machinery made its way into the county.

In the early 1900s, the first tractors began to appear and take over many of the jobs done earlier by livestock. It was truly part of the industrial revolution in agriculture. After World War I, home generators and wind generators equipped farms with some electricity, but it was not until the 1930s and 1940s that the Rural Electric Association brought permanent electricity to farms. People could now throw out the old coal and wood cookstove, kerosene lanterns, battery radio, and hand-crank phonograph. Also, pumping water, cleaning the barn, milking cows, and doing a vast assortment of other tasks became easier. The agricultural community had truly progressed and brought more settlers with these innovations.

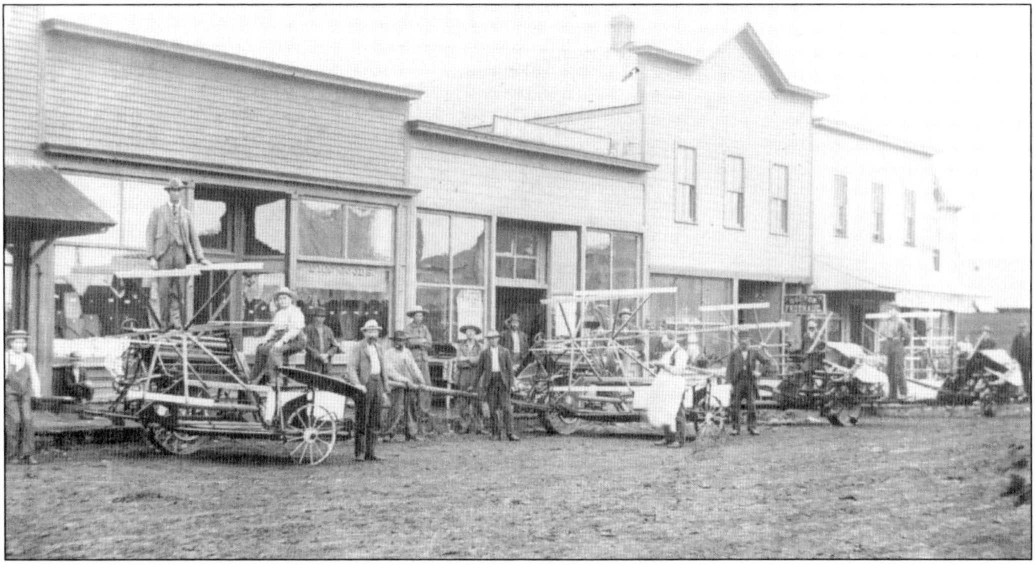

Pictured is a new line of machinery on display in downtown Luverne. This was a major event in the community, with streets being blocked off and farmers coming to town. With the coming of the railroad, more mechanized machinery became available to farmers and Rock County. The newer equipment was pulled into town by tractors rather than horse and oxen.

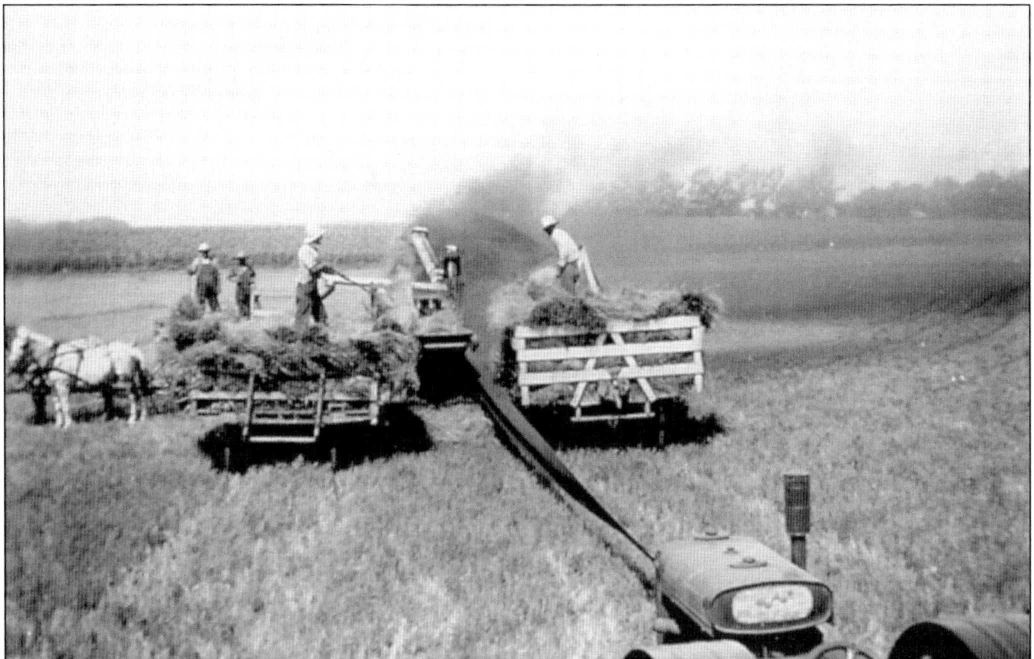

The early threshing was done by tractors, which drove threshing machines. In this photograph, one can see the tractor and thresher. The stacks behind the machine had been harvested earlier. When it was time to thresh, the stacks were run through the threshing machine where grain was separated from stalks and husks, and the leftover straw was blown out the back of the machine.

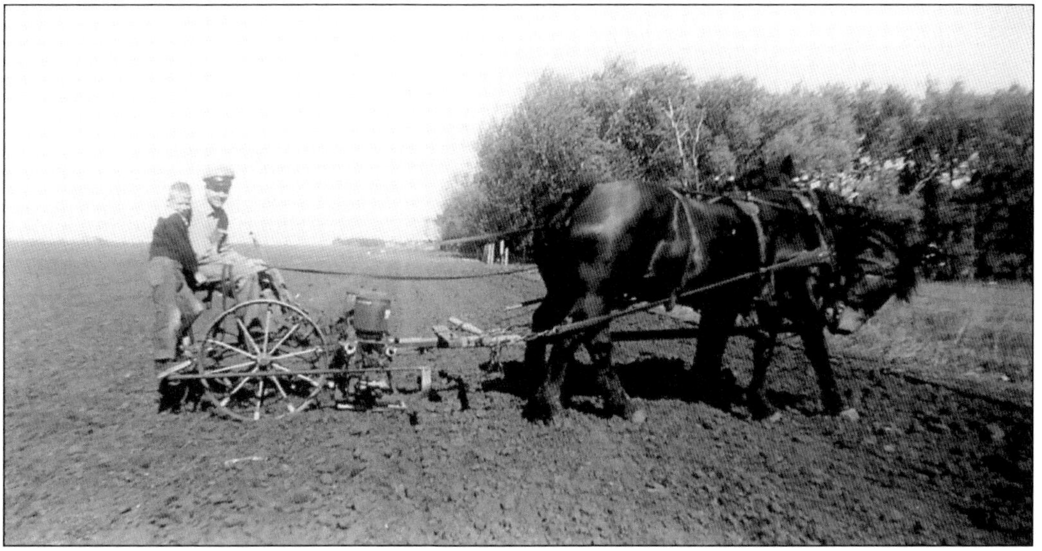

The planting of various crops was originally done by hand. With the introduction of machinery, this task became much easier, as noted in this image. Horses were used to pull the planter; pictured is a two-row planter. With modern machinery, planting became more accurate and less time consuming. With the introduction of the mechanized planter, the number of rows that could be planted at any one time increased greatly.

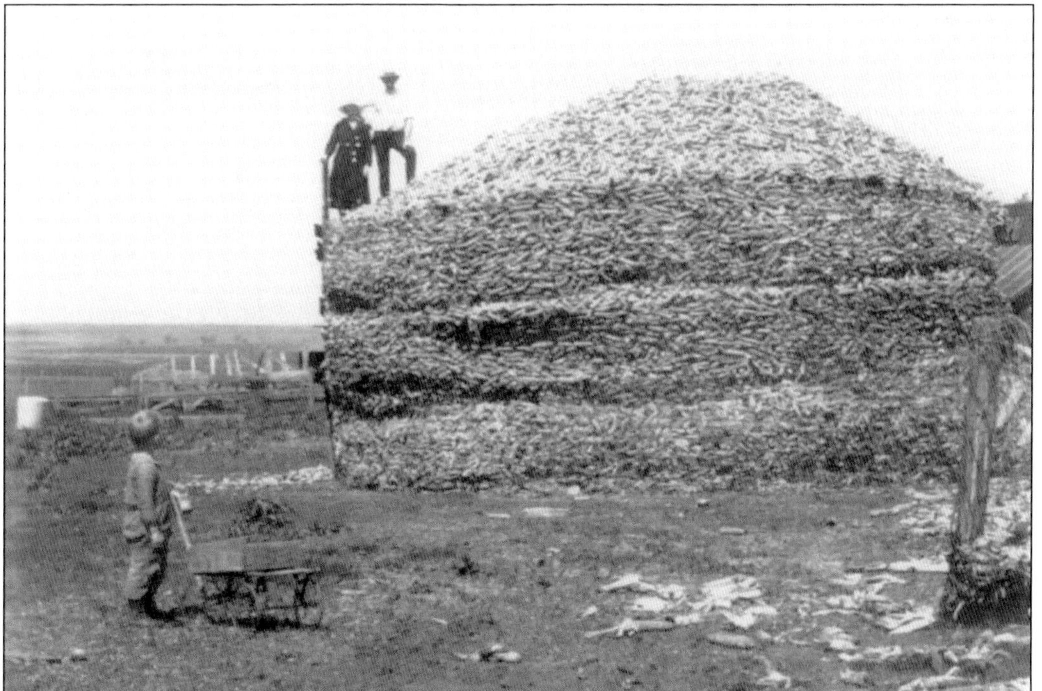

After the annual corn crop matured, it was harvested, and the stalks and ear corn were separated. Here is a large corncrib made out of fencing where ear corn was stacked and dried. The corn was left in these bins to dry and was then either fed to livestock or was shelled and sold on the open market.

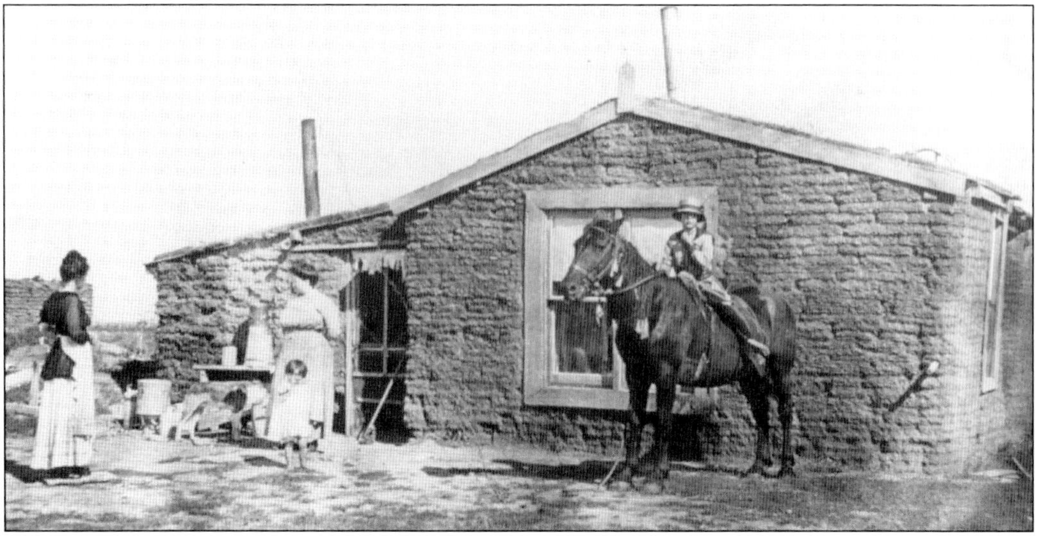

This is one of the early sod huts in Rock County. The foundation was made of dried sod bricks that were sealed with dirt.

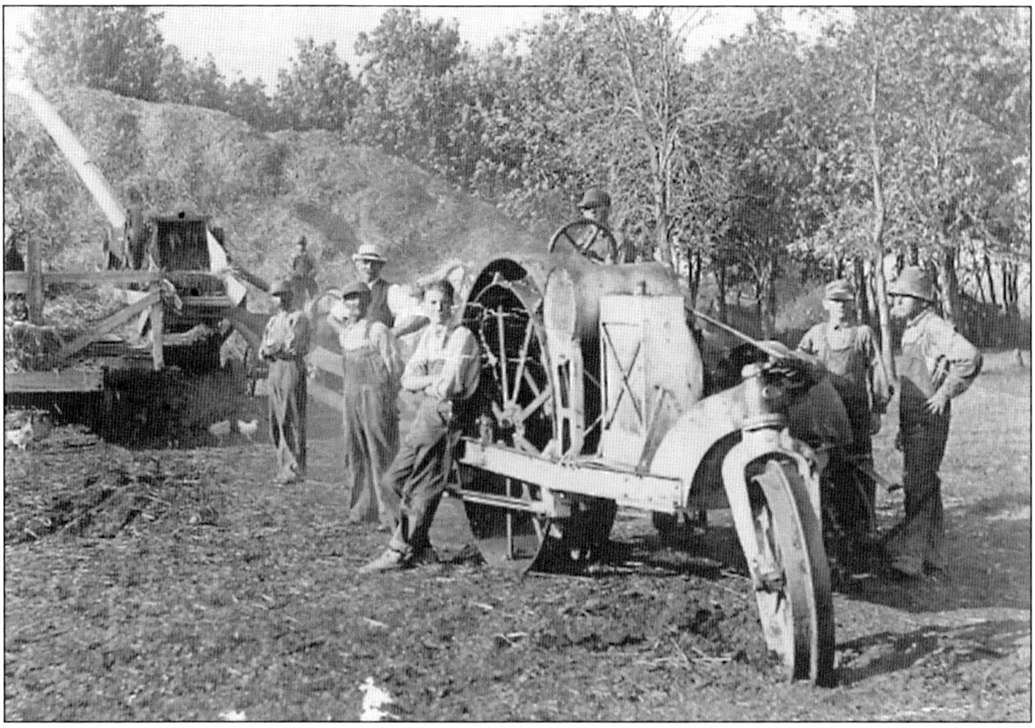

Pictured is a tractor-driven thresher. This type of tractor replaced the huge steam-engine tractors like the one the cover of this book. Even though the tractor reduced some of the work, it was still necessary to have a number of field hands to help out.

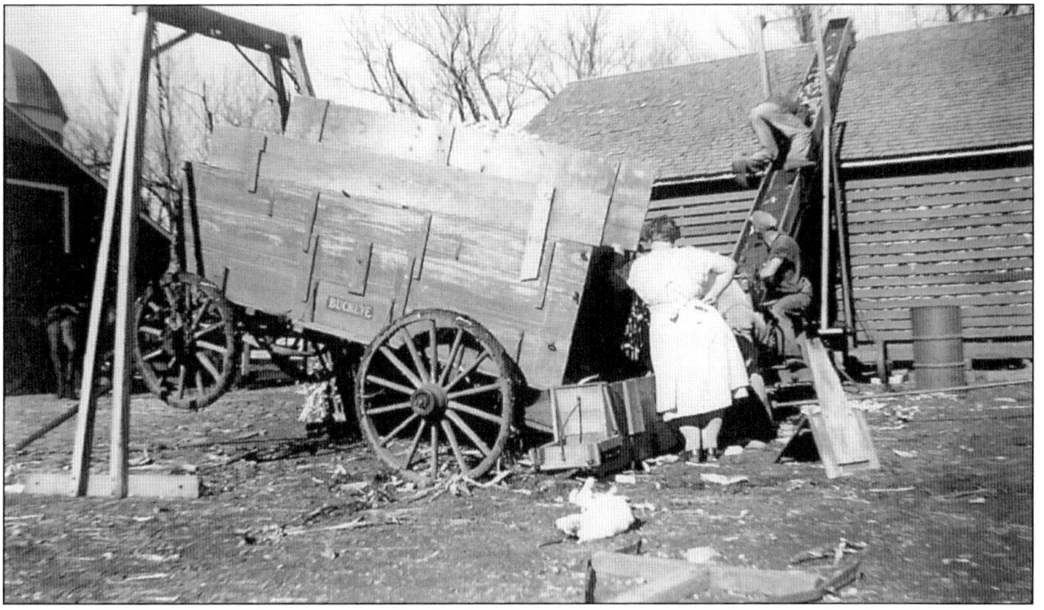

Harvested ear corn was also placed in covered corncribs, usually located on the farm homestead. In this photograph, one can see a wagon full of ear corn. The ear corn is being placed onto a conveyor that takes it to the top of the wooden corncrib. Note the corncrib has open slats, which allow air to pass through to the corn and dry it.

Many farmers raised hogs, one of the more important livestock in the area. Every farmer had hogs for their own consumption and also for market. Most farmers, with the help of family members, processed their own animals, as seen here. Hogs were processed and then either smoked, canned, or frozen to provide food for the farmer's table.

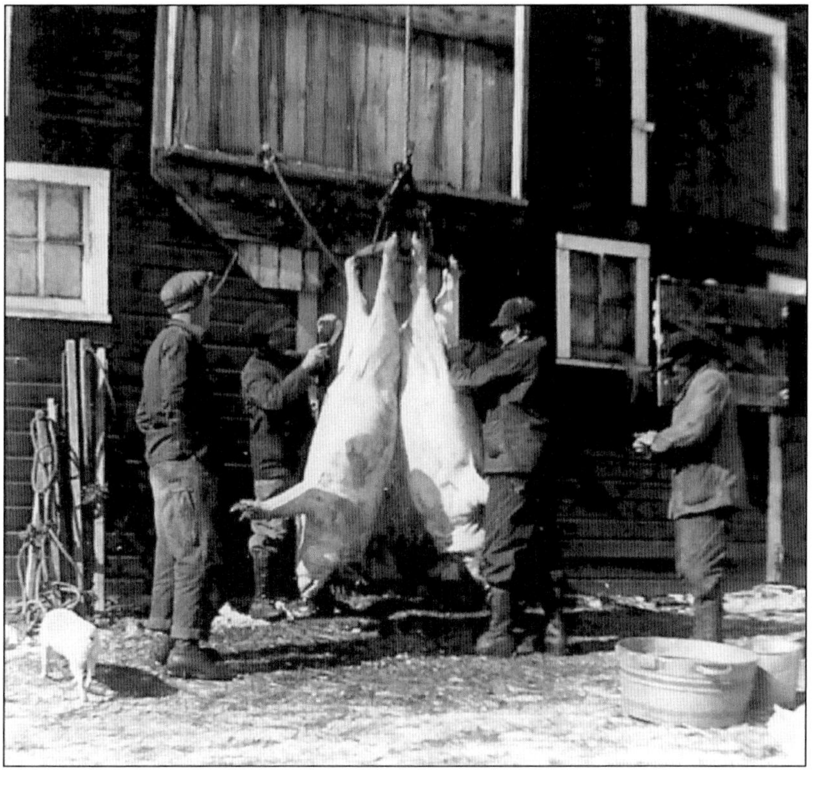

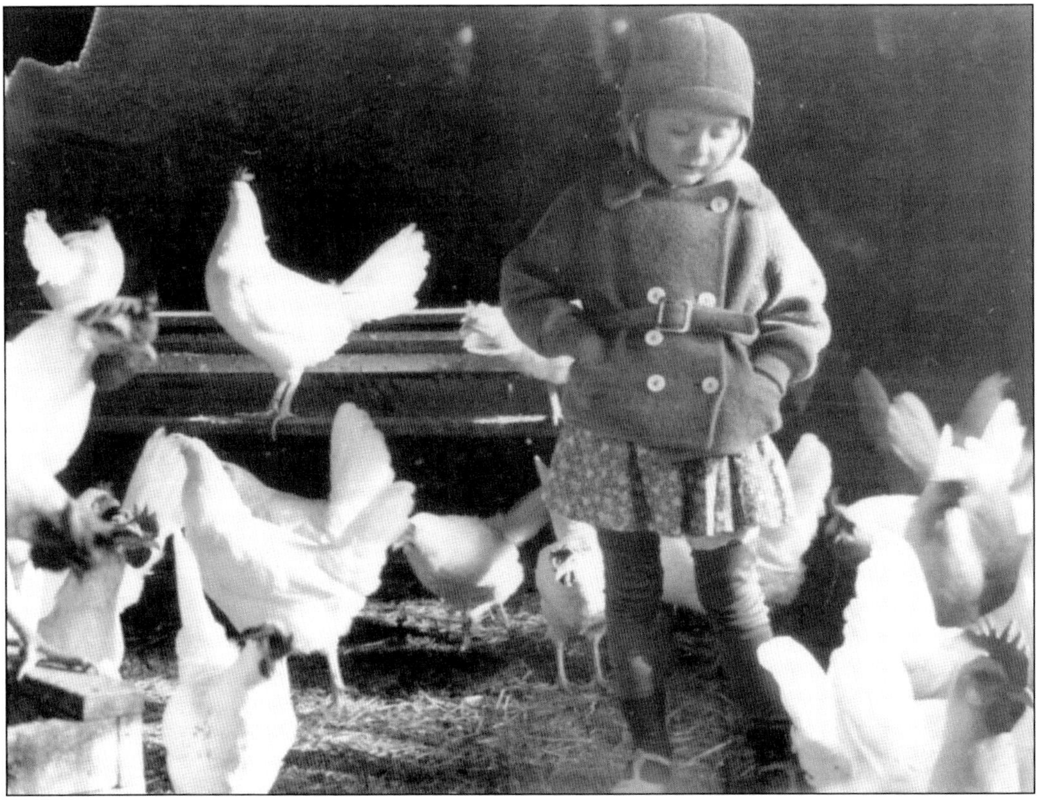

Farmers also raised chickens for their meat and eggs. In many cases, the children in the family gathered eggs and fed the chickens. The girl seen here appears to be checking out her chickens or looking for eggs. She may be on guard in case one or more of the chickens decides to turn on her.

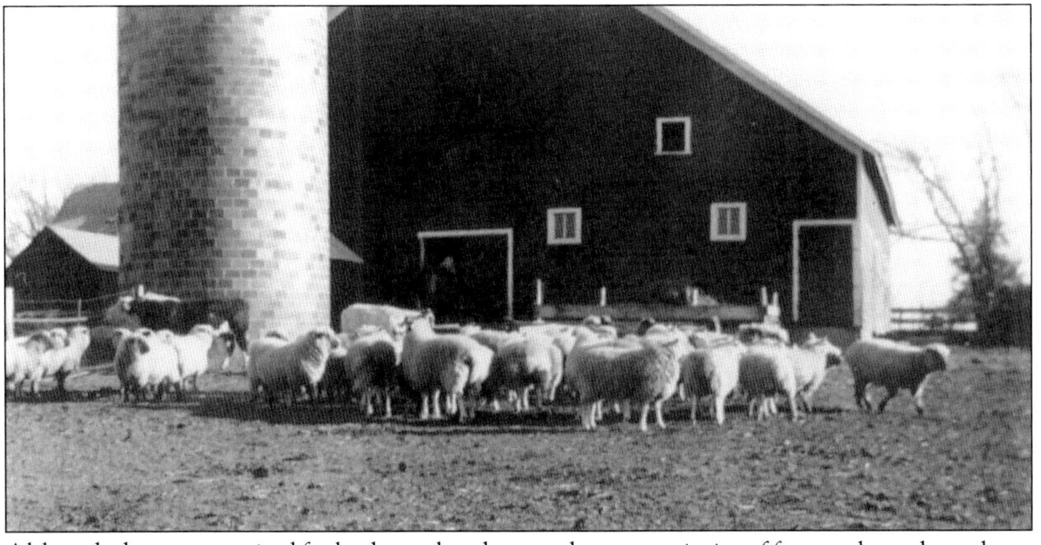

Although sheep were raised for both wool and meat, the vast majority of farmers kept them sheep primarily for wool. In another photograph in this chapter, a group of farmers has gathered for the shearing of sheep.

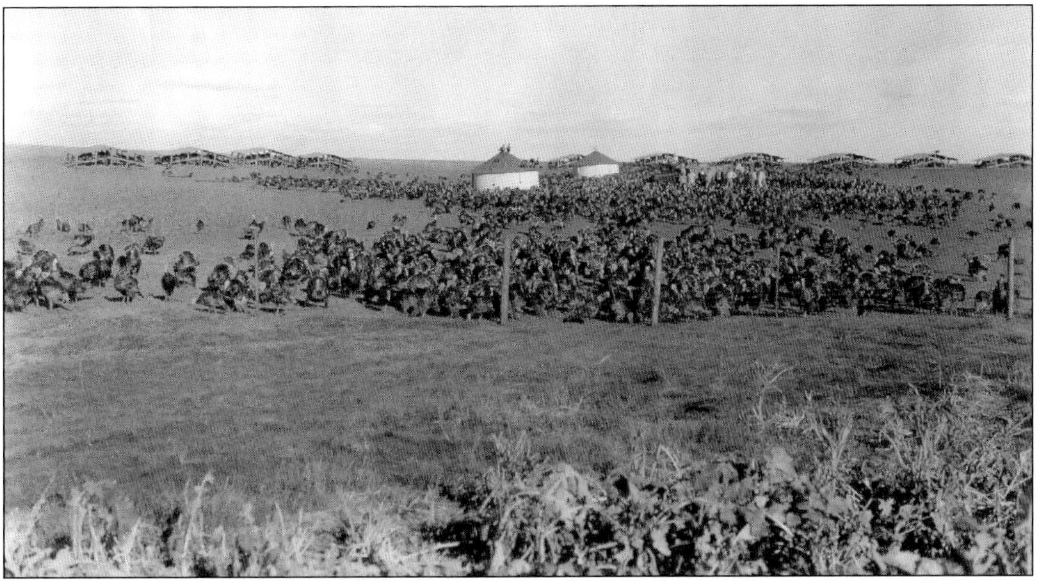

For a number of years, Rock County was considered the "turkey capital of Minnesota." At its height, more than 20,000 turkeys were raised in Rock County. There were several outlets within the state of Minnesota for the animal, which brought about a number of farmers who entered the turkey business. It gained in popularity from the 1940s to the 1960s.

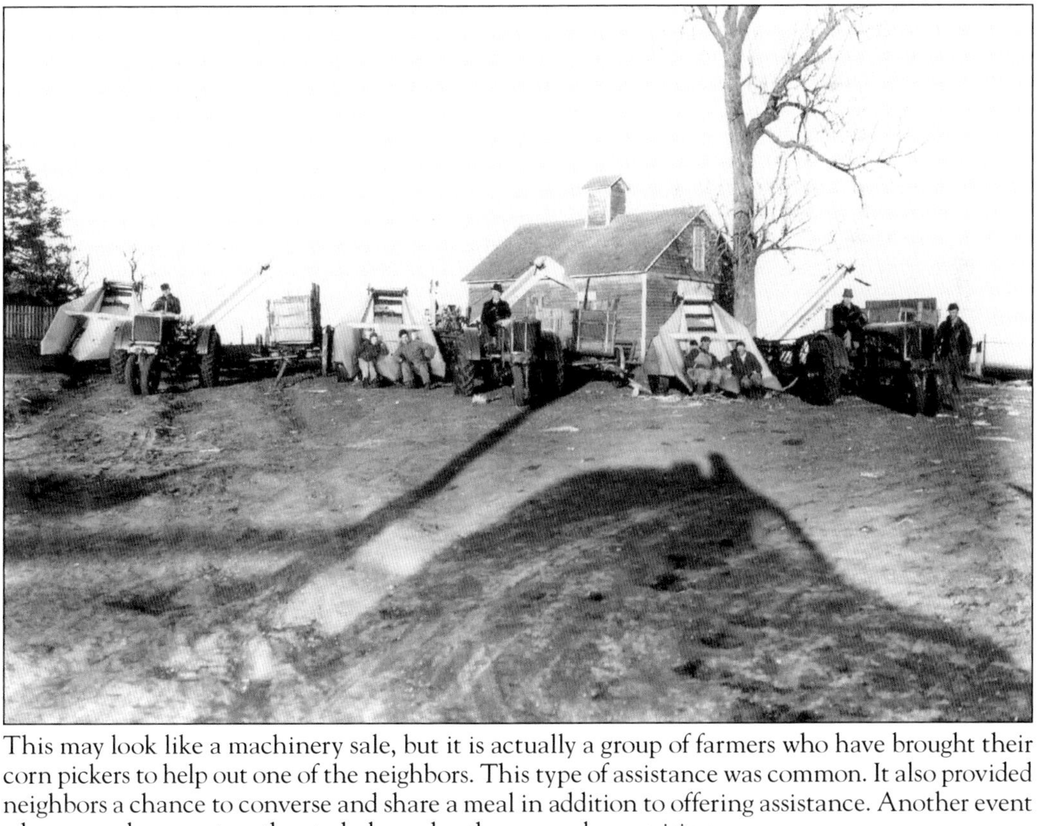

This may look like a machinery sale, but it is actually a group of farmers who have brought their corn pickers to help out one of the neighbors. This type of assistance was common. It also provided neighbors a chance to converse and share a meal in addition to offering assistance. Another event where people came together to help each other was a barn raising.

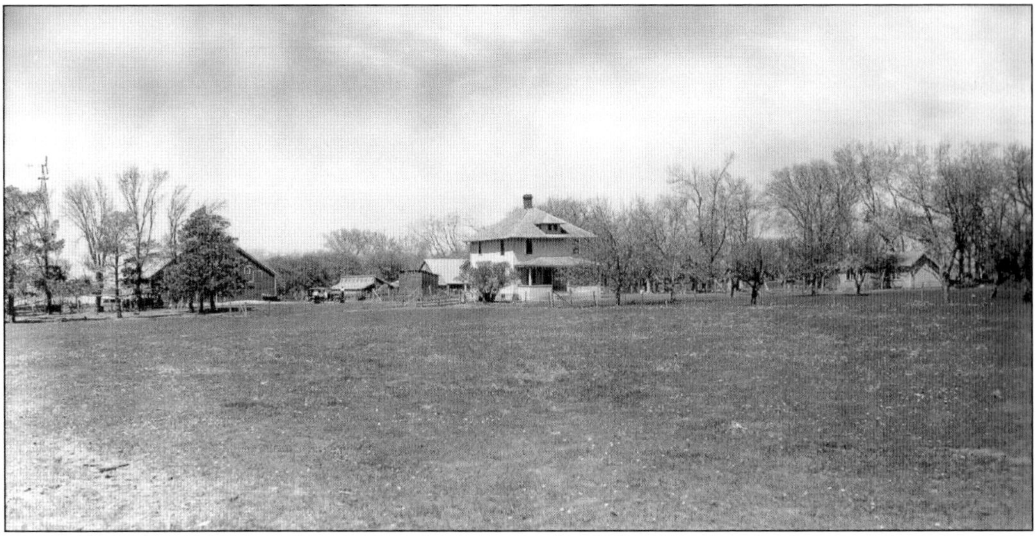

This photograph shows a typical farmstead in Rock County. A typical house was usually two stories high and had a front porch. Many were ordered from Sears, Roebuck & Co. Often, a barn, chicken coop, hog and cattle pens, corncribs, and a machine shop for the storage of equipment and repair were found on the property. Tree shelterbelts were planted around the homesteads to protect them from the wind and snow that were prevalent in Rock County.

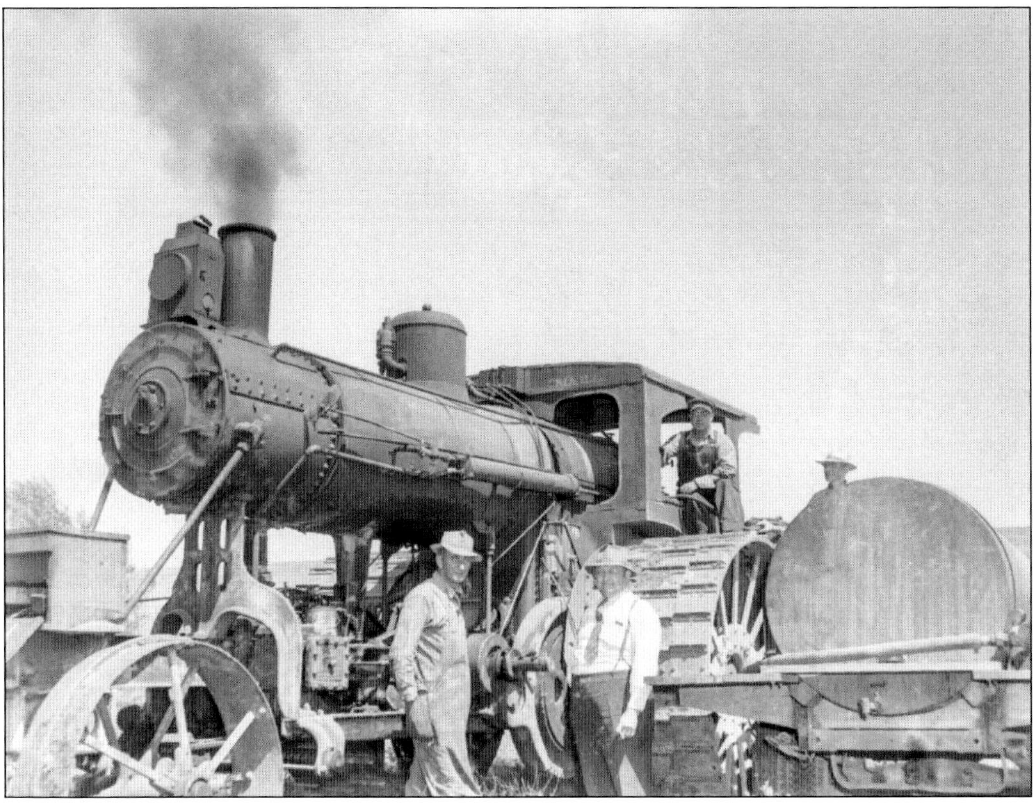

Here is an early steam-engine tractor. Note the truck to the right of the tractor bringing water for the engine. Many of the early steam-engine tractors were similar to steam-engine trains.

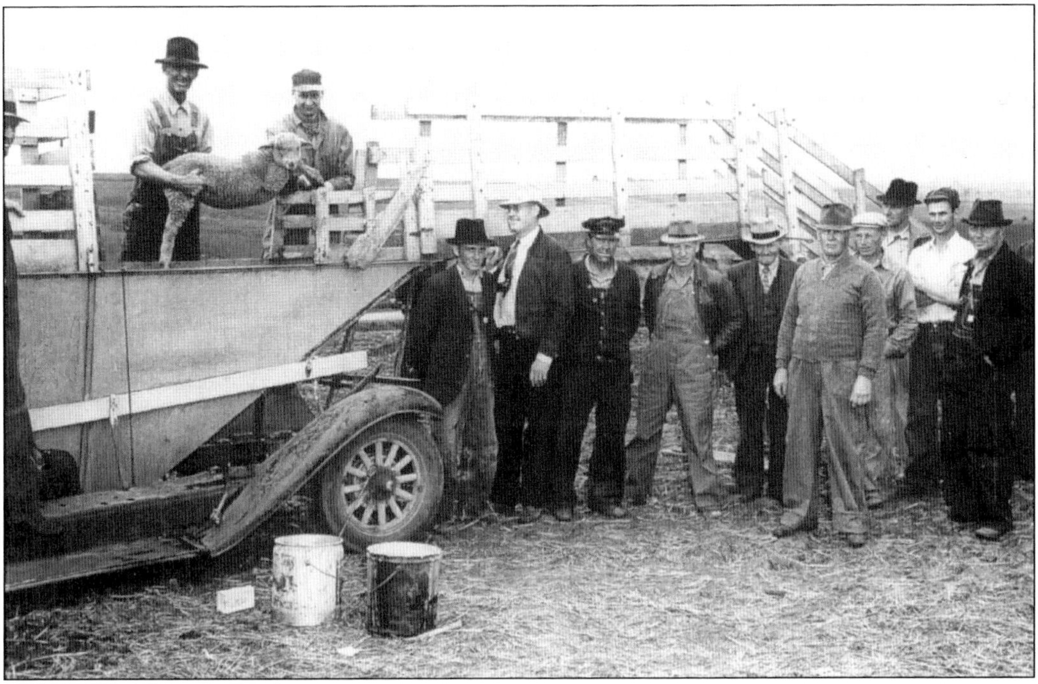

Many events in the agricultural community brought people together. Men would help gather sheep for shipment. Pictured is Bill Perkins bringing his sheep to the Kenneth stockyards to be shipped by rail.

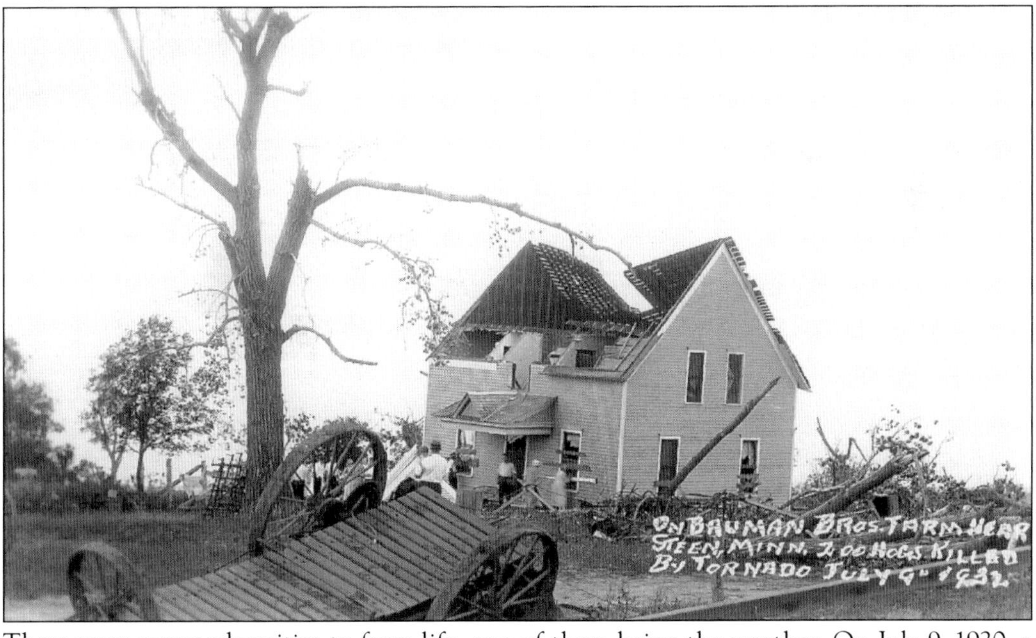

There were many adversities to farm life, one of them being the weather. On July 9, 1920, a tornado appeared near Steen and inflicted serious damage to the Bauman Brothers farm. In this photograph, the family surveys damage to their home and property. The house, along with other outbuildings and trees, had extensive damage. Note that the majority of the roof of the house is missing and that the building itself is somewhat twisted.

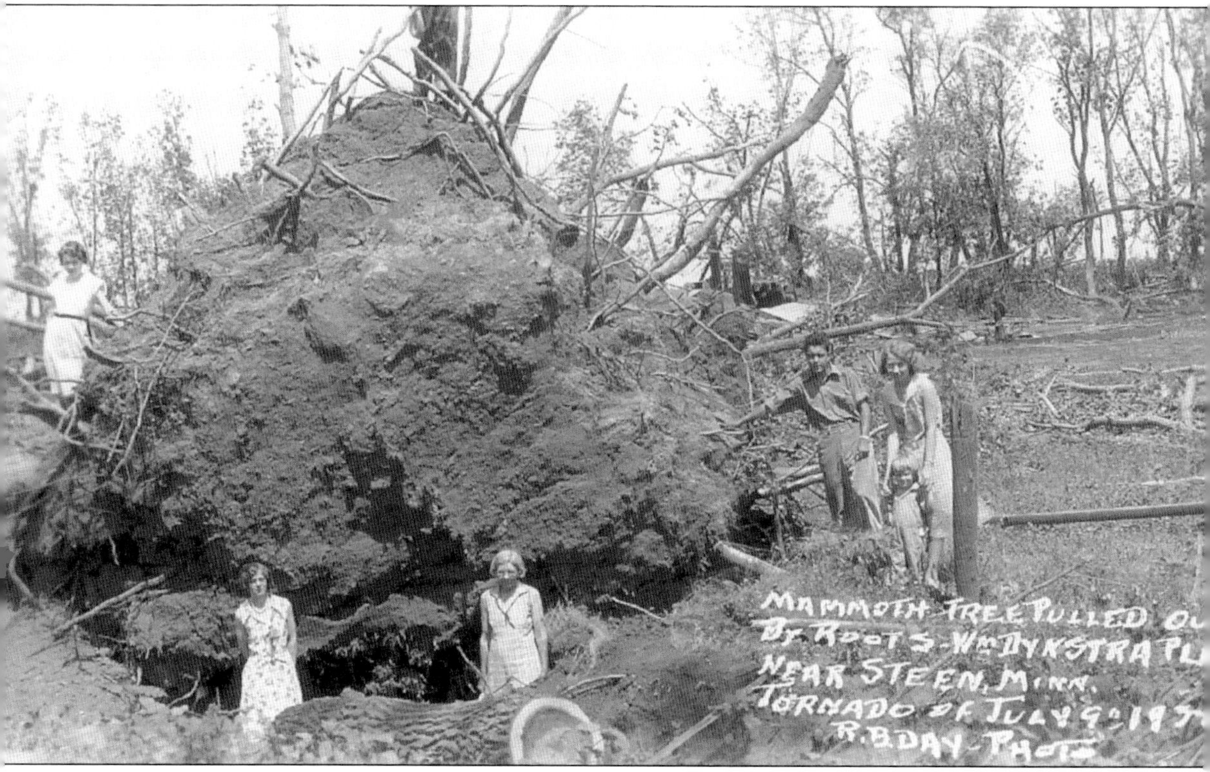

The same storm that passed through in 1920 also damaged a number of trees. The large root ball of this tree is evident. The area was fortunate that the storm was not widespread and did not take many of its trees, which served as windbreaks for farmsteads.

Two

Main Street Memories

This chapter deals with the communities located in Rock County. Each one was founded for a number of reasons and at different times in history. They are briefly described here.

Luverne was founded in 1867 by Philo Hawes and platted in 1872 by Philo Hawes, William Van Epps, and Edward McKenzie. P.J. Kniss did the original survey that made up the original 16 blocks of the community. Hills was formed in 1872 with the creation of Immanuel Norwegian Evangelical Union Church. The community was named in honor of Frederick C. Hill, president of the Sioux City & Northern Railroad. Beaver Creek was founded in 1877 as a result of the extension of the Worthington & Sioux Falls Railroad. Ash Creek started as a railroad station in 1879, when the Doon Branch of the Omaha Railroad needed a location for a post office. Magnolia, in 1884, was selected by the Burlington Railroad as a depot for shipping farm products. Kanaranzi, the community and township, was named for Kanaranzi Creek. Again, because of the Burlington Railroad, a townsite was established in September 1885. Hardwick was where the Burlington Railroad established a station in 1886. In 1887, the town was named to honor J.L. Hardwick, a master builder of the Burlington Road. Steen was established in 1888 as a town named Virginia. The name changed to Steen in 1893. The Illinois Central Railroad laid trackage from Chicago to Sioux Falls with a depot in Steen. Kenneth was founded in 1899, when the Burlington Railroad extended its line from Worthington to Hardwick, Minnesota. The town was named in honor of the son of Jay A. Kennicott. Manley was located close to the South Dakota border at the junction of the Great Northern and Chicago, St. Paul, Minneapolis and Omaha Railways.

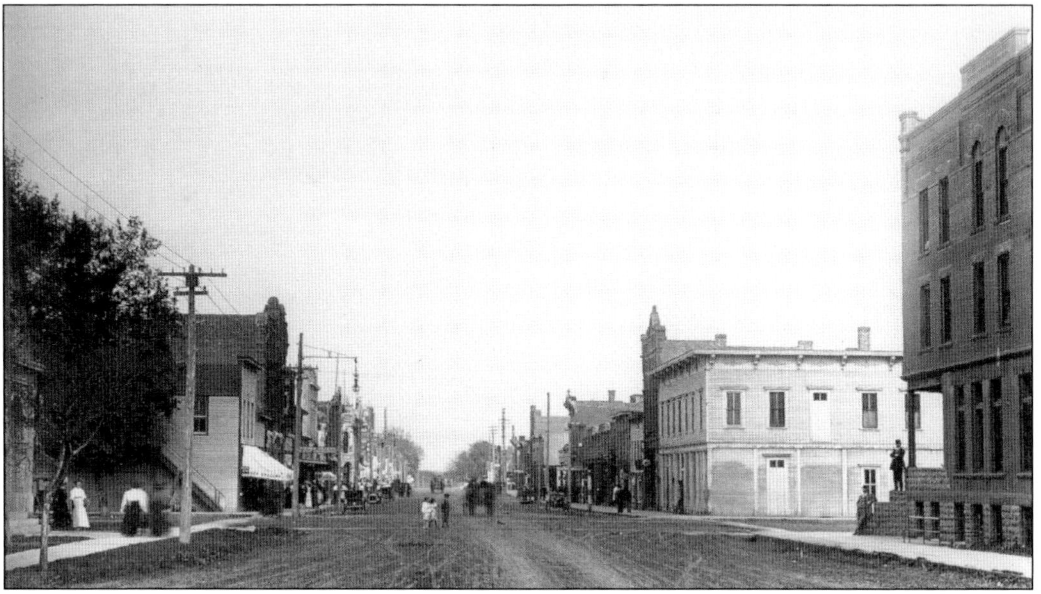

This photograph of downtown Luverne is looking east at Freeman Avenue down Main Street. The Manitou Hotel is on the right, and across the street is the Union Building, which was later torn down and replaced with the Palace Theatre. Farther down is the Independent Order of Odd Fellows (IOOF) hall with its prominent stone peak. On the left side of Main Street on the corner is the Wright Grocery Store, and to the right of it is the Arcade Building with a large Sioux quartzite front. The Arcade Building housed two businesses.

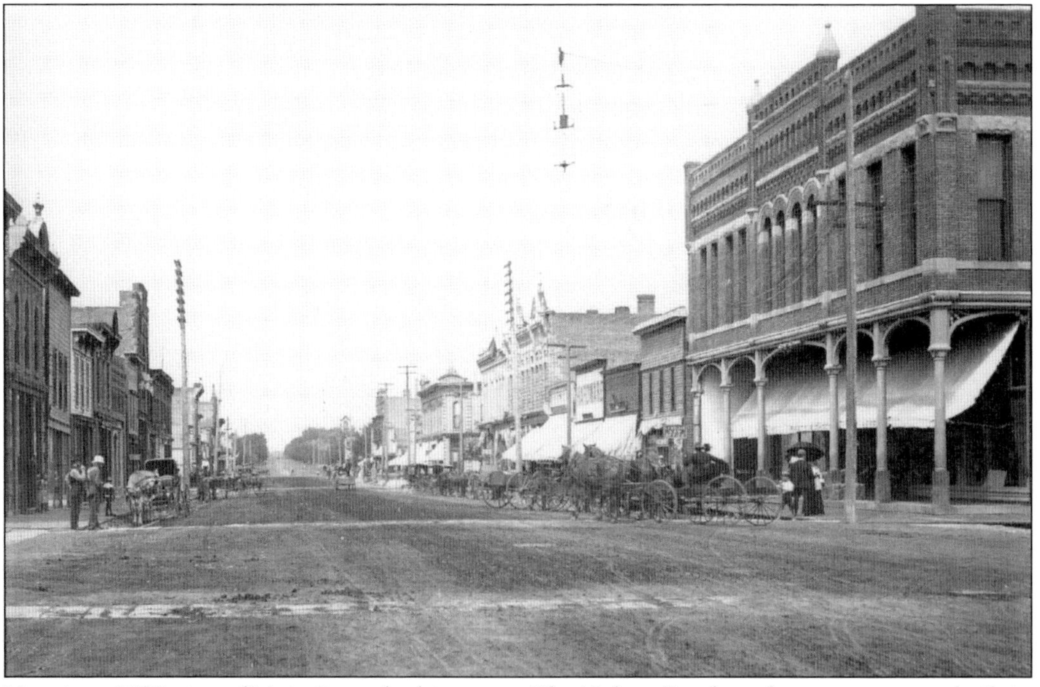

Here is an 1893 view of Main Street looking west. The Nelson Brothers department store, built in 1892, can be seen on the right. On the left side in the middle of the block is the Gerber Building, with a large stone front made of Sioux quartzite. Note the gas-vapor light on the corner.

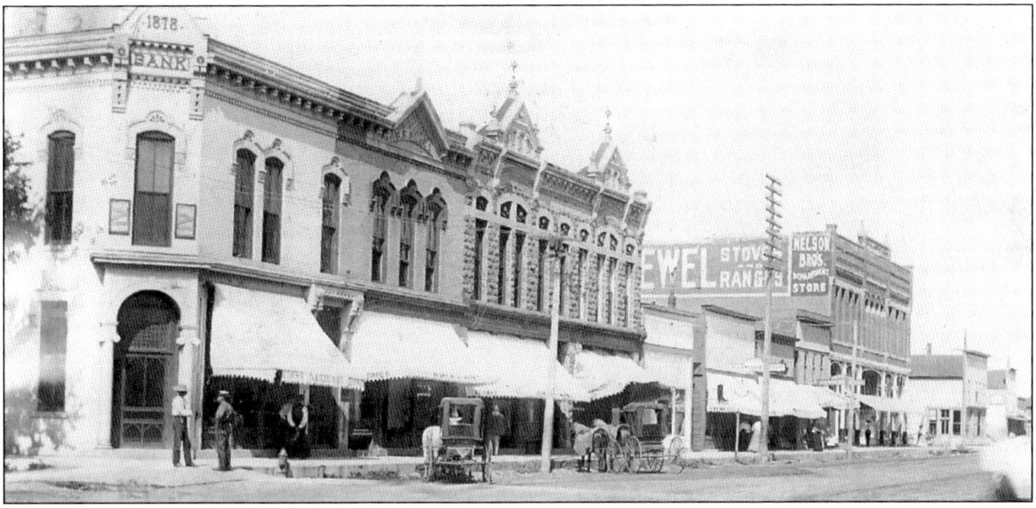

This shows the north side of Main Street from Cedar Street to McKenzie Avenue. The Bank of Luverne was built in 1878. To the right of the bank are the Hawes and Howe General Merchandise, I.I. Smith Furniture, and the Smith mortuary. These stores are followed by the S.S. Walters dry goods store, W.E. Wilson feed store, and Nelson Brothers.

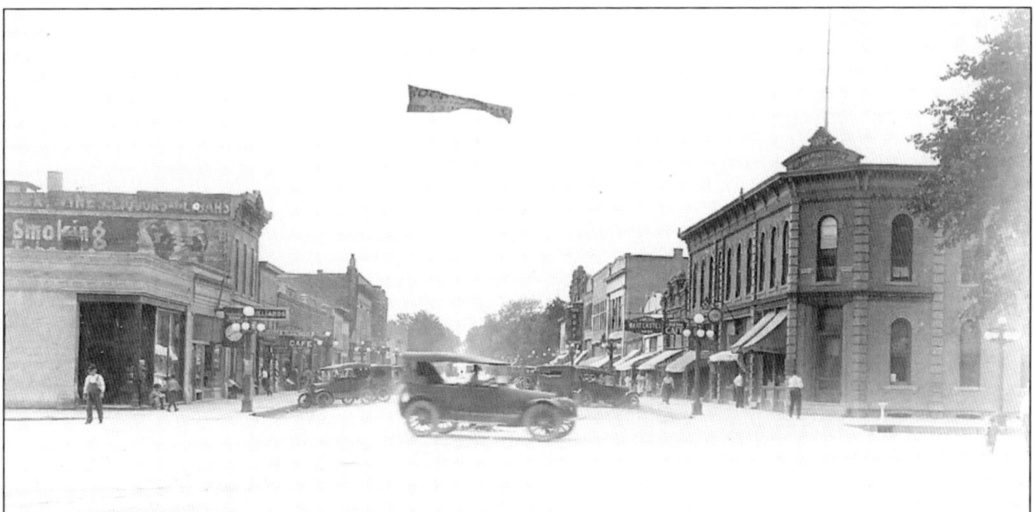

Downtown Luverne was bustling in the 1920s. Note the electric streetlights and concrete curbs and sidewalks.

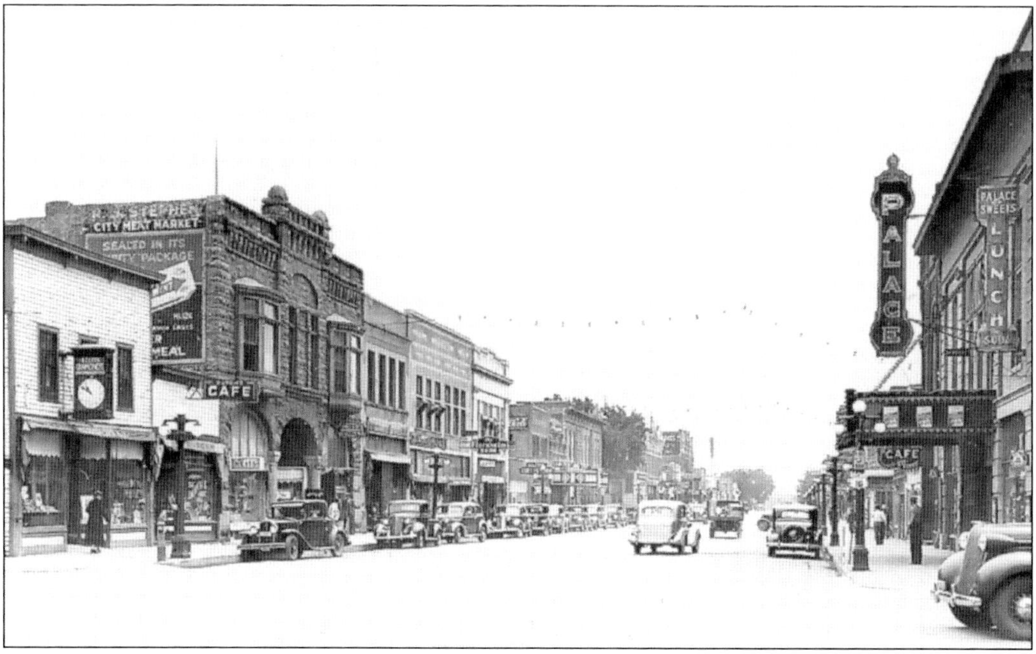

This image looks east from Freeman Avenue in the late 1930s. The Palace of Sweets and Palace Theatre are on the right. Across the street are, from left to right, the B.E. Lezs Jewelry Store, Dutch's Café, the Arcade Building, a general store, clothing store, shoe store, grocery store, drugstore, and the Pix Theater.

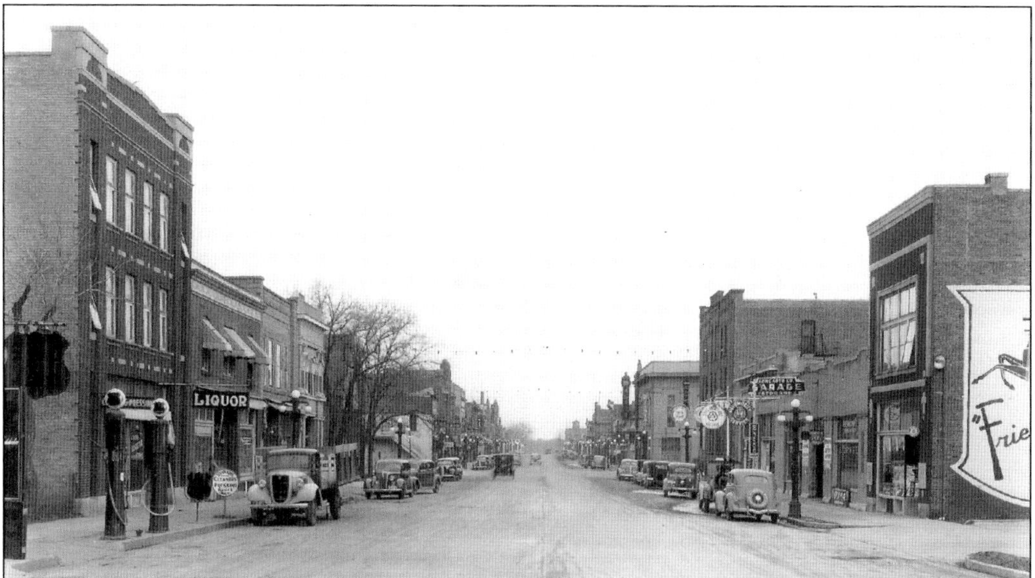

Pictured is Main Street looking east from Estey Street. On the left side of the street is the Luverne Liquor Store. On the right side, a sign is painted on the Rock County Herald Building for a gas station on the corner. To the left of the newspaper office is a garage with an auto dealership. The Manitou Hotel is located on the corner at the end of the block.

This view is looking west on Main Street in the 1930s. On the right side of the photograph are, from front to back, Nelson Brothers, a hardware store, dime store, Creeger's Clothing, and Smith Furniture. On the left side of the street are, from front to back, T.H.'s Café, a bakery, Kash Savings, and Gerber's Hardware. Note that streets and sidewalks have been constructed.

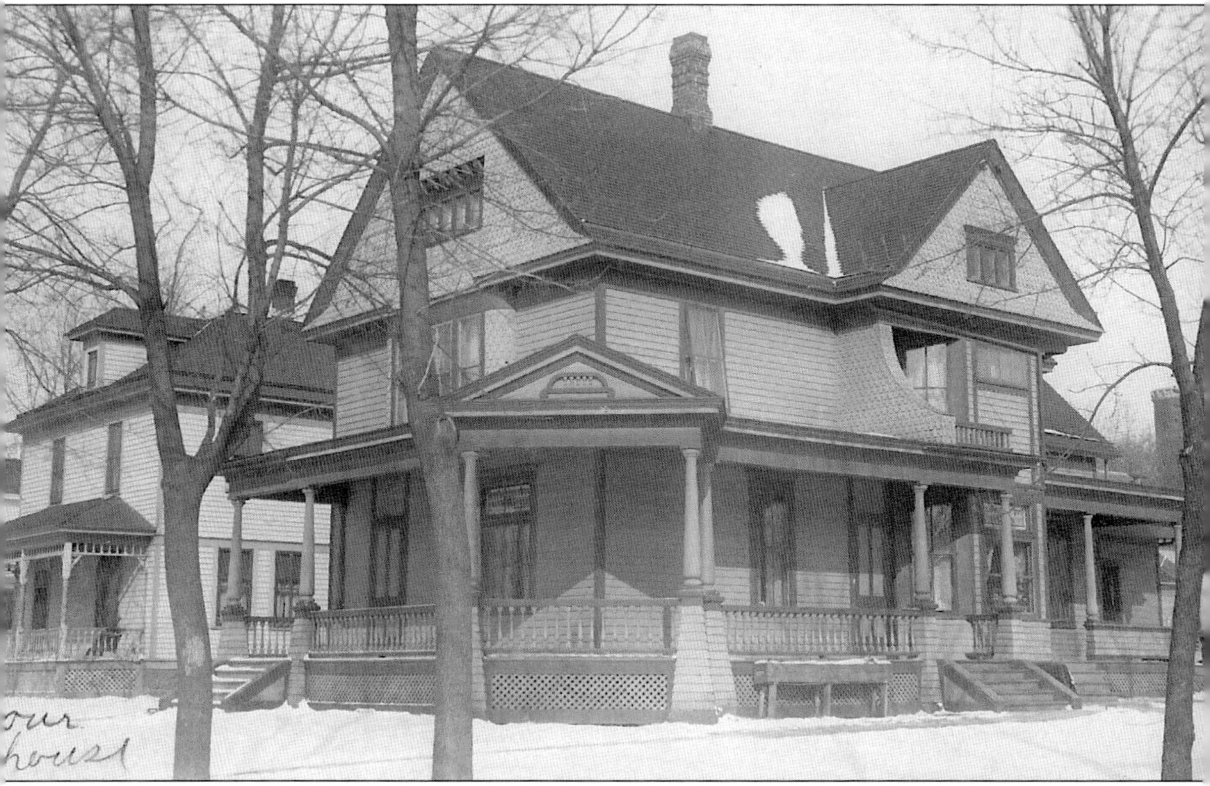

Seen in the early 1900s is one of the beautiful old homes of West Main Avenue. A number of historic homes were built in this area.

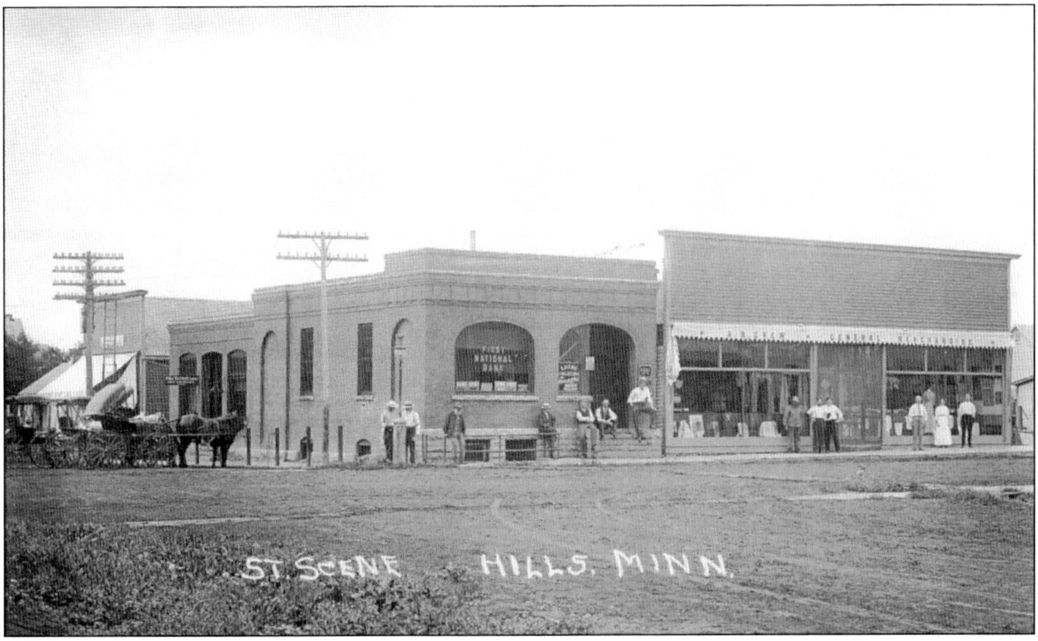

First National Bank of Hills was located toward the south end of Main Street. Behind the bank is an office space. To the right of the bank is the Crew General Merchandise. Both of these buildings were constructed in the early 1900s.

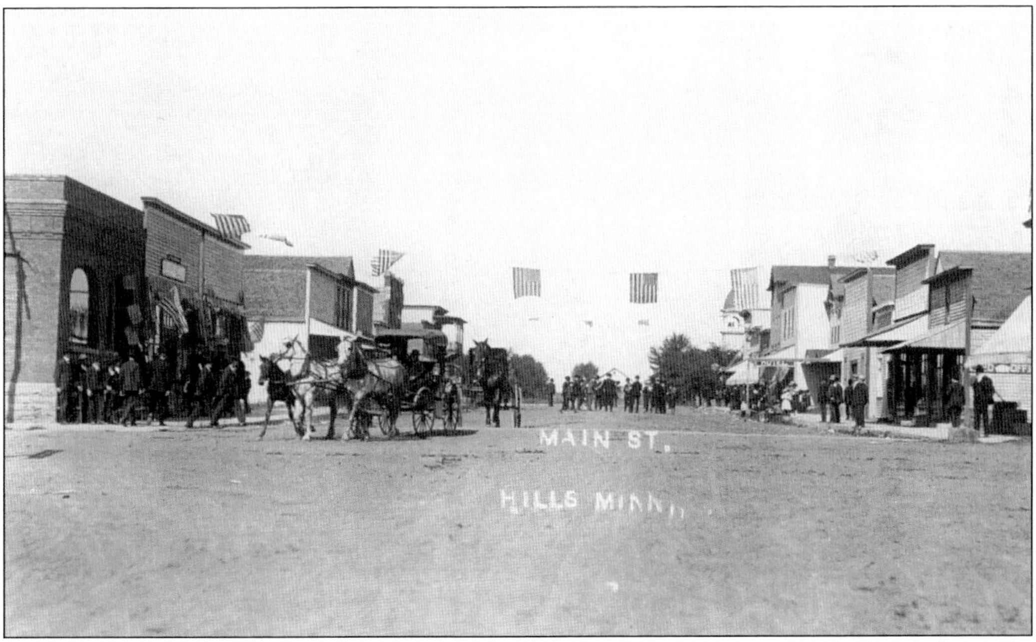

Here is Main Street of Hills in the early 1900s. Some of the businesses identified include a café, Sundem Drugstore, a funeral home and furniture store, the harness shop, and the bank on the left side of the street. On the right side is a hardware store, and in the middle of the block is Rudd's General Store.

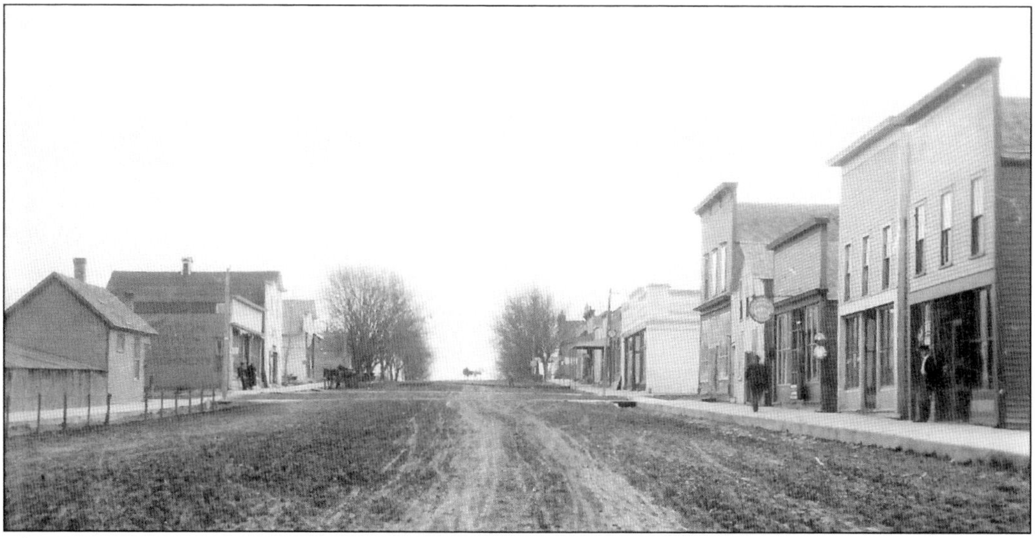

This is Main Street in Beaver Creek looking east. Many of the former businesses were destroyed by two different fires in the downtown area. Businesses identified include the Tuthill Lumber Company, Henton Blacksmith & Wagon Shop, Alfred Morgan's Pool Hall, Vopat Café, the post office, Ott & Grant's Grocery, brick garage, Dunbar Grocery, and First National Bank.

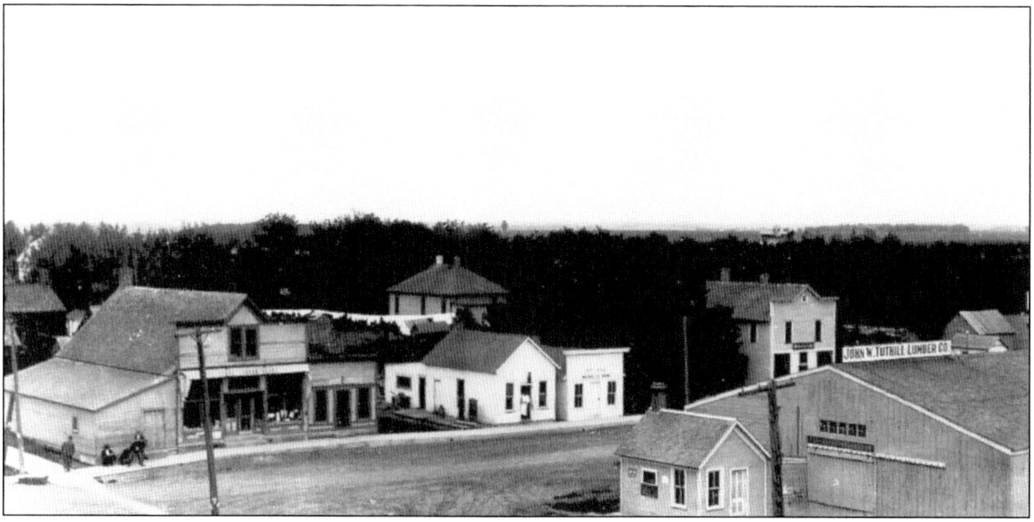

This is downtown Magnolia. The country store is visible on the corner (far left), and to the right of it are the creamery buying station, the post office, the livery, and the hotel. The John Tuthill Lumber Co. is in the right foreground.

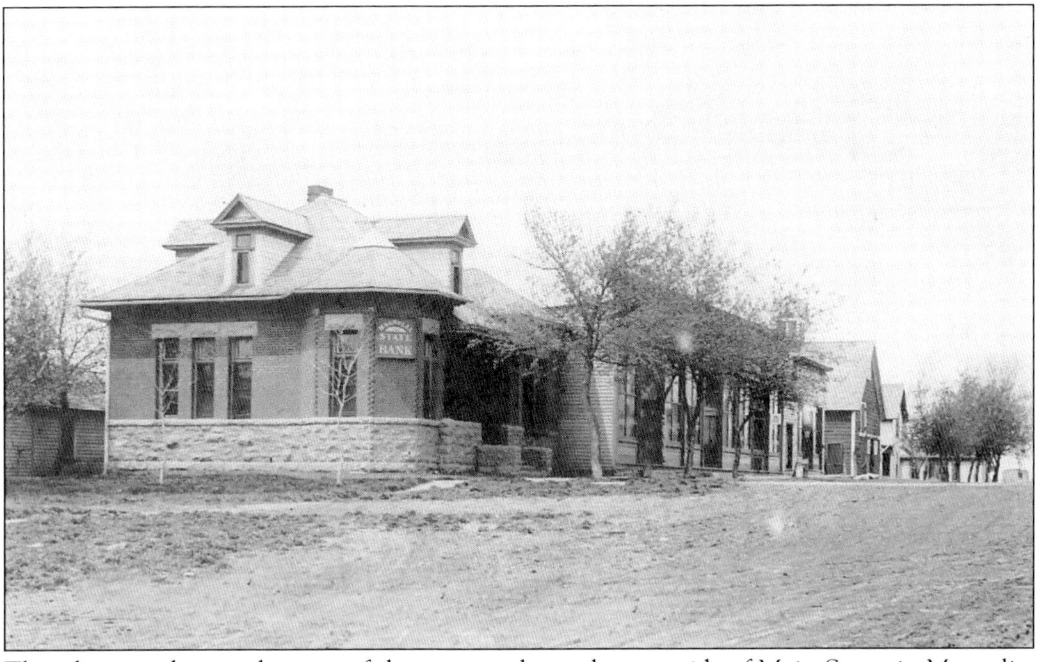

This photograph near the turn of the century shows the west side of Main Street in Magnolia. Pictured is Magnolia State Bank, and to the right of it are a pool hall/barbershop, hardware store, grocery store, and a smaller building for machinery. Local residents claim this is the first strip mall in the country. The next block includes the Pemberton Garage.

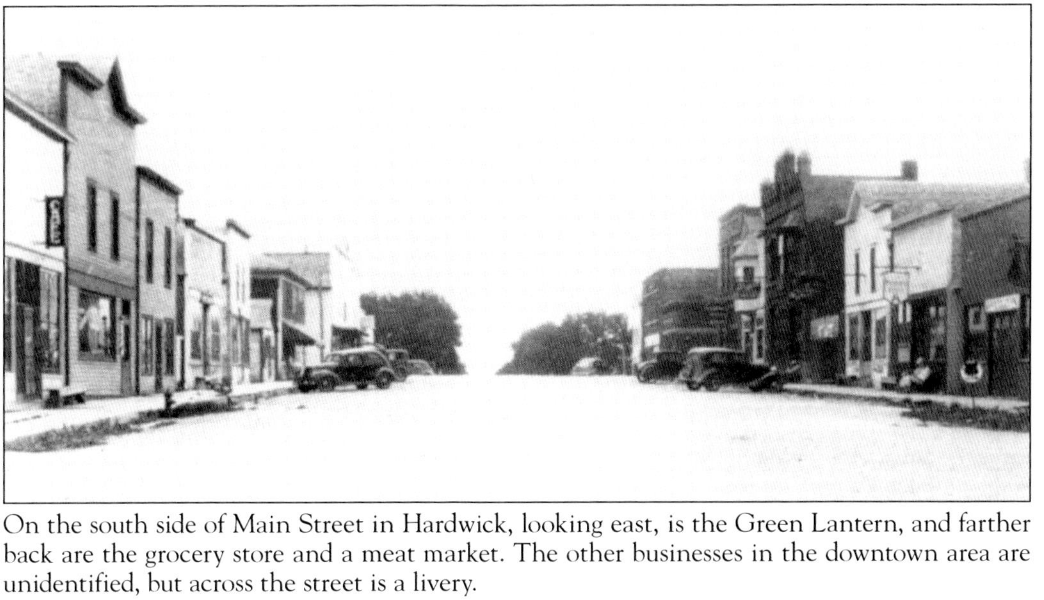

On the south side of Main Street in Hardwick, looking east, is the Green Lantern, and farther back are the grocery store and a meat market. The other businesses in the downtown area are unidentified, but across the street is a livery.

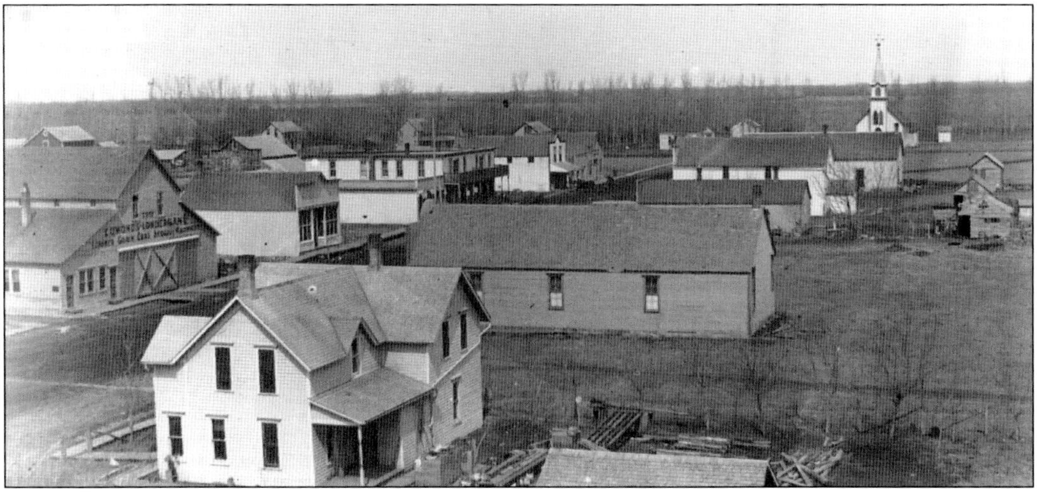

Downtown Steen in the early 1900s had a variety of businesses, including a hotel, garage, harness shop, and the first Schoon Motors in Rock County. This auto-repair and dealership business moved to Luverne and is still an active under the Papik Auto name.

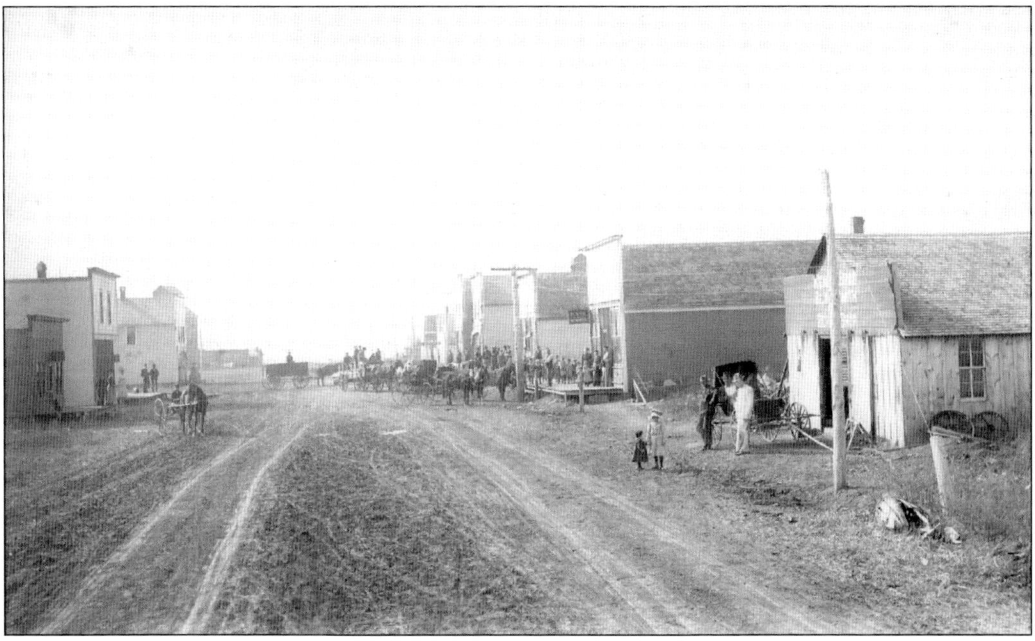

Downtown Kenneth in the early 1900s was a bustling community. Businesses started up and were expanded with the introduction of the railroad into town. Some of the early businesses included a bank, hardware store, and a general store. Kenneth also had a feedlot where livestock were loaded on trains and shipped for processing.

Three

Providing for Community Needs

As the rural population began to grow, the need for goods and supplies became extremely important. Wagons, buckboards, and horses could travel about 20 miles in a day. Entrepreneurs and businessmen recognized the opportunity in offering goods and services to these homesteads, and towns naturally developed to supply these farmers within an approximate 10-mile zone.

Mills were among the first businesses developed. They provided a market for farm grain so that it could be screened and ground into flour. Flour was not only used by farmers and residents, but it was also sent to markets elsewhere.

Lumberyards and hardware stores were also among the first businesses established in the county. As the prairie was settled, the only stands of trees were typically along streams, rivers, and creeks. Lumber in a natural setting was a scarce resource, and as farmers needed to build wagons, homes, barns, and fences, lumberyards would have the wood and building supplies needed for these projects.

Post offices and train depots were constructed at strategic points in the county. As they took hold, entrepreneurs opened mercantile stores, hardware stores, hotels and boardinghouses, harness shops, livery stables, saloons, and other businesses around them.

Entrepreneurs identified the needs of the community and developed a business model to meet those needs. That same entrepreneurial spirit lives on in Rock County today.

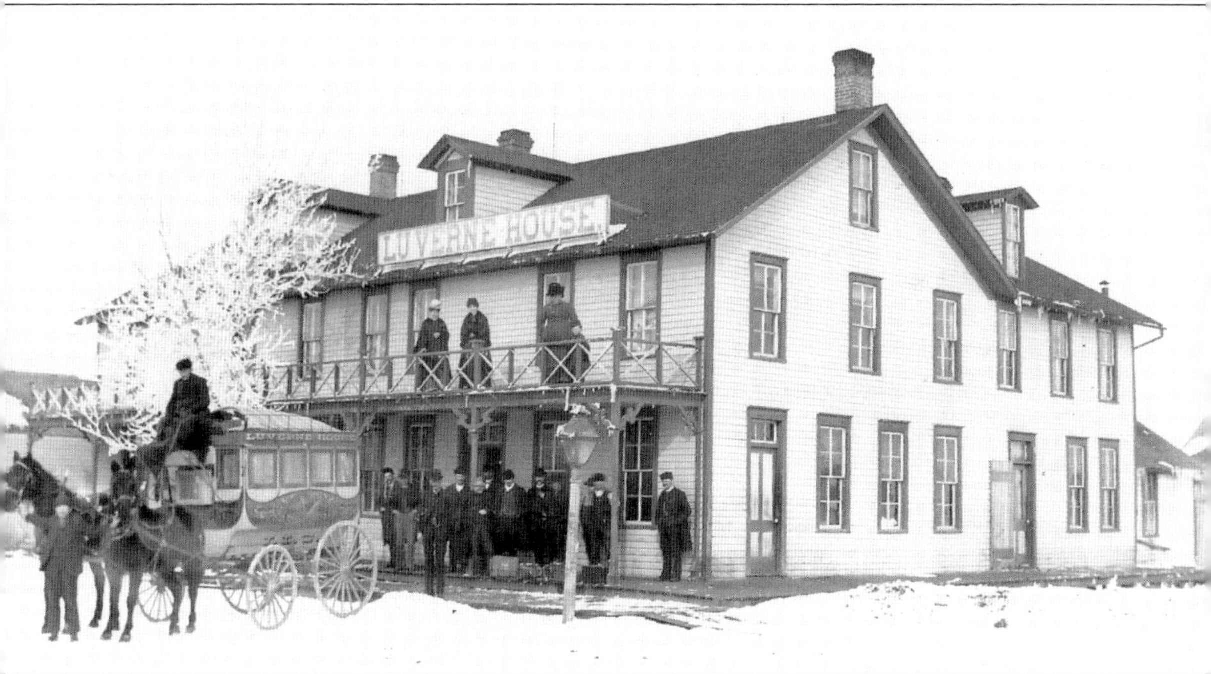

One of the early businesses in Luverne was the Luverne House boarding facility. In 1872, Dr. Vary moved to the area to invest in land and other business ventures. He built the structure to provide a facility for travelers venturing to Luverne. The second story was added in 1883, but in 1886, the entire structure was destroyed by fire. Dr. Vary eventually moved to Sioux Falls.

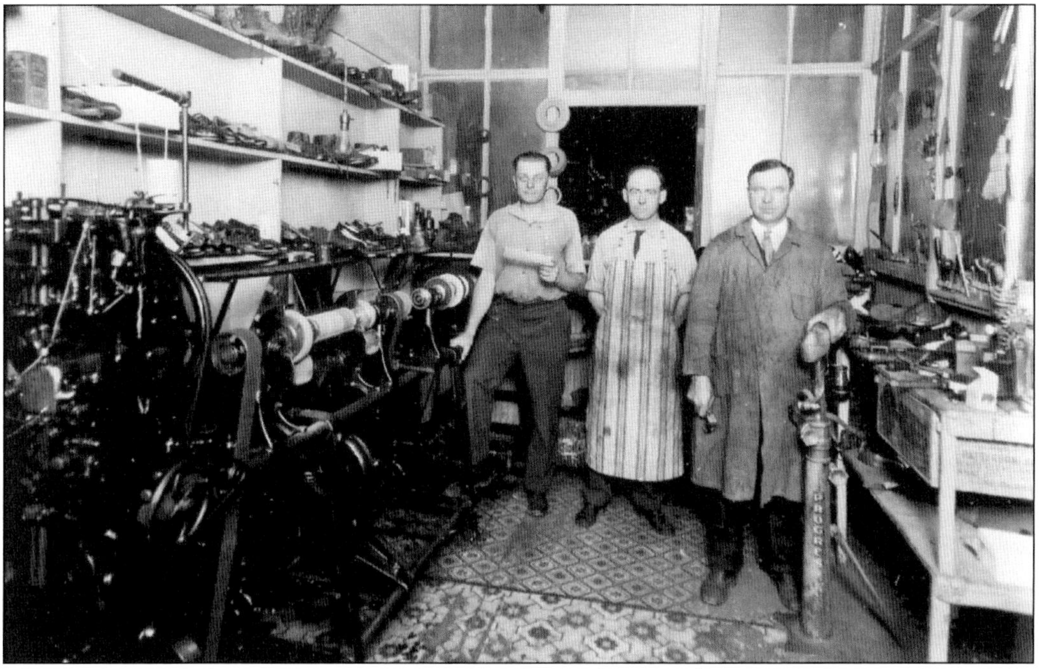

A very important business in any community was its harness shop. This photograph is of the Ed Hudson harness shop located in downtown Luverne. It provided a number of services and products, including men's and women's shoes and boots.

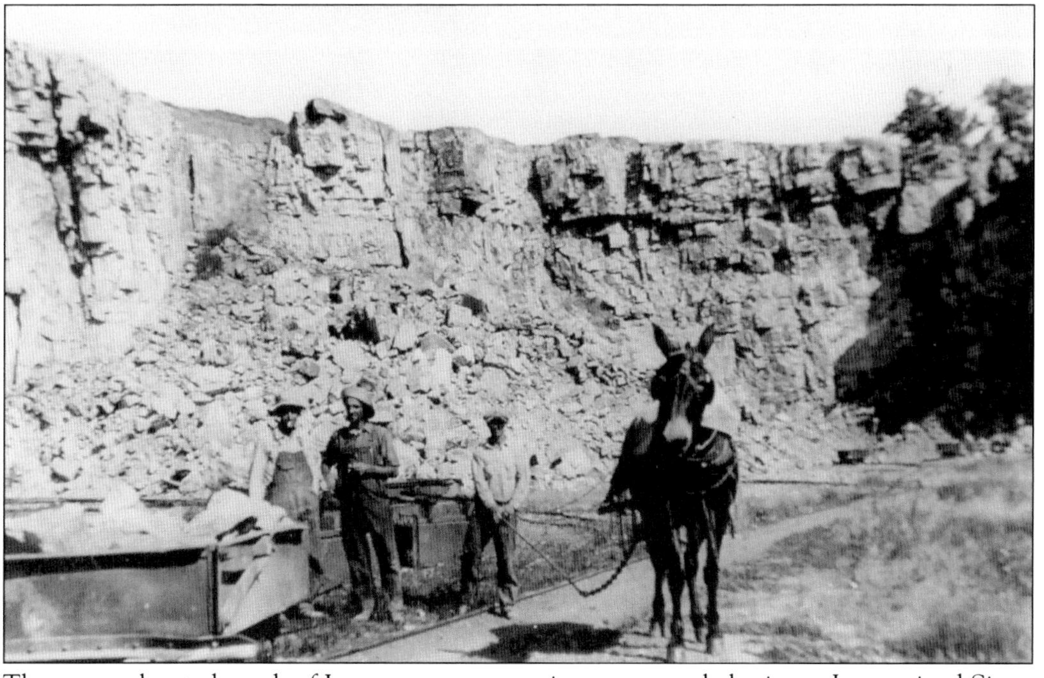

The quarry, located north of Luverne, was a very important early business. It contained Sioux quartzite, which was used in many of the buildings in Luverne and outside the area. This image shows stone being collected, put into carts, and hauled by mule down the hill to a crushing plant that eventually shipped it.

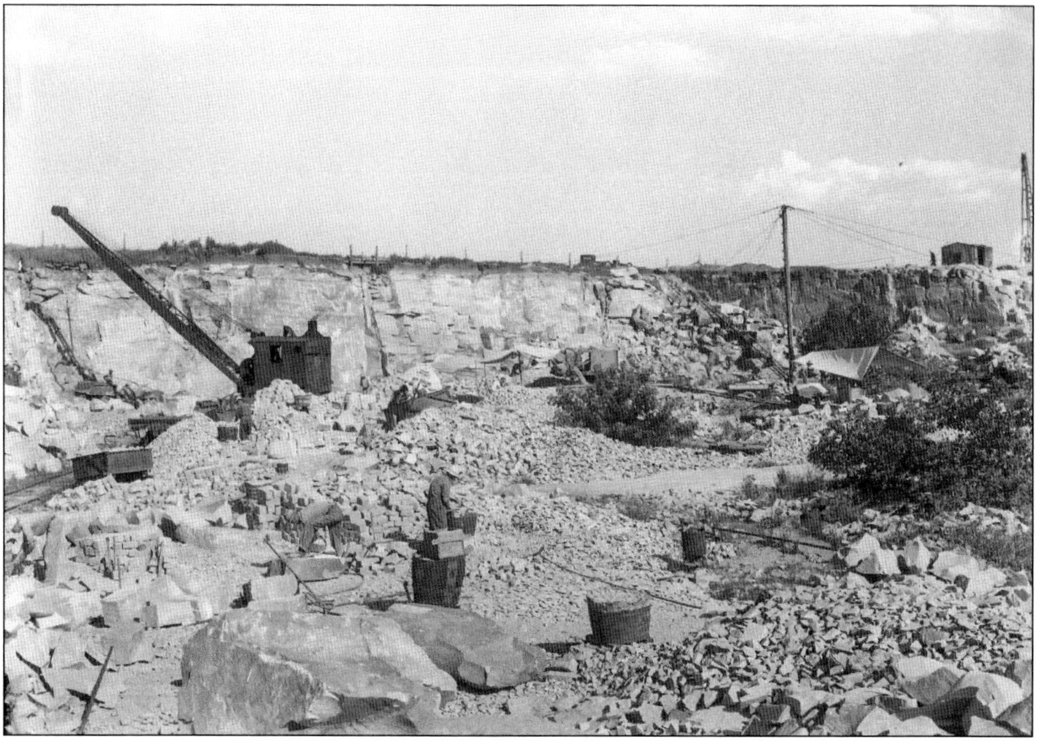

This photograph of the quarry depicts workers inside the quarry, cutting and shaping the stone to be used for buildings and other projects.

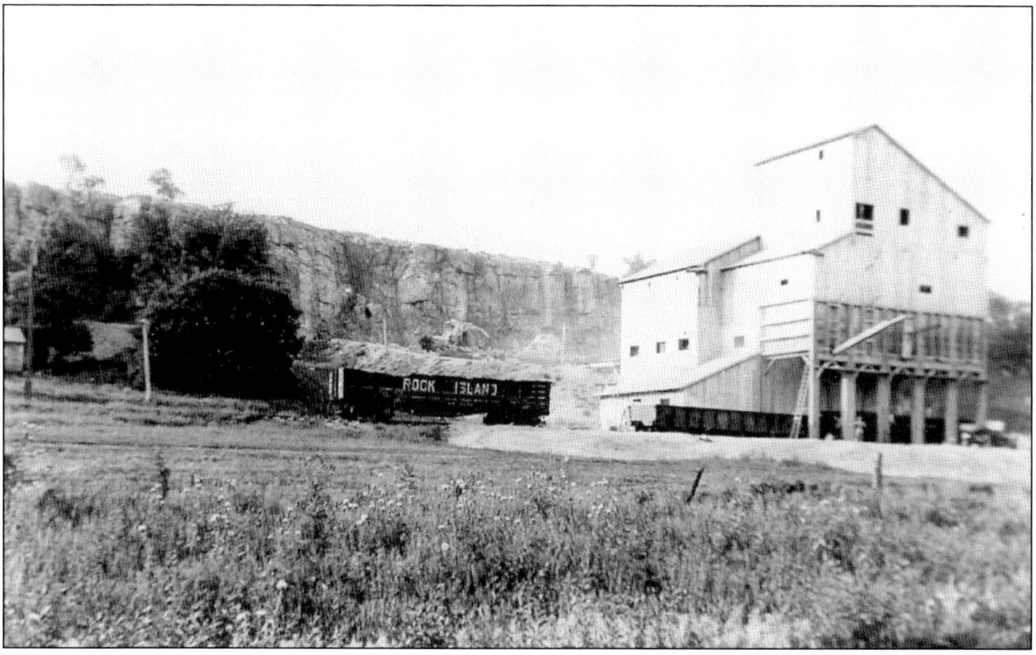

As the Rock Island Railroad built its line north from Luverne toward Hardwick, a supplemental line was constructed to the quarry processing plant, shown here. Railcars were then loaded with the Sioux quartzite and distributed to customers.

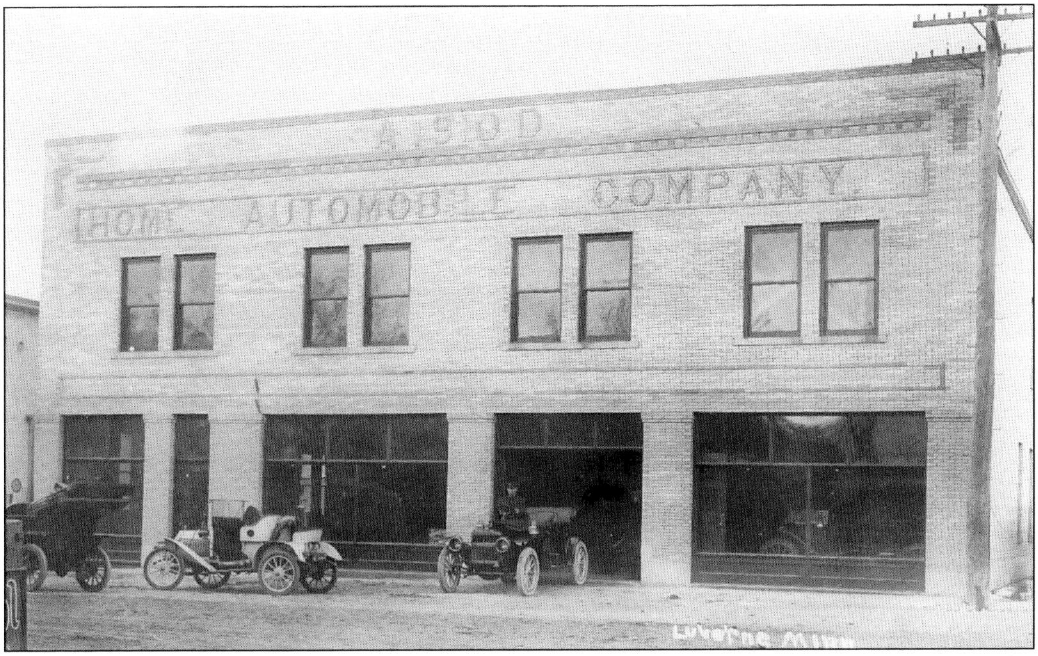

The Home Automobile Company began in 1910 and remained in Luverne for many years. The building in this photograph was located on the corner of Lincoln and McKenzie Streets and contained an automobile showroom and also an early elevator that could bring cars from the street level up to the second floor.

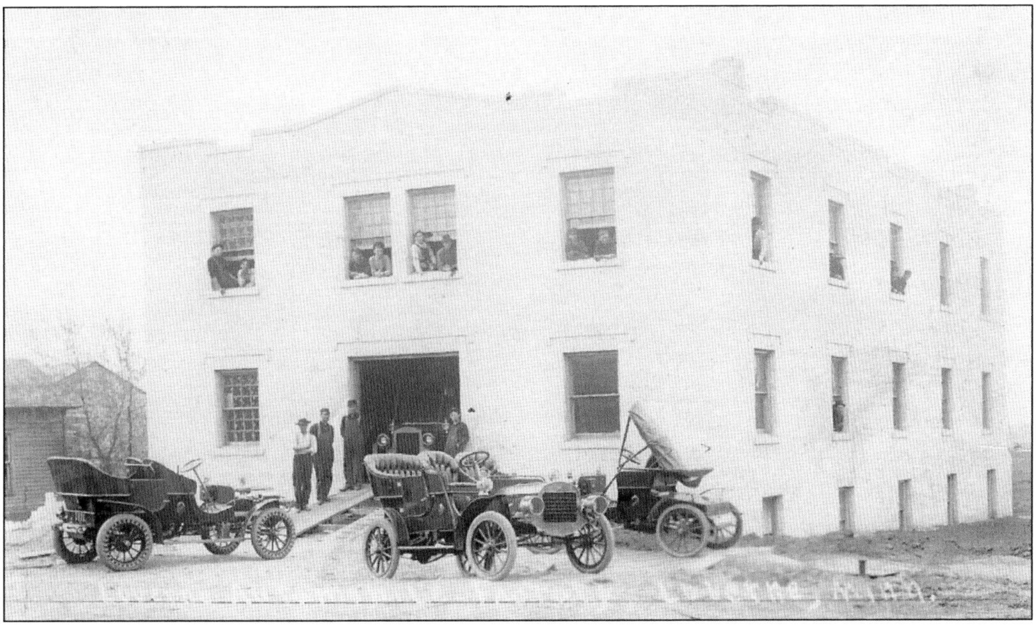

Starting in 1909, the Luverne Automobile Company began manufacturing automobiles; today, the company continues with the manufacture of fire equipment. Seen here are three floors of the manufacturing plant where automobiles were assembled. Parked outside the building are several of the models the firm manufactured. The Luverne automobile had a reputation of being one of the finest of its time.

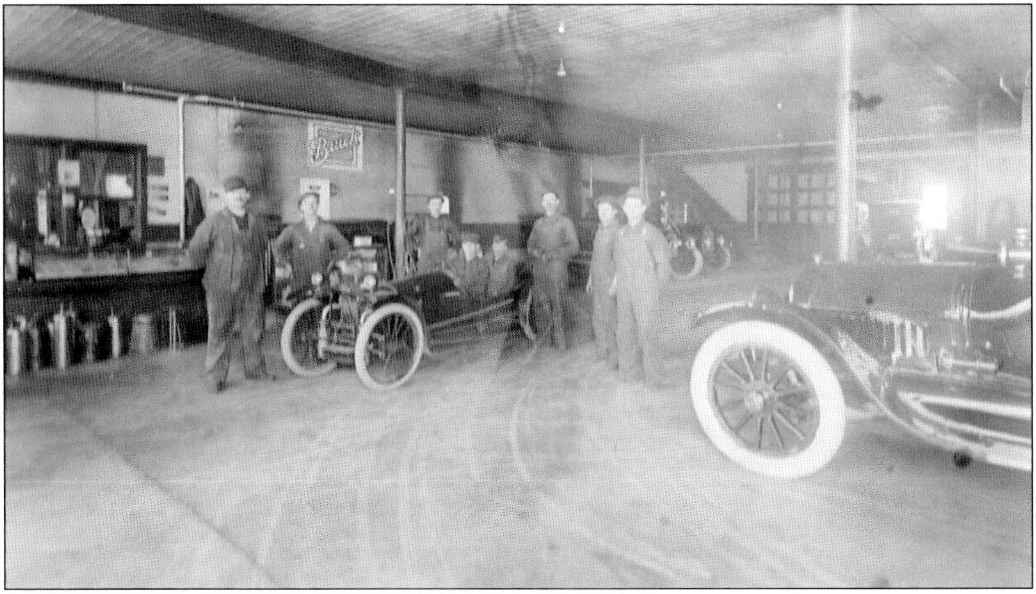

This photograph was taken in the basement of the Luverne Automobile Company, where workers installed engines to Luverne automobiles. Note the Buick sign on the wall in the background. Normally, engines that were put into early automobiles came from a limited number of suppliers, and many of them were Buick engines.

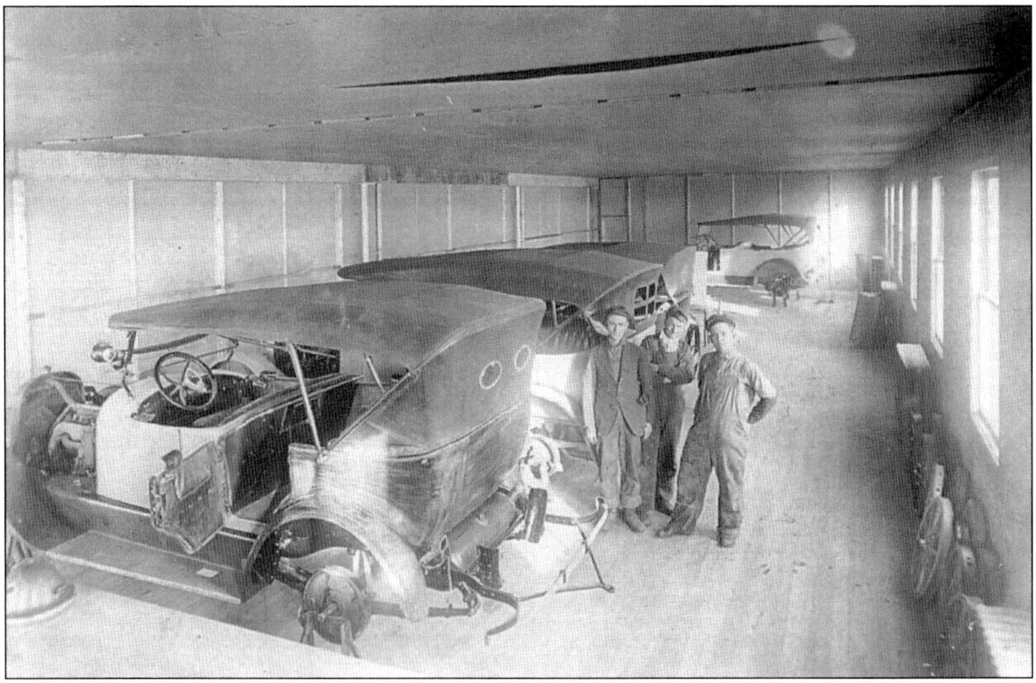

The upper floor of the Luverne Automobile Company was used more for the finishing of autos. It was where seats were installed, rims and tires became part of the vehicle, and other polishing and finishing were done. Once completed, the vehicles were taken down from the top floor to the street-level floor by elevator. They were then sent to dealers or made available for residents at the downtown sales area.

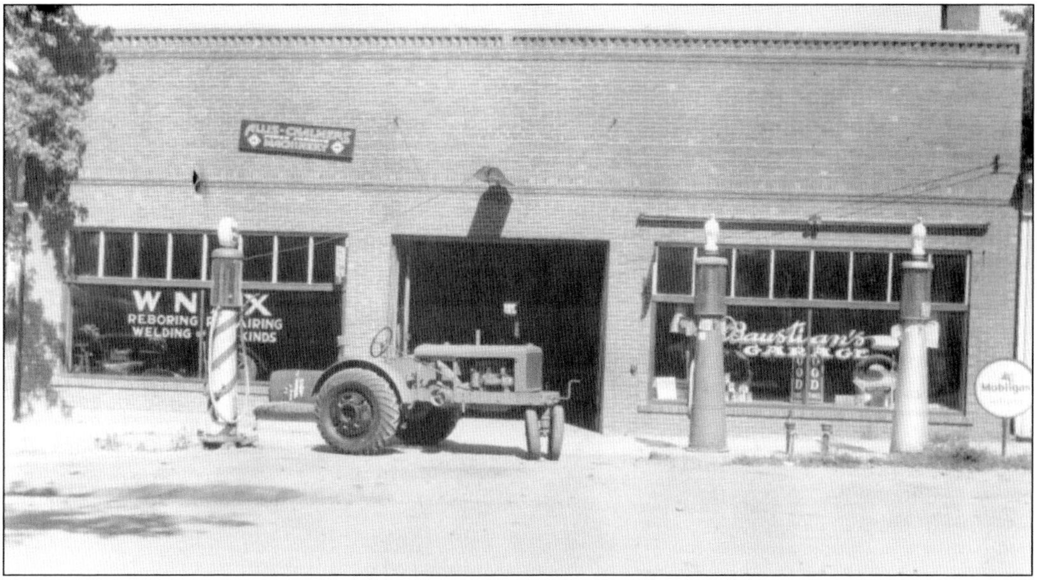

Here is a typical garage in Luverne during the 1940s and 1950s. Note that there are several businesses within one building. In this instance, there is a garage, implement dealer, and boring and welding shop.

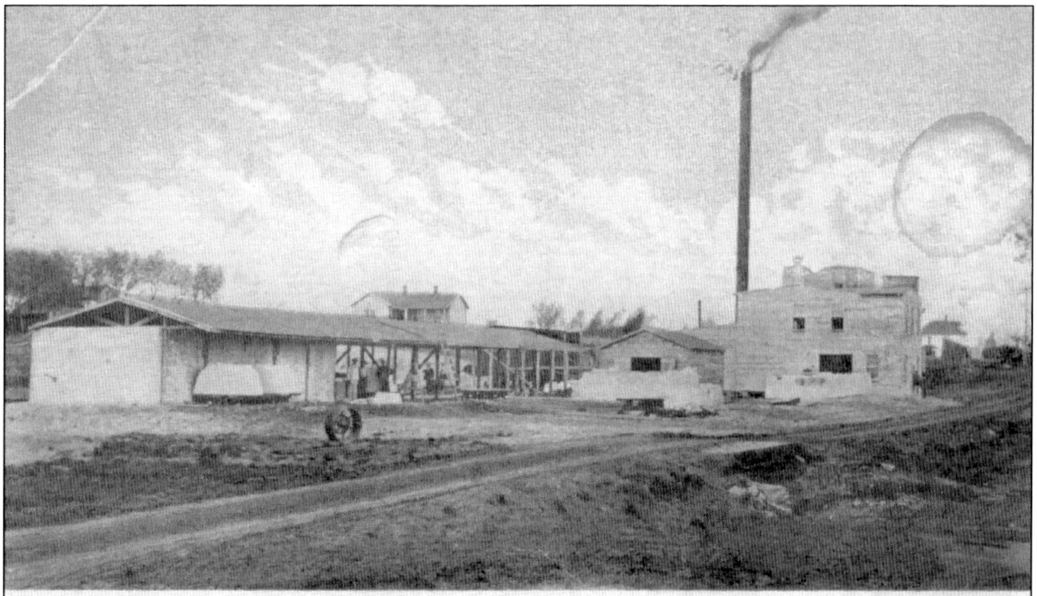

Sand Lime Brick Factory, Luverne, Minn. Pub. by J. A. Harronn

Another unique business in Luverne was the Luverne Block Company, which manufactured concrete blocks and bricks. The manufacturing process was similar to that of the Luverne Brick and Tile Company, but the type of product manufactured here was smaller than the items at the plant outside of Luverne. The block company provided a large number of foundation blocks used in commercial as well as residential properties.

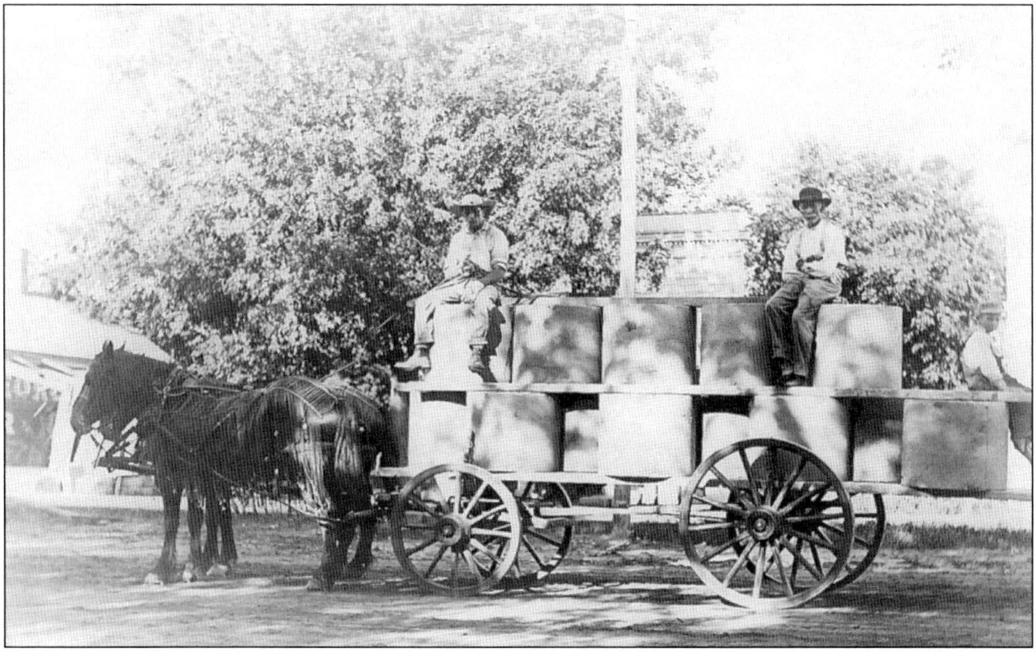

This photograph shows a wagonload of concrete tile from the Luverne Block Company. The horse-drawn wagon delivered the large concrete blocks to builders constructing many of the businesses in Luverne. With the close proximity of the block company to the railroad, the company was able to deliver its blocks and bricks to areas outside of Luverne.

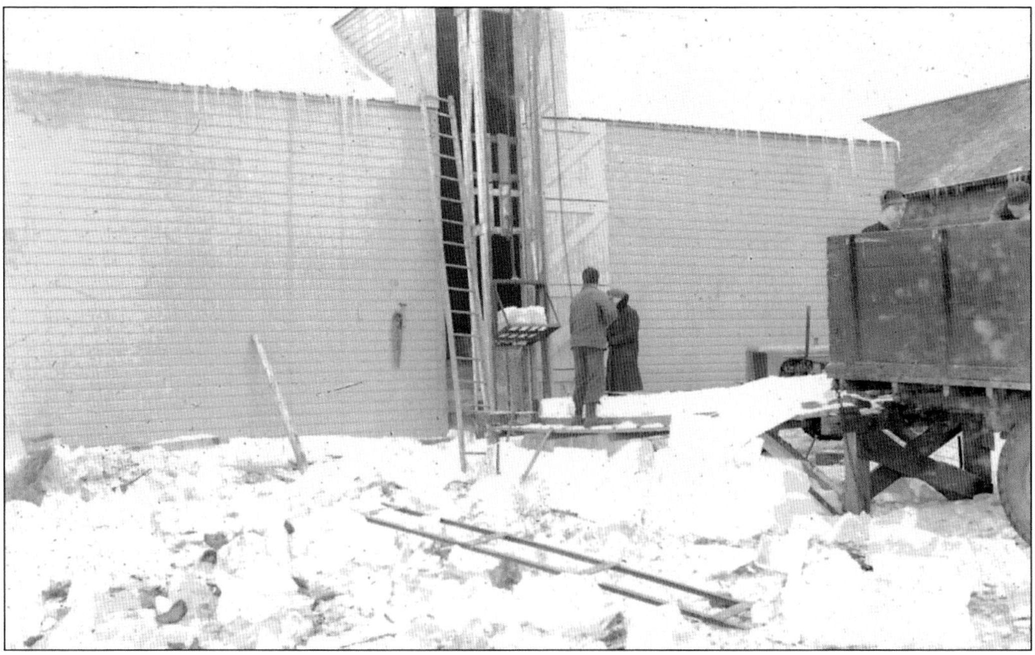

Another business that was very important to the community of Luverne was the local ice plant. Before there were refrigerators, people used iceboxes to keep perishables cold. A local business would deliver ice and place it in iceboxes of residences throughout town. Individuals cut ice from the river, conveyed it to trailers, and then hauled and loaded it into an icehouse in town.

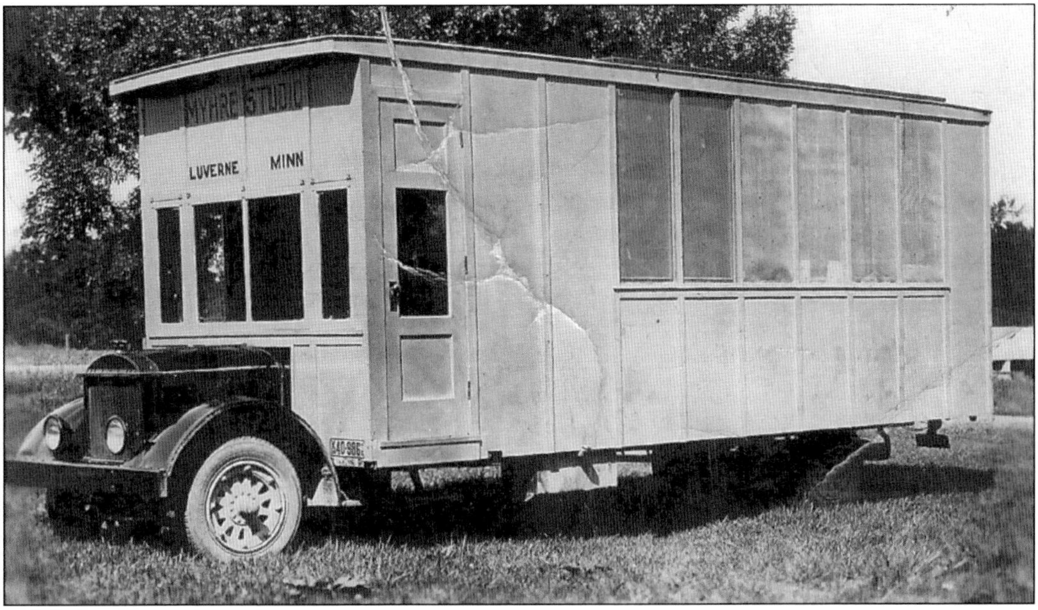

Myhre Studio was responsible for photographing much of Luverne's past. This truck contained cameras and other equipment and traveled throughout the county taking photographs of families and other items of interest. Carrying the equipment in a truck allowed Odin Myhre to travel to families and farms rather than have them travel into town to have their photographs taken.

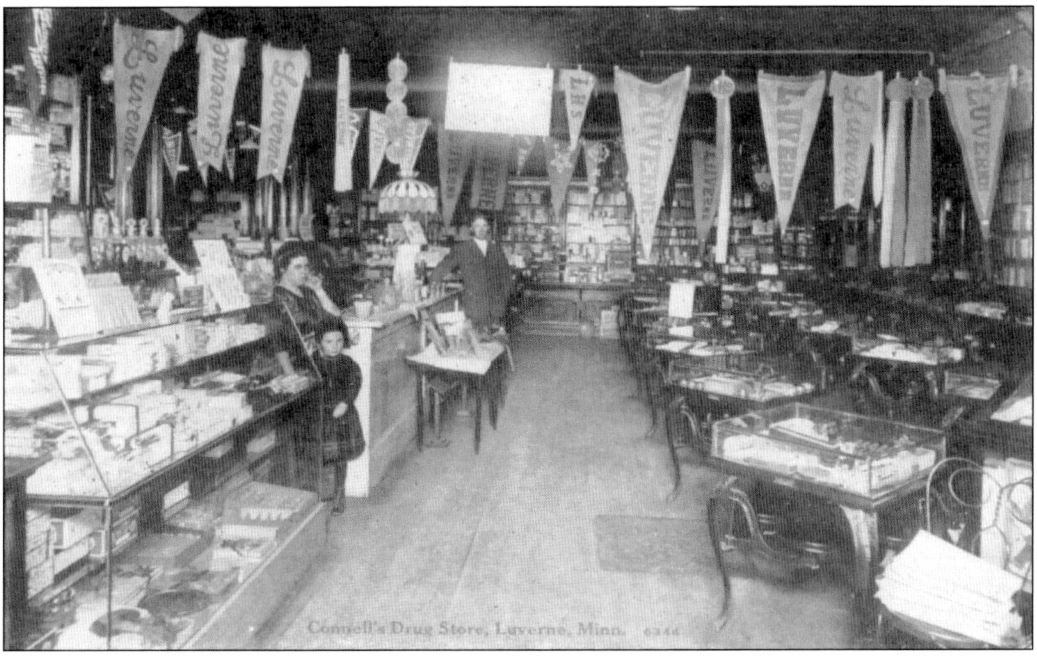

The Connell Drugstore, one of the early drugstores in Luverne, served the needs of Luverne for many years. Although the store was primarily for the distribution of medicines, the photograph shows that the business had a variety of items to meet the needs of customers. Notice the banners promoting Luverne hanging from the ceiling in the building.

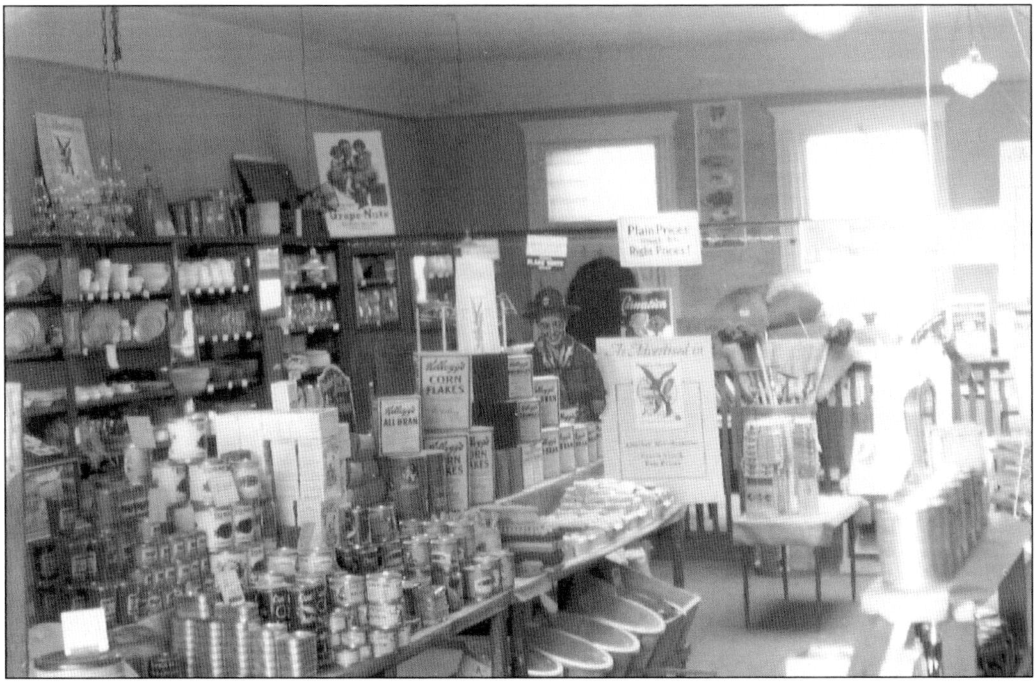

Many communities had a general merchandise store similar to the one in this image. Available at this store were groceries, cleaning items, dishes, and other necessities for any home.

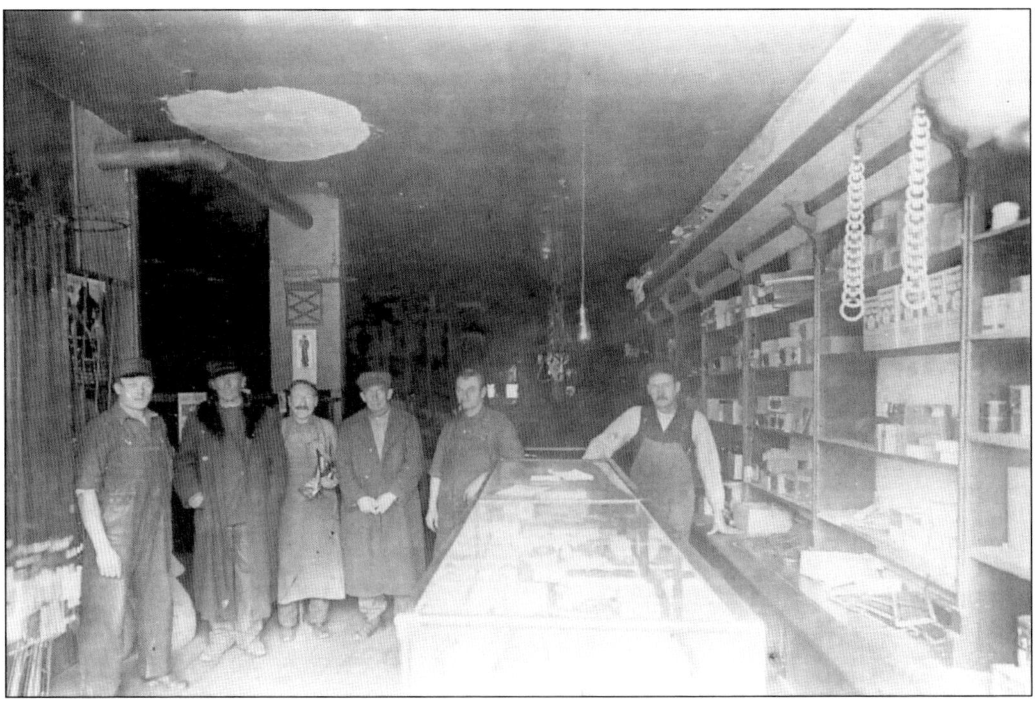

The hardware store, and in some cases a harness shop, contained a variety of items for both the farm and home. If nothing else, it served as a gathering place for locals.

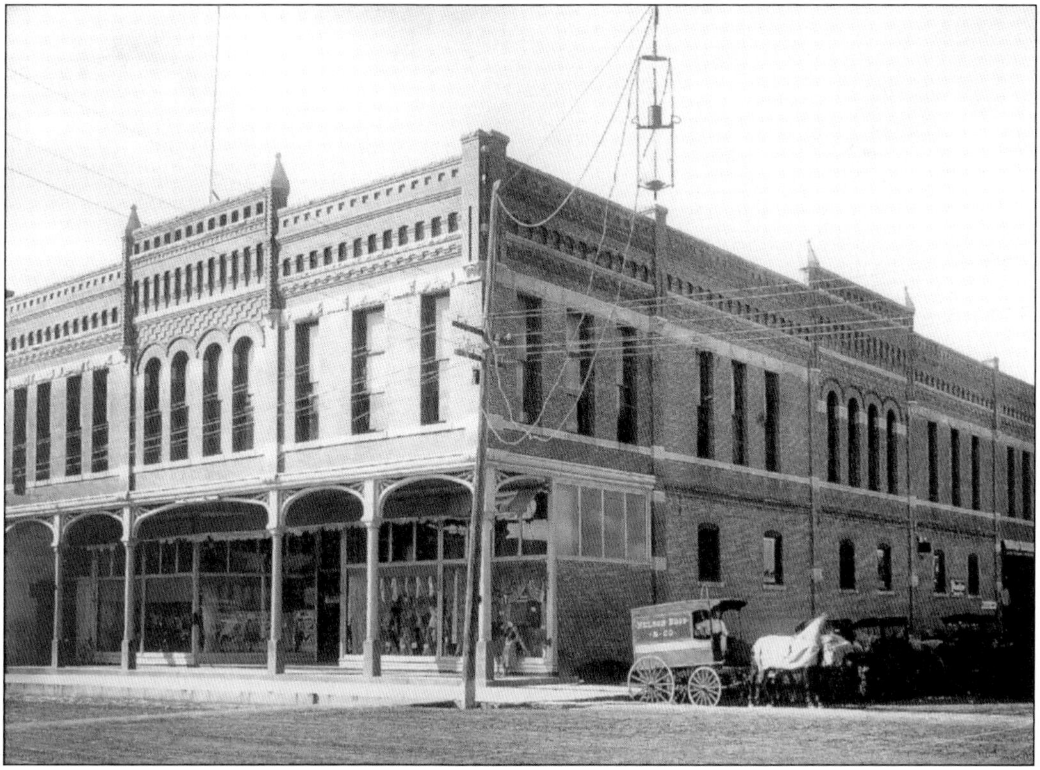

One of the larger retail businesses in Luverne was Nelson Brothers department store. Built in the early 1900s, this two-story structure handled a variety of retail needs for the community. Clothing, groceries, dry goods, furniture, hardware, and many other items were available at Nelson Brothers. Note the horse-drawn wagon; it allowed the store to make deliveries, which was another unique service of the time.

This photograph shows the interior of a typical hardware store. Bins containing bolts, screws, nails, fasteners, and other items can be seen on the left. On the right side are wood-burning stoves, furnaces, gas lanterns, and other hardware items.

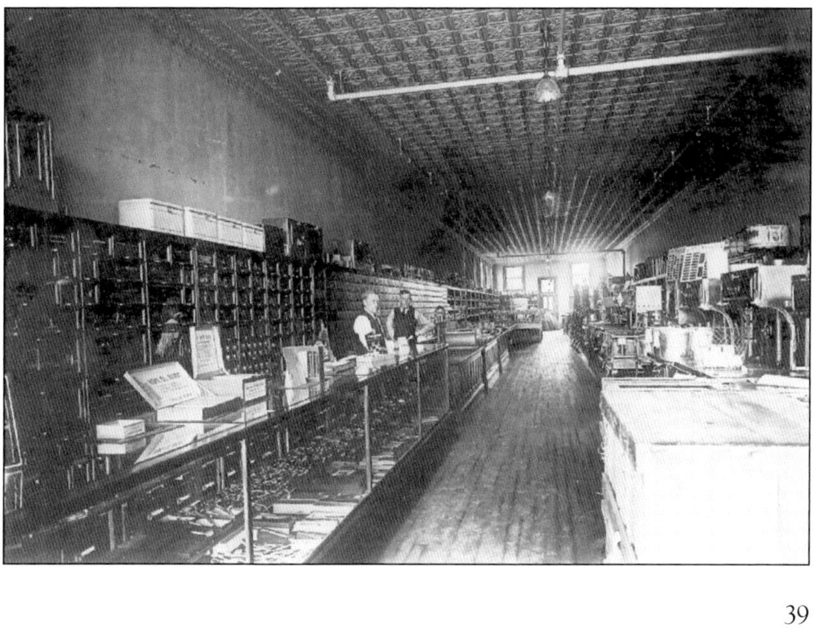

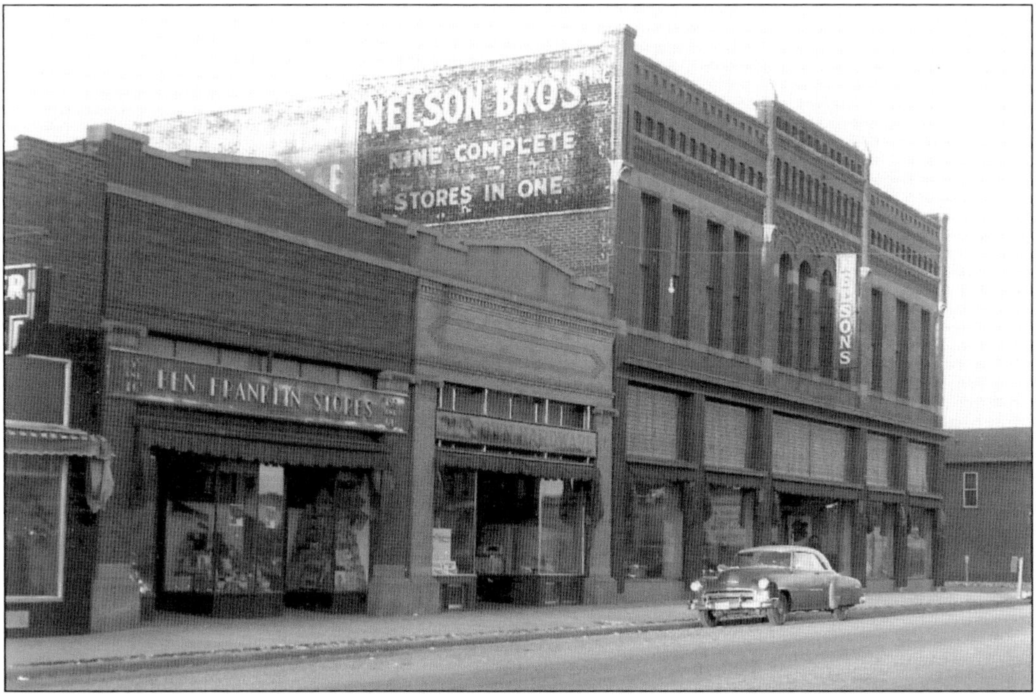

Here is the Nelson Brothers department store at a later date. From left to right are the Ben Franklin variety store, the Our Own Hardware store, and Nelson Brothers. The advertisement on the wall boasts that Nelson Brothers had nine complete stores in one. This is a good depiction of the local shopping experience at the time.

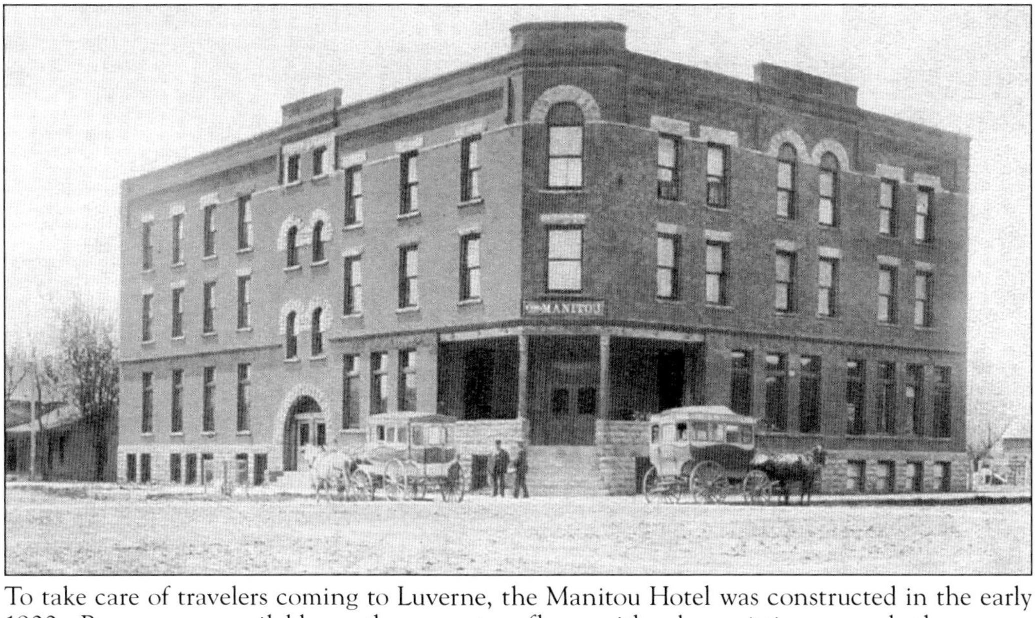

To take care of travelers coming to Luverne, the Manitou Hotel was constructed in the early 1900s. Rooms were available on the upper two floors with a large sitting room, bathrooms, a dining room, and a kitchen on the main floor. There were other smaller businesses located in the basement of the structure. Many travelers arriving by train took a wagon from the depot three blocks north to the Manitou.

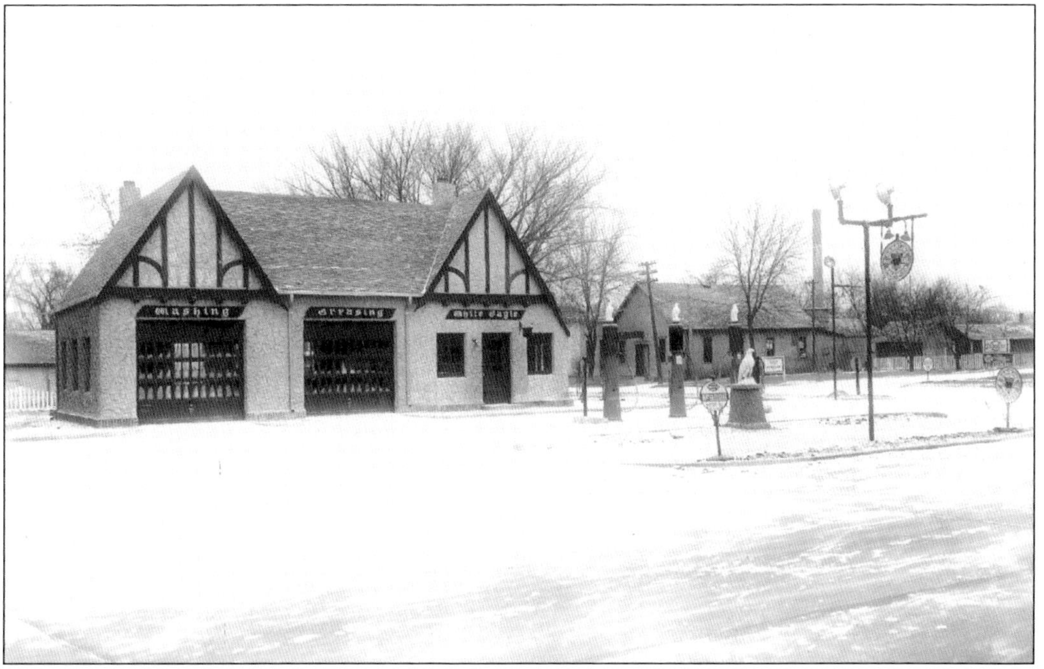

With the development of the automobile, there was also a need for service stations to maintain vehicles. This White Eagle gas station was located on the corner of Main and Estey Streets. Built with a stucco exterior and decorated with white eagles on top of the gas pumps, the gas station was a very attractive business for the time. The white eagle eventually changed to the flying red horse of the Mobil Oil Company.

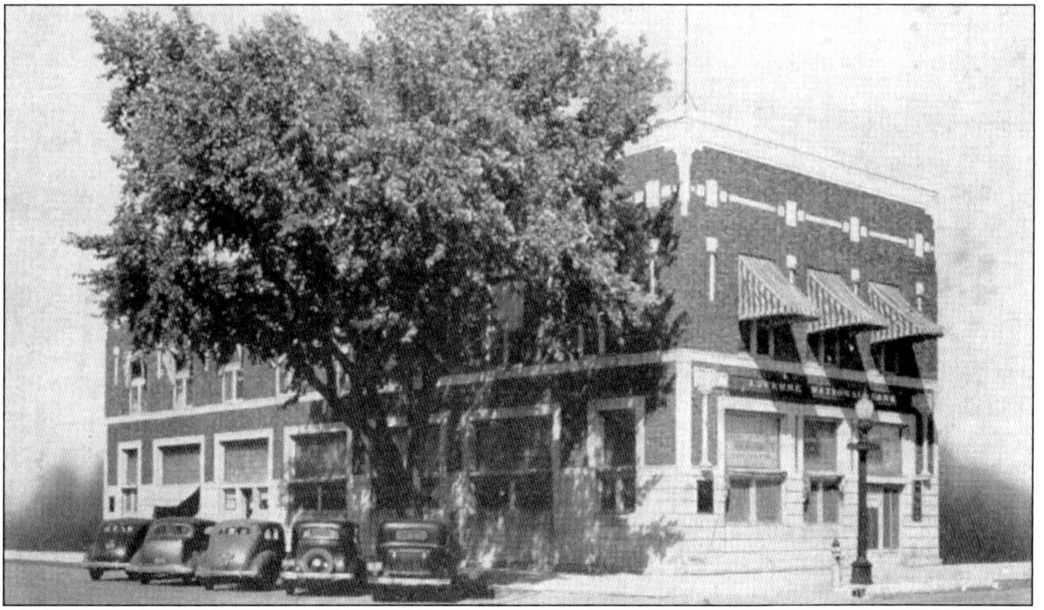

The Luverne National Bank, built in 1917, was on the corner of Main and Cedar Streets. The building exists today, but the tree next to it, labeled a "Century Tree" in 1967, is gone. It was very large and one of the few trees found in downtown Luverne. In addition to the bank, the upper story of the building contained medical and business offices.

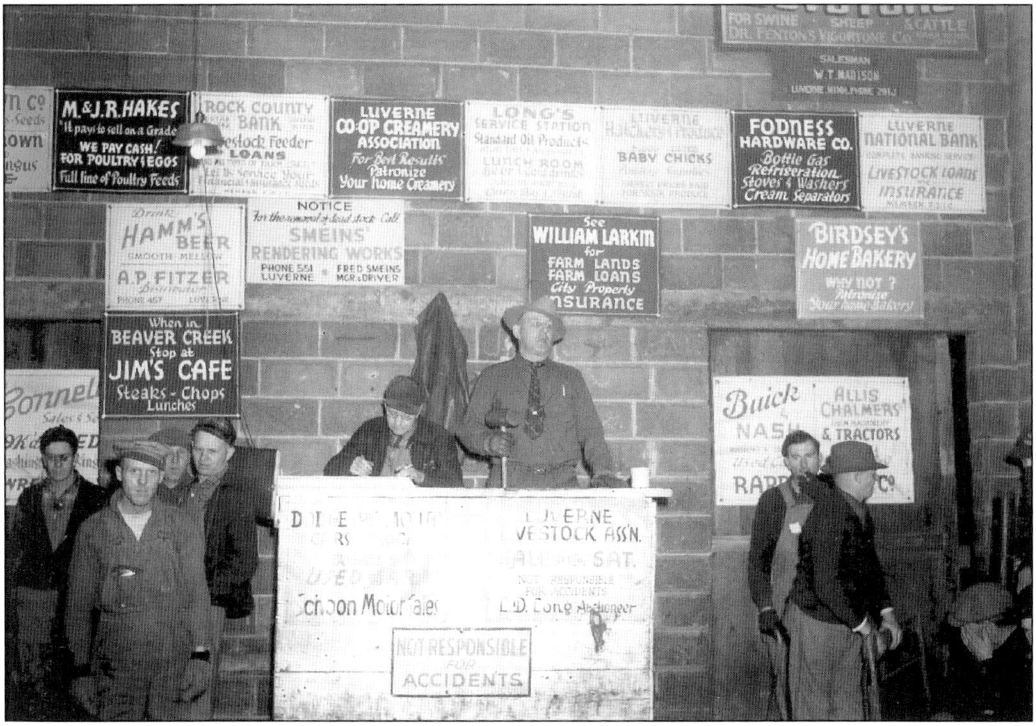

This photograph shows Col. Lloyd Long as auctioneer at the local sales barn for the weekly Saturday auctions. Weekly auctions provided a service for farmers in the sale of their livestock and brought farmers and others throughout the county together for socializing. In addition to his auctioneering, Colonel Long also owned a service station and restaurant.

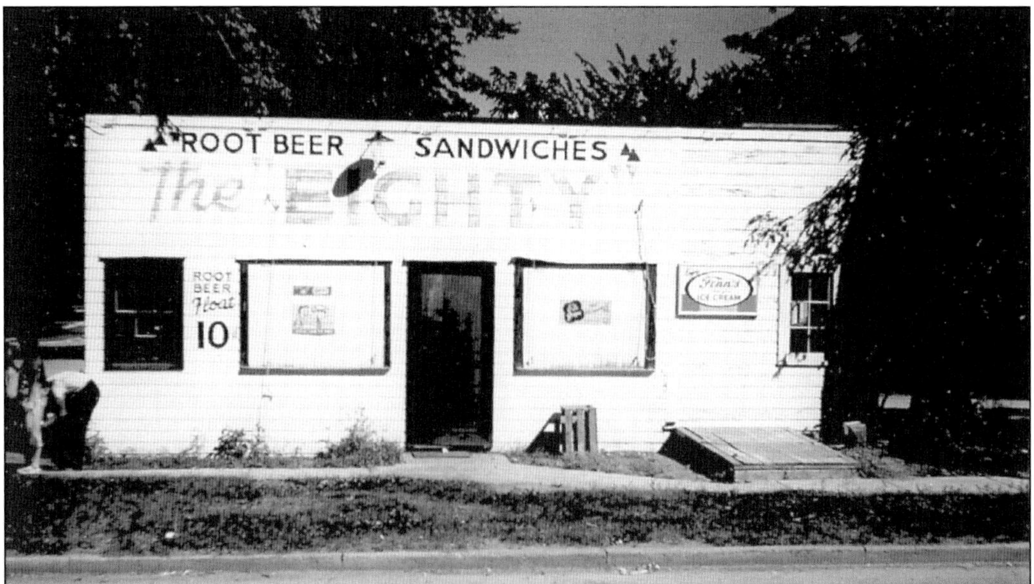

A small but unique part of Luverne Americana was the Eighty drive-in. Located on North Highway 75, this drive-in was a popular eatery for kids and families alike. The building was moved to the local fairgrounds to make room for the present Grace Lutheran Church at this location.

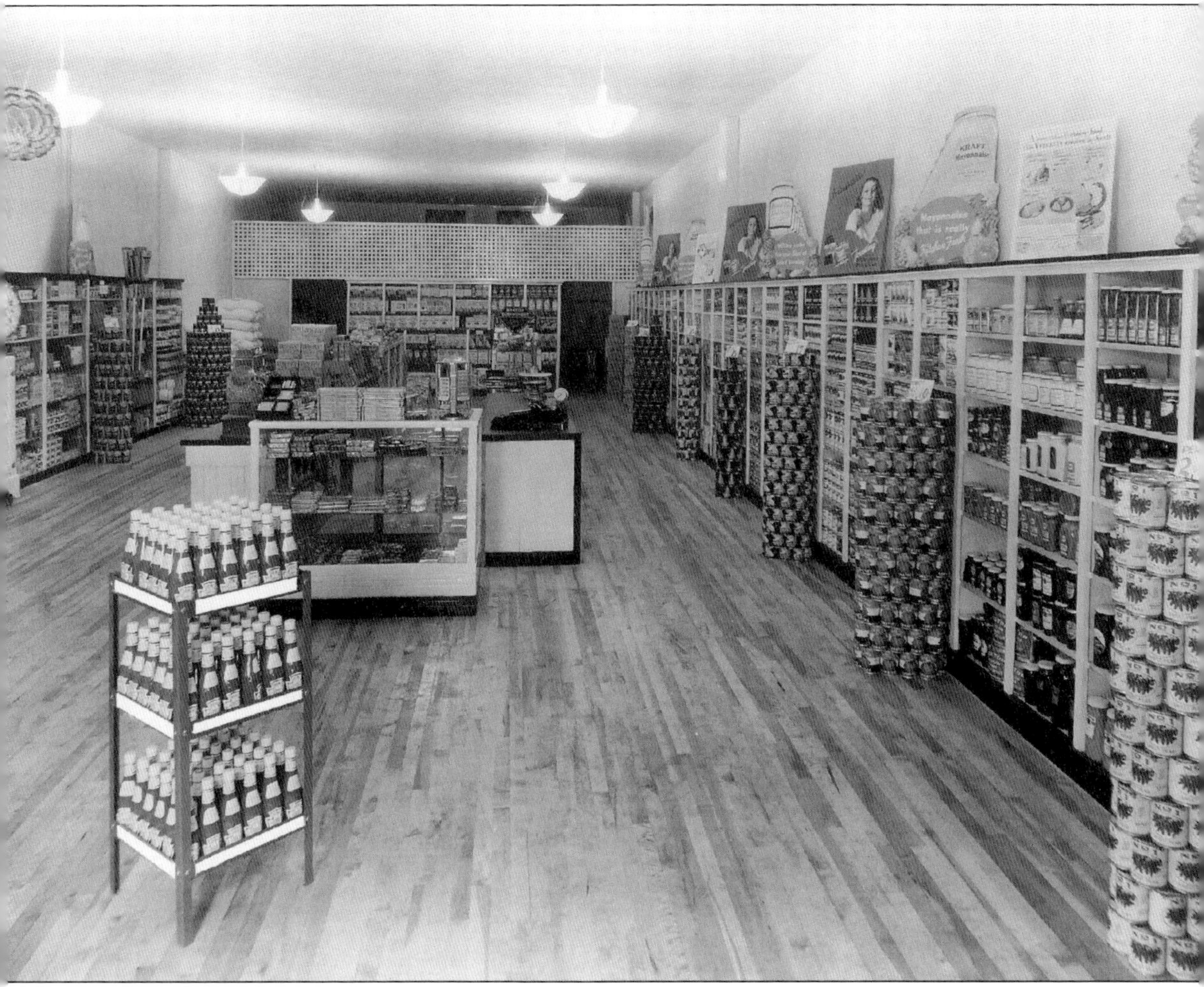

Groceries were a necessity for any family. Pictured here is the interior of a typical grocery store found in the early to mid-20th century. Compared to the grocery stores of today, there are considerably fewer items; although, it appears that there is much more room to see the items that were available.

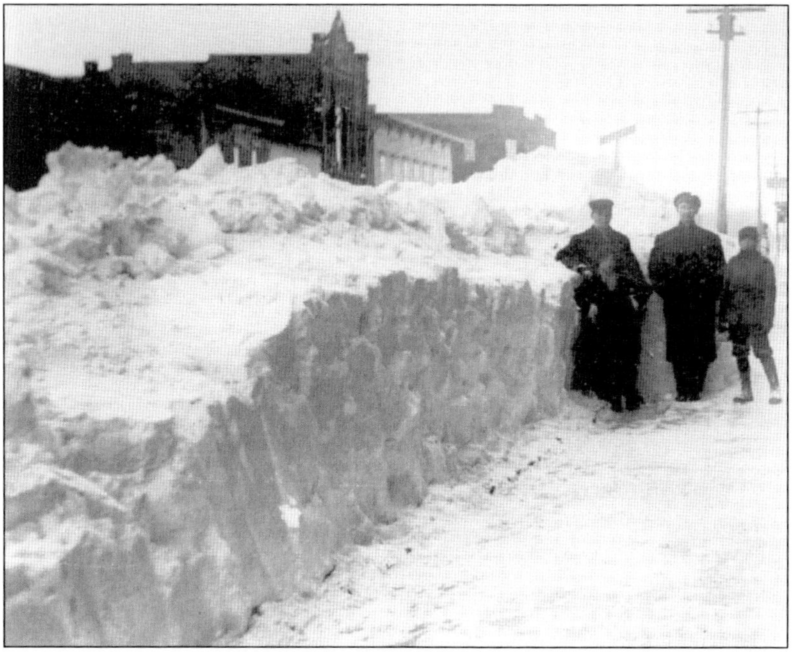

A number of things can hamper business in the community. In 1909, a blizzard struck Luverne and made it virtually impossible for people to get to town for a number of days. This photograph shows the size of the drifts that accumulated on Main Street after the storm.

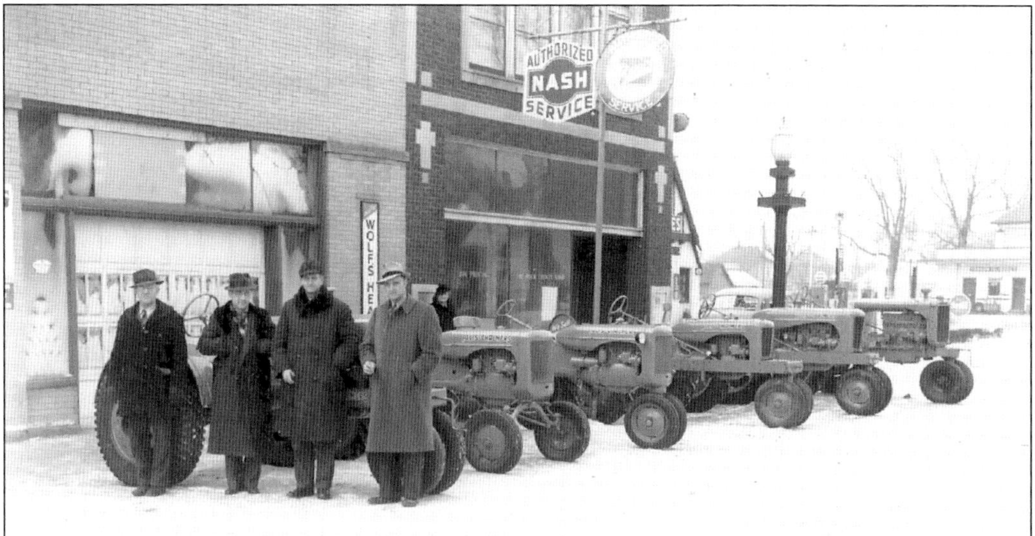

Introducing the newest line of machinery available to farmers was always a big event in a small community. Shown here is the latest in Allis Chalmers machinery, along with owners and salespersons ready to sell the machinery to those who are interested. The sign for Nash automobile service indicates that many of these farm machinery dealers also handled automobiles.

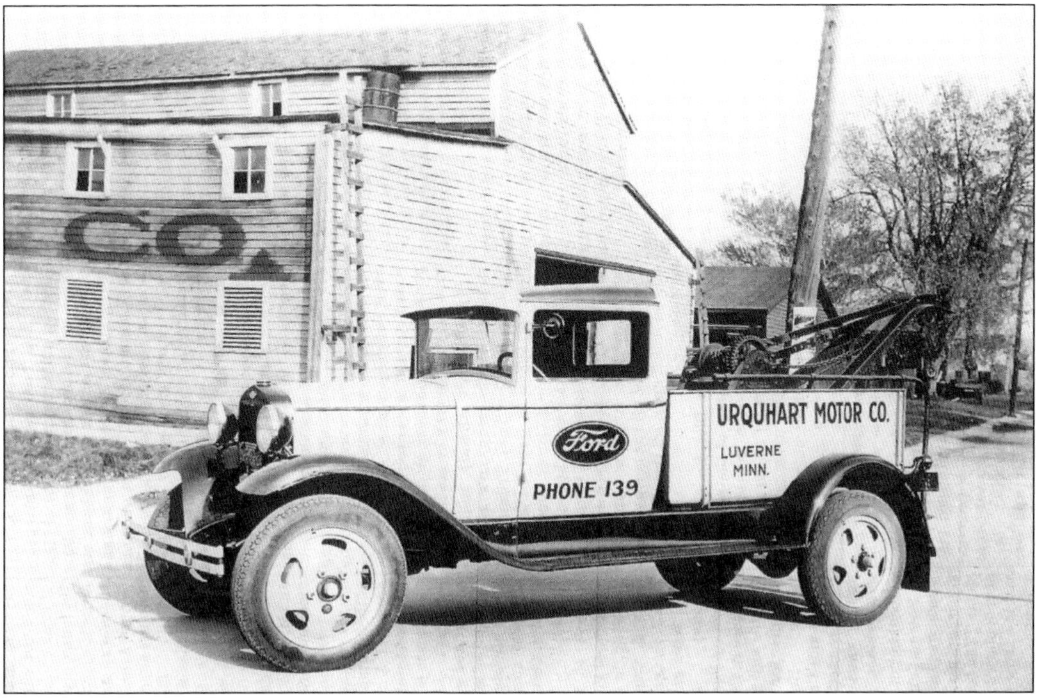

The Ford motor dealership has been a part of Luverne for many years. Shown here is the 1930s wrecker for Urquhart Motor Company.

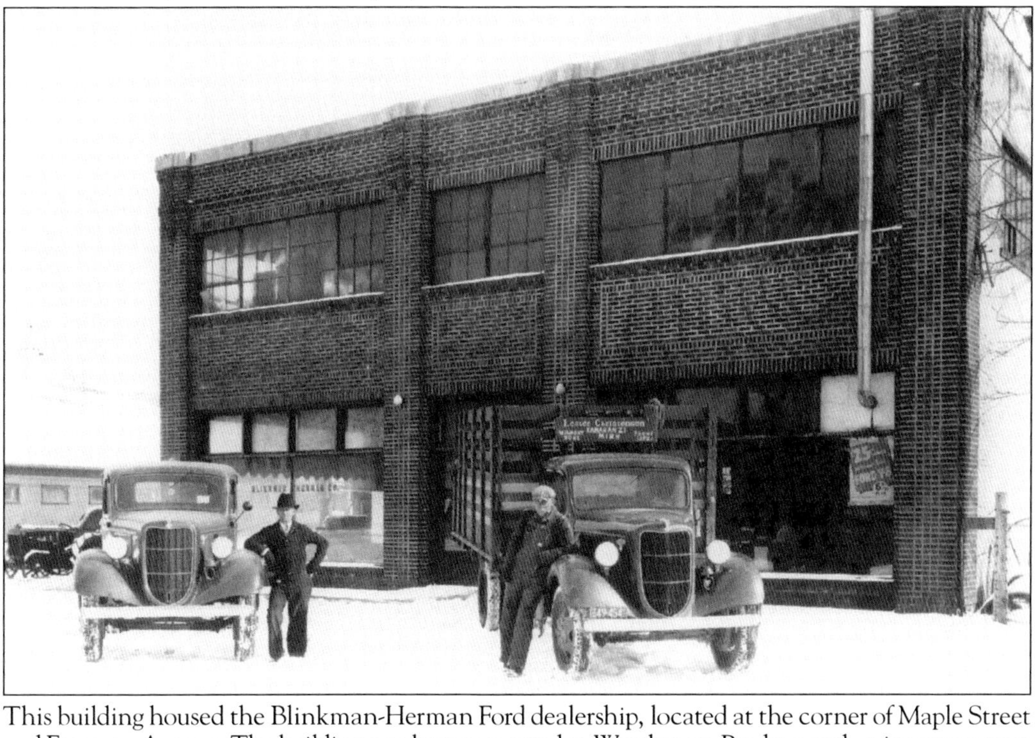

This building housed the Blinkman-Herman Ford dealership, located at the corner of Maple Street and Freeman Avenue. The building was later converted to Worthmore Produce and an ice cream store and meat locker. It was then changed to housing and is now the home of Camelot apartments.

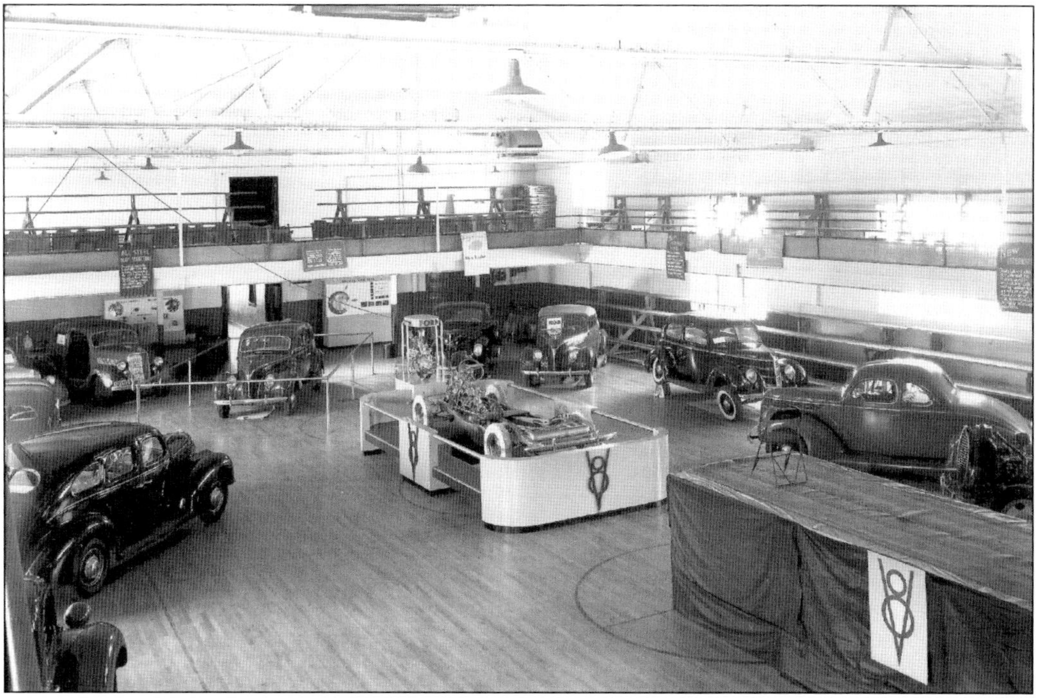

The local armory was used for a number of business events. This particular event was the introduction of the new Ford V-8 engine. Because the space available at the dealership was too small, the vehicles were moved to the local armory, and the center display was set up to promote the introduction of the new Ford engine.

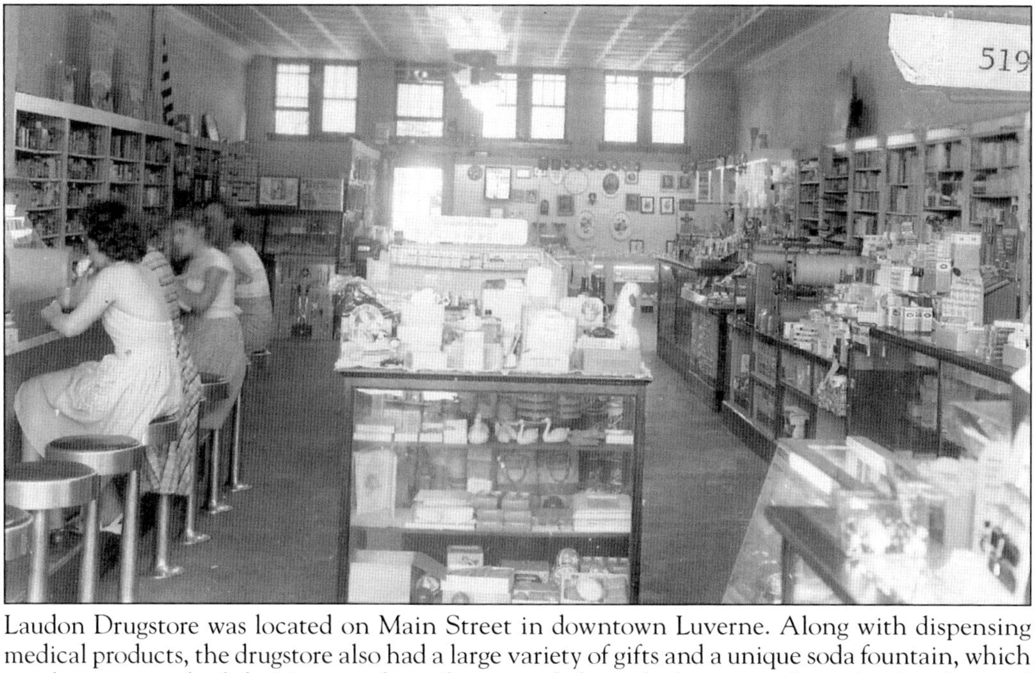

Laudon Drugstore was located on Main Street in downtown Luverne. Along with dispensing medical products, the drugstore also had a large variety of gifts and a unique soda fountain, which can be seen on the left. Many students frequented the soda fountain after school and school events. It was a great place to meet friends and share some ice cream.

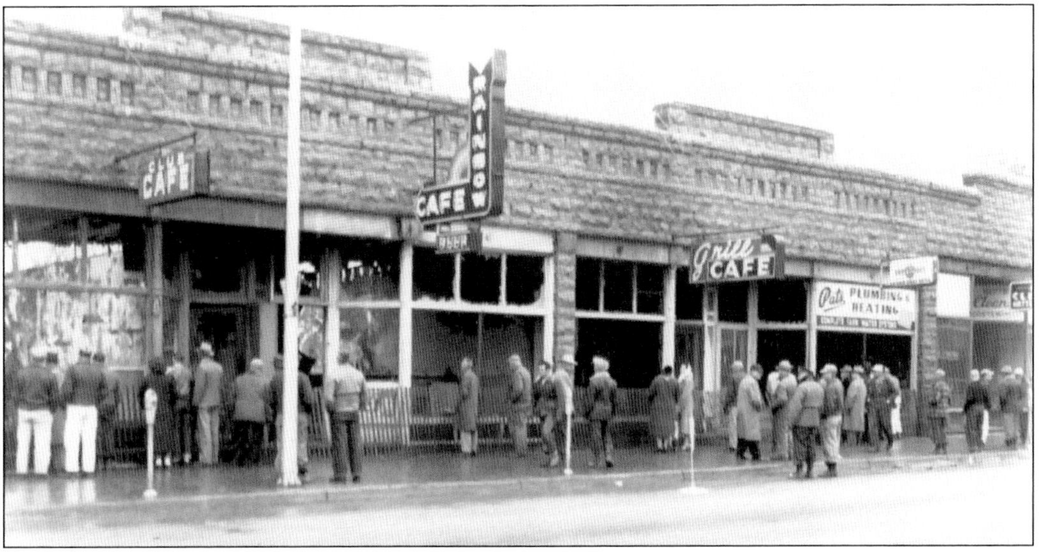

Downtown Luverne was dealt a severe blow caused by a fire on Main Street. This photograph shows, from left to right, Club Café, Rainbow Café, Grill Café, Pat's Plumbing and Heating, and United Cleaners totally gutted from the fire. The blaze likely started in one of the basements and spread quickly to the other businesses. Eventually, the Rock County Bank with a drive-through window replaced this row of storefronts.

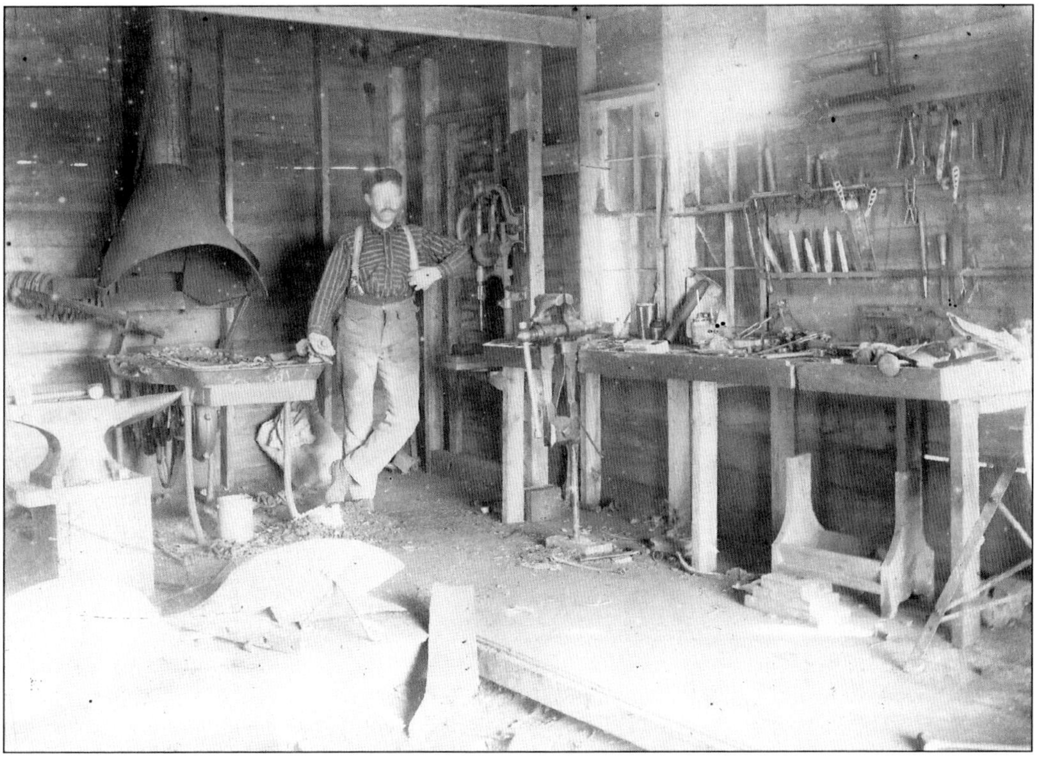

One of the early businesses in Magnolia was the blacksmith and wagon shop. This two-story building was used for the manufacture and repair of wooden wagons, with the lower floor used as the blacksmith shop.

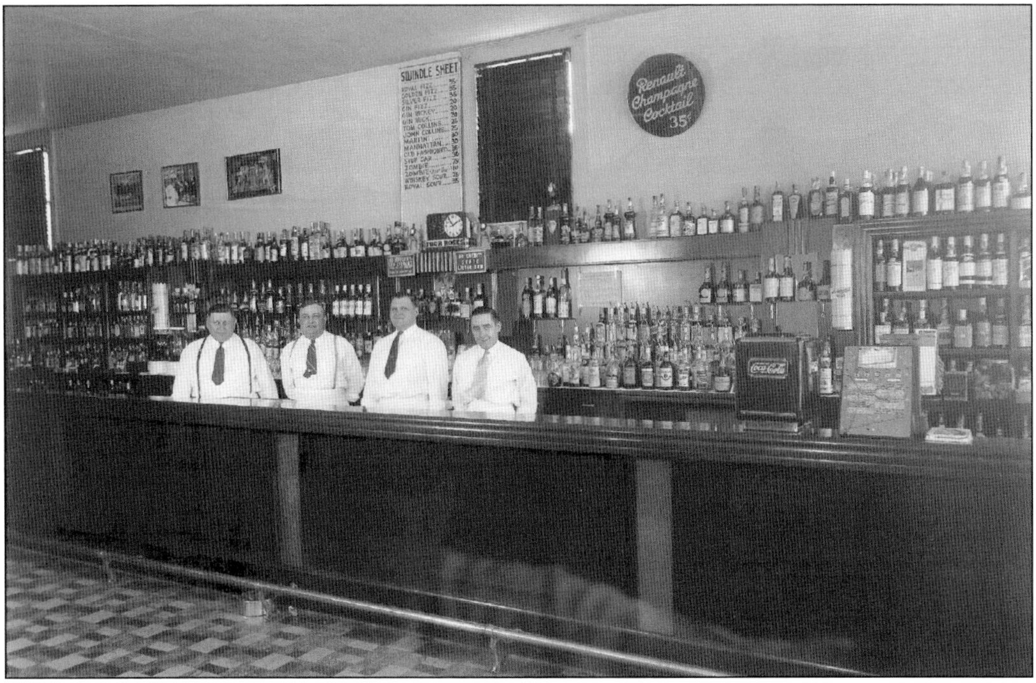

Another business in Magnolia that gained popularity over the years was the Magnolia Bar. Four bartenders are seen here posing for the camera. The bar remained a popular gathering place in Magnolia for many years.

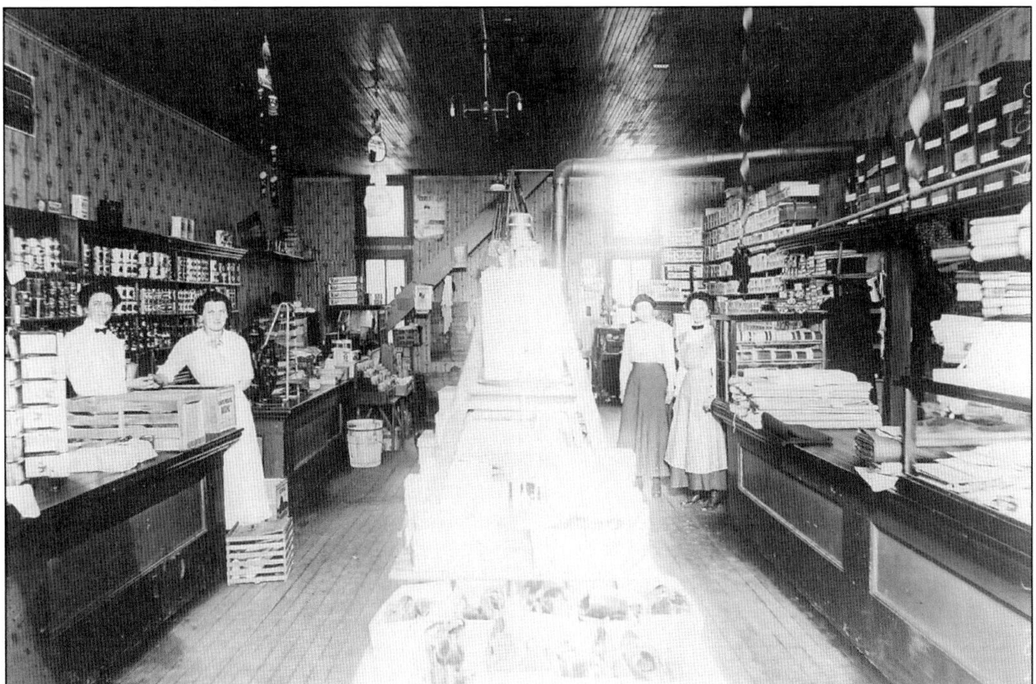

This photograph shows the country store in Magnolia. At the back of the store is the stairway used by the store owners to access their residence.

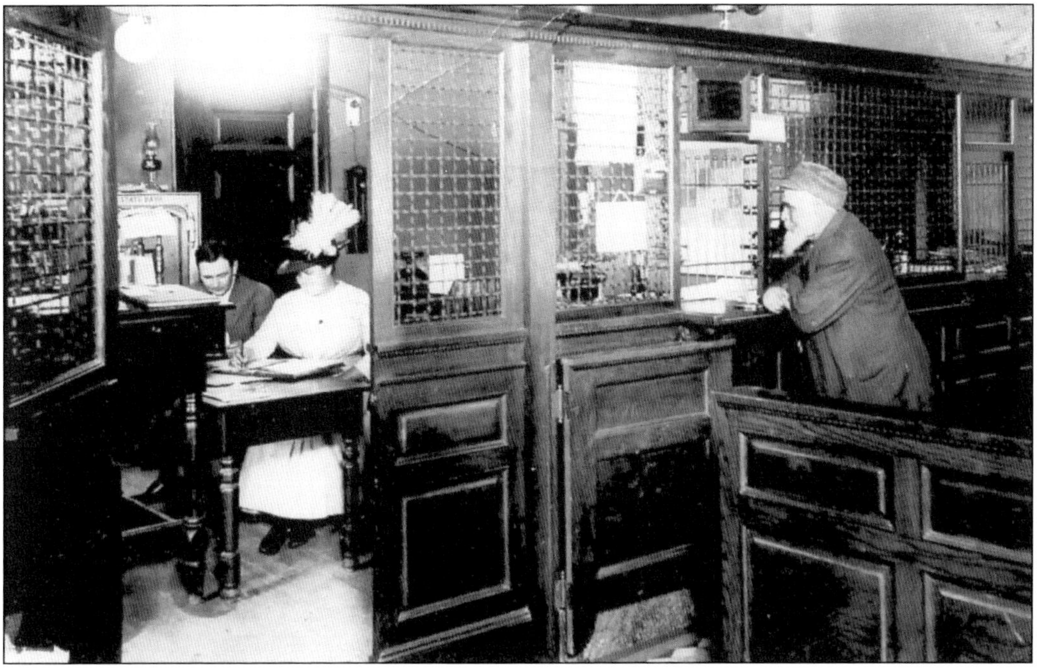

The Magnolia State Bank provided not only financial services but also a place to gather in the community. The structure was fairly simple, with a wooden wall and grated windows separating the outer lobby from the business office and safe in the back of the building.

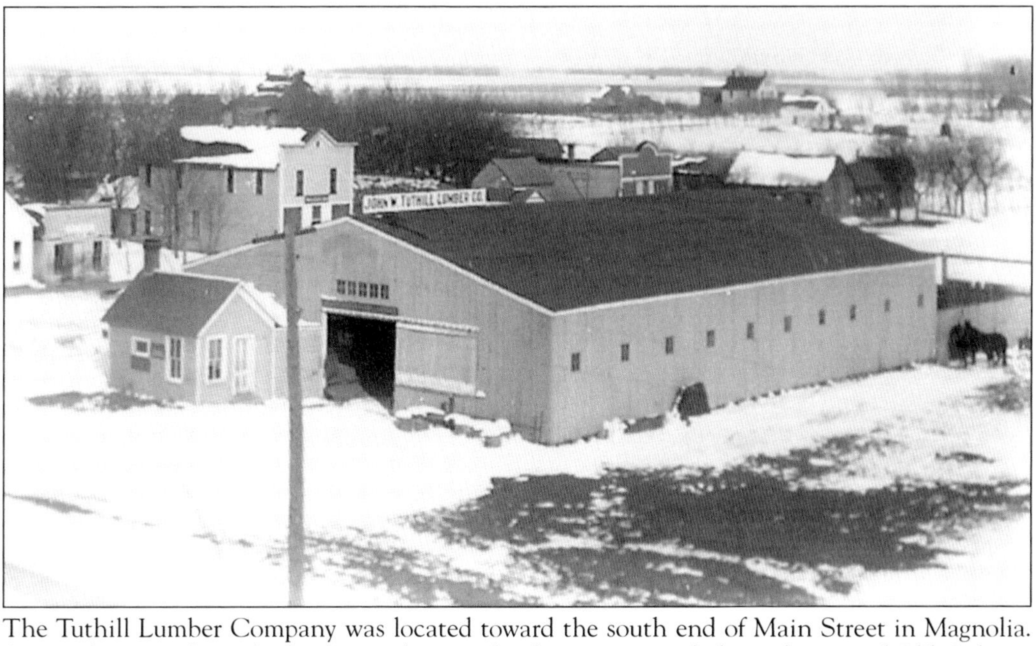

The Tuthill Lumber Company was located toward the south end of Main Street in Magnolia. Across the street from the lumberyard were other businesses, including a livery and Olds Saloon. The lumber company was a large building with openings at both the east and west ends. The office is on the left side of the building.

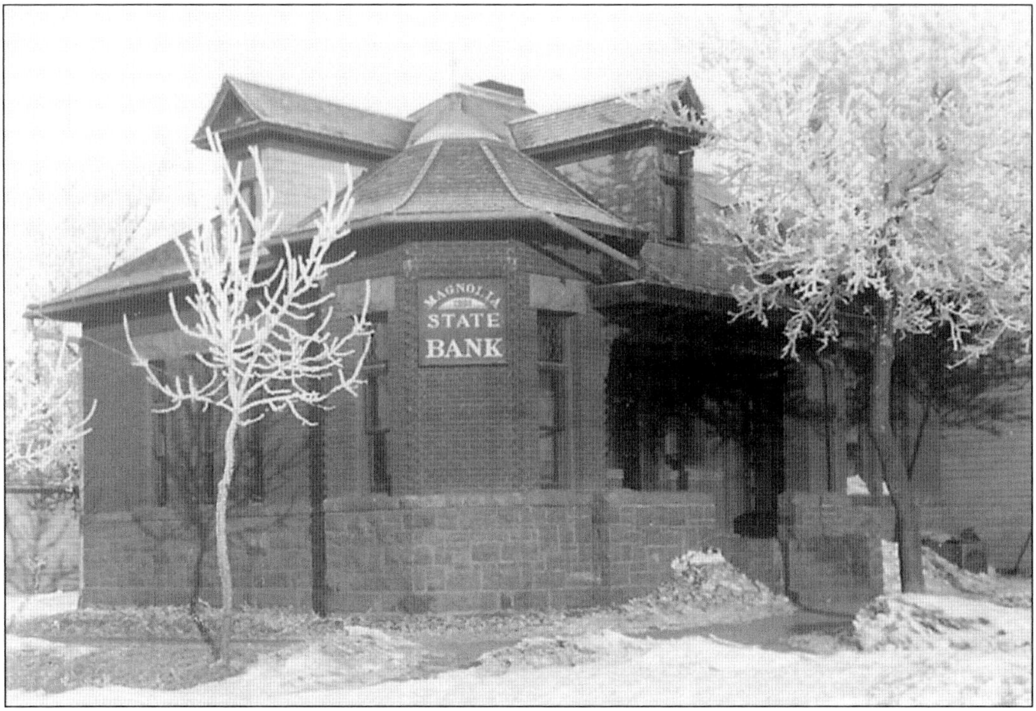

The Magnolia State Bank started in 1901 and moved into this brick building in 1902. Though a few changes have been made, the structure remains on the south edge of Main Street. At the time this beautiful building was constructed, it was the first of its kind in Magnolia made of brick.

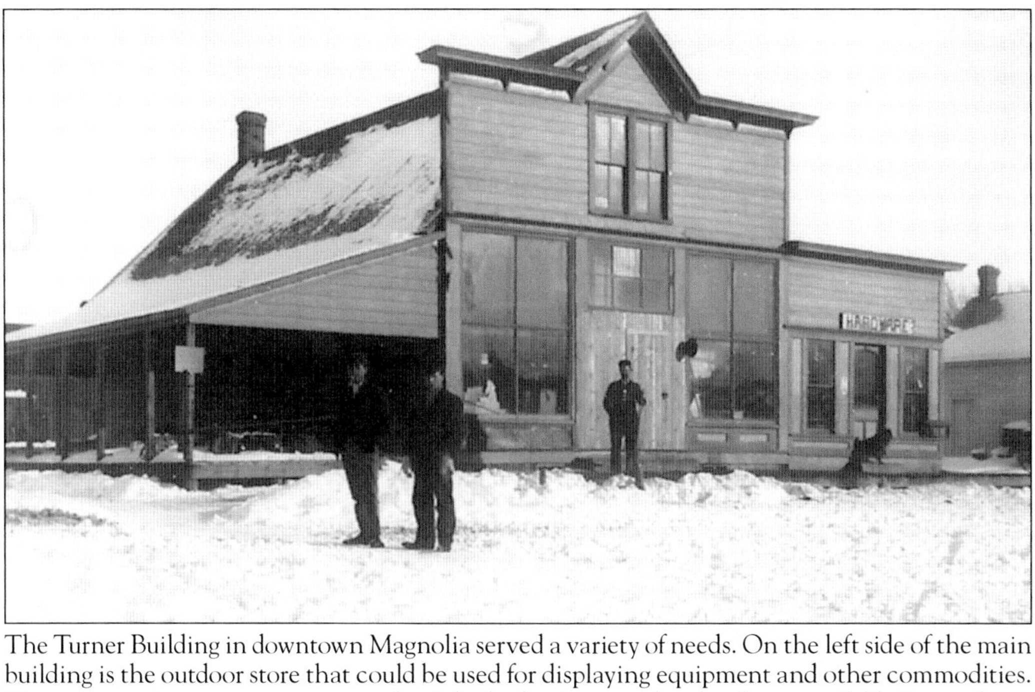

The Turner Building in downtown Magnolia served a variety of needs. On the left side of the main building is the outdoor store that could be used for displaying equipment and other commodities. The main portion was a grocery store, but it had other items such as hardware available for purchase. The smaller building on the right side of the structure was the owner's residence.

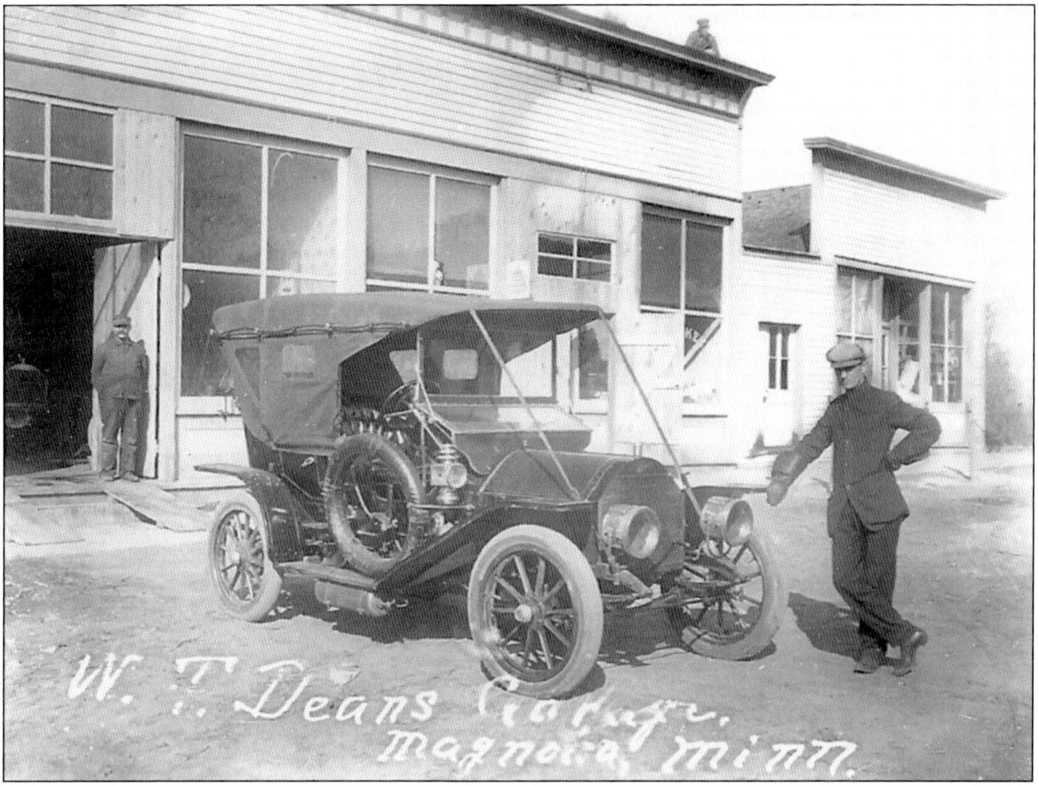

Another early business in downtown Magnolia was Dean's repair shop. Pictured is one of the vehicles repaired there. Dean also built three vehicles in the shop that were sold to others.

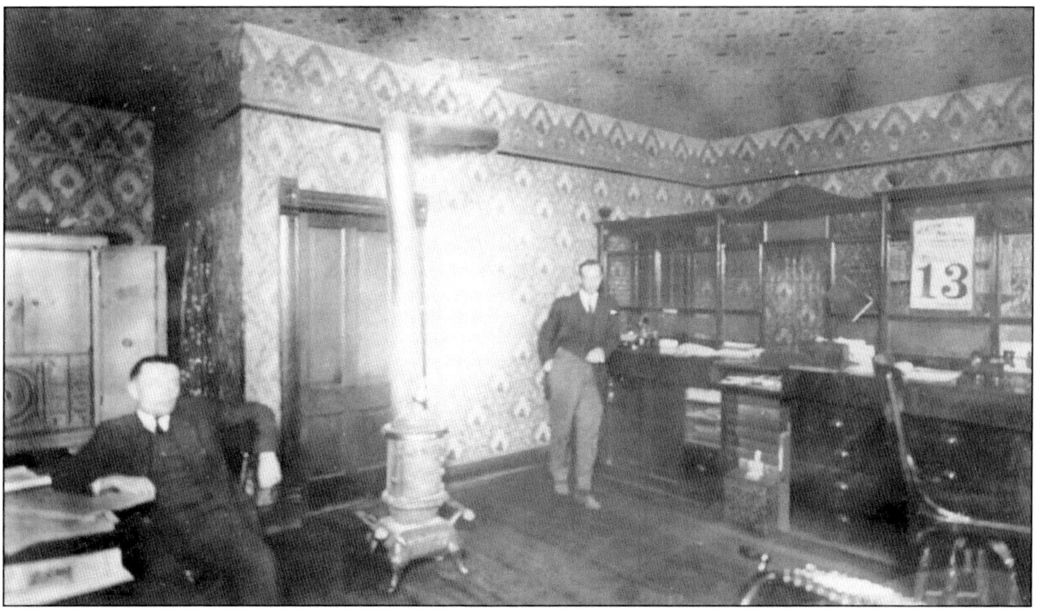

The Kenneth State Bank was built in 1903. It started as part of another business in 1901 with R.B. Hinkly as president and A.D. Parker as cashier. This image, taken in the early 1900s, shows Parker (left) and assistant cashier John Engebretson.

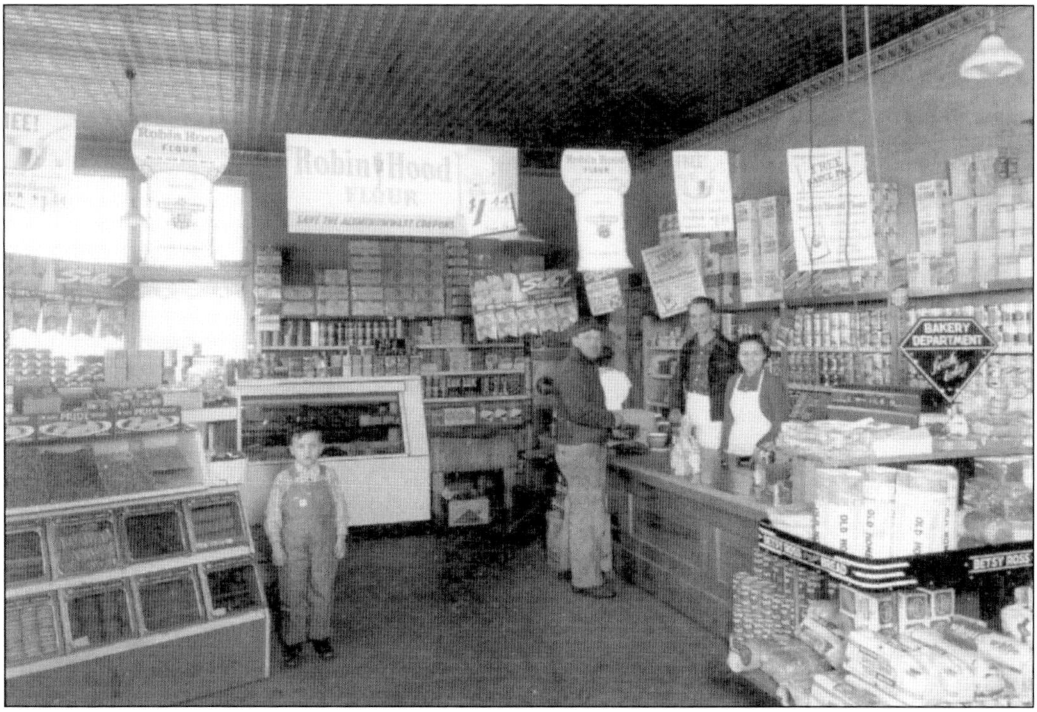

An early business in Kenneth was the Garner store. The Frank Garner Egg, Grocery, and Locker Plant was located in the front of the E.L. Rogness blacksmith shop. Pictured serving customers are owner Frank Garner and clerk Martha Abel.

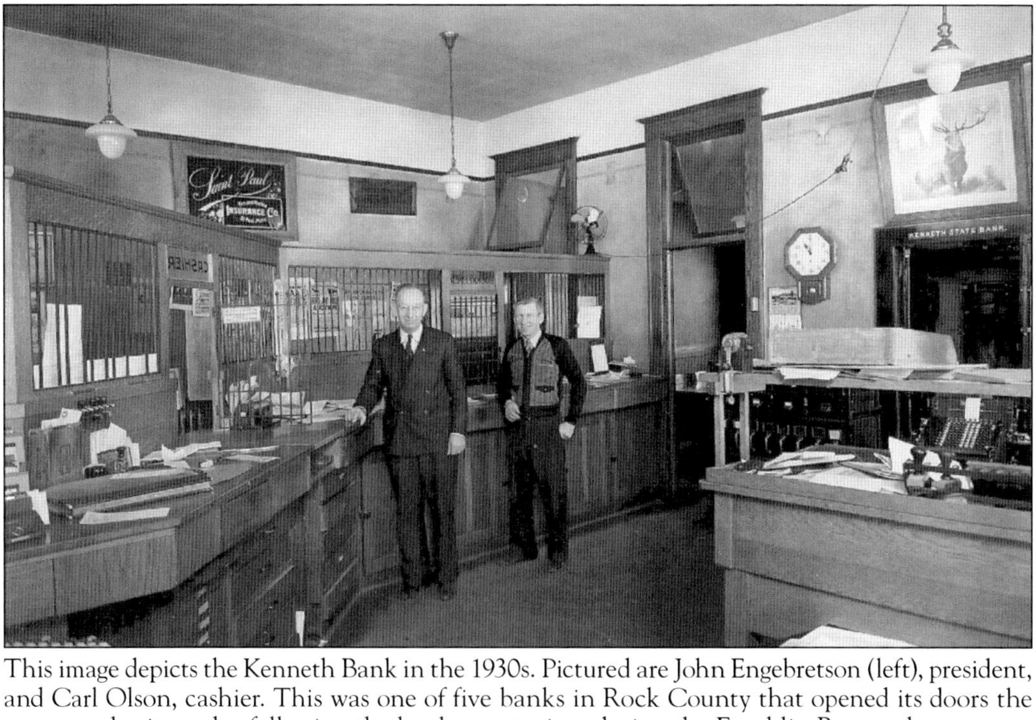

This image depicts the Kenneth Bank in the 1930s. Pictured are John Engebretson (left), president, and Carl Olson, cashier. This was one of five banks in Rock County that opened its doors the very next business day following the bank moratorium during the Franklin Roosevelt era.

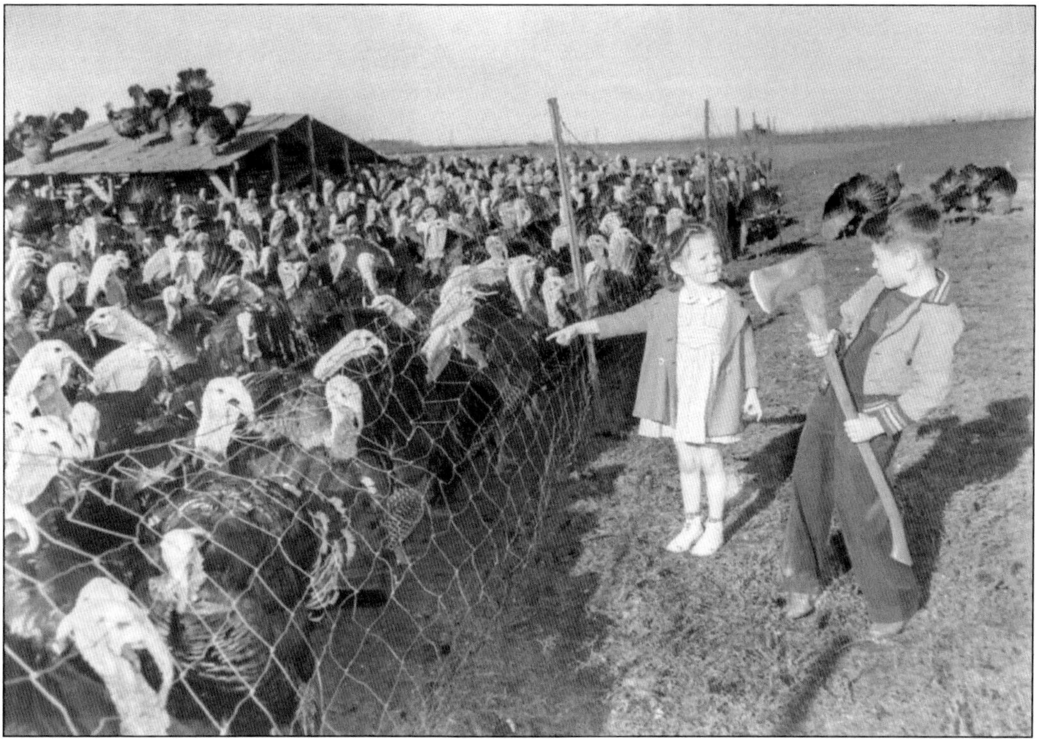

The turkey business was good in Rock County. Thousands were raised every year and shipped out for processing throughout the country. The boy and girl in this photograph are demonstrating the turkeys' fate—especially during the Thanksgiving holiday.

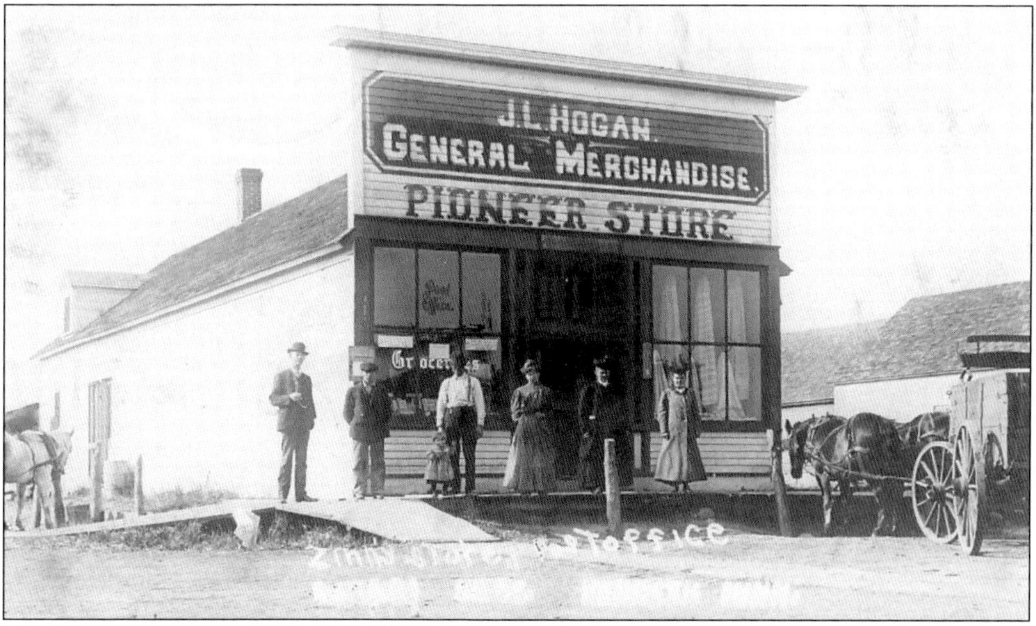

The J.L. Hagan general merchandise store was the first of its kind in Kenneth, built in 1901. In addition to the store, the business also served as the local post office. It was popular and busy enough to keep three people busy waiting on customers.

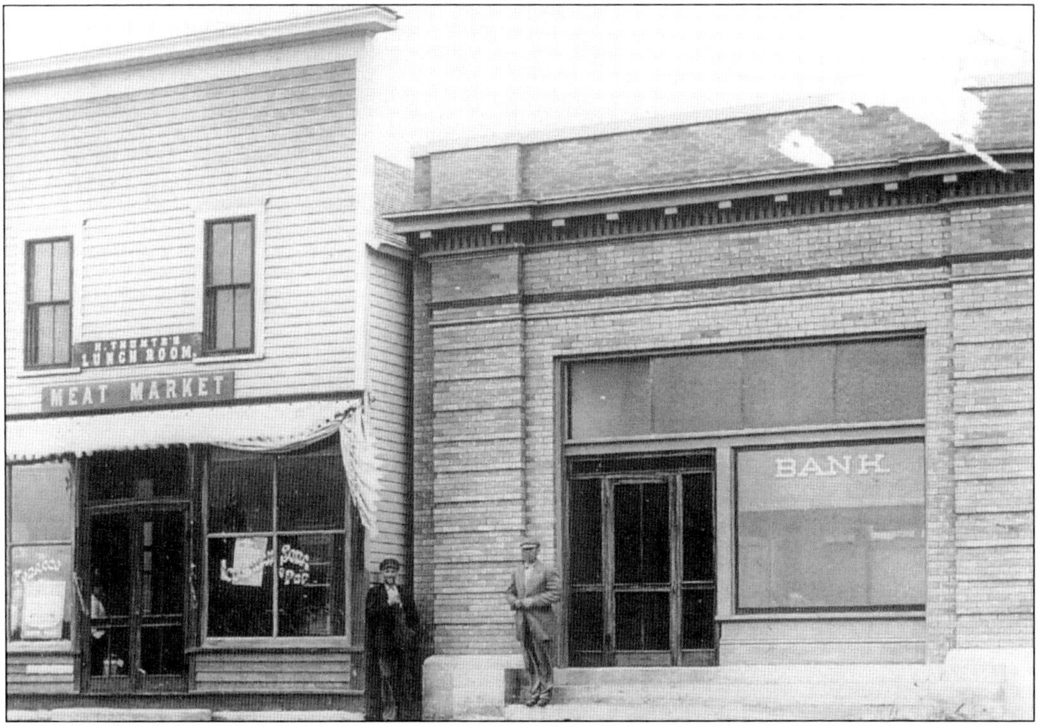

Pictured here is the new Kenneth Bank, which was built in 1903. To the left of the bank is the Herman Thomte meat market and lunch counter. Thomte also started the first livery barn and hotel in Kenneth.

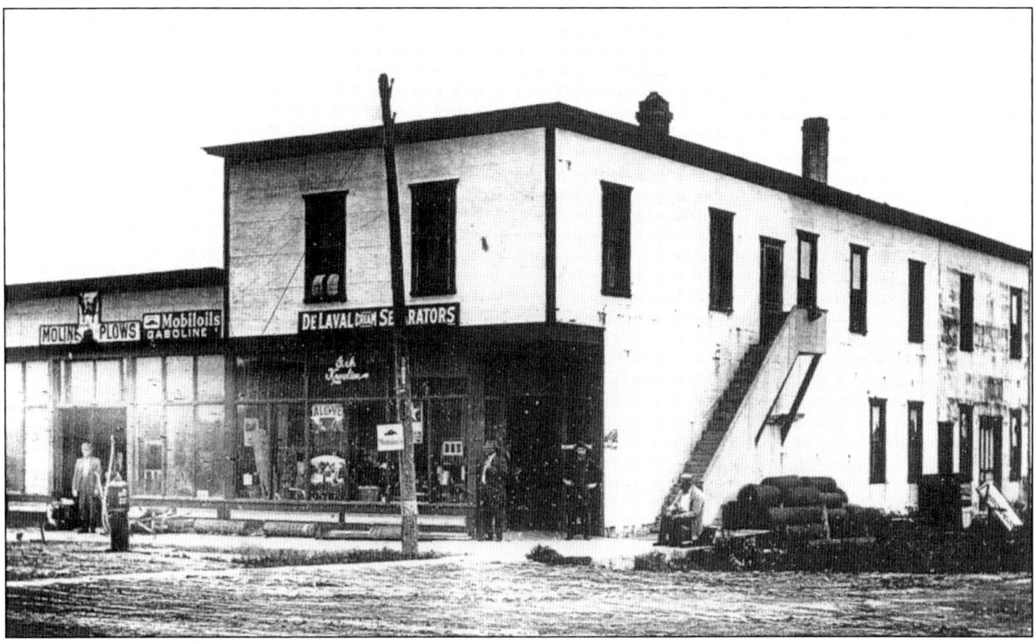

The Knowlton store was built in the early 1900s. This hardware store also provided a line of farm machinery and dairy products. Rolls of wire fencing can be seen along the side and in front of the building. It later became the VandeVelde Hardware Store.

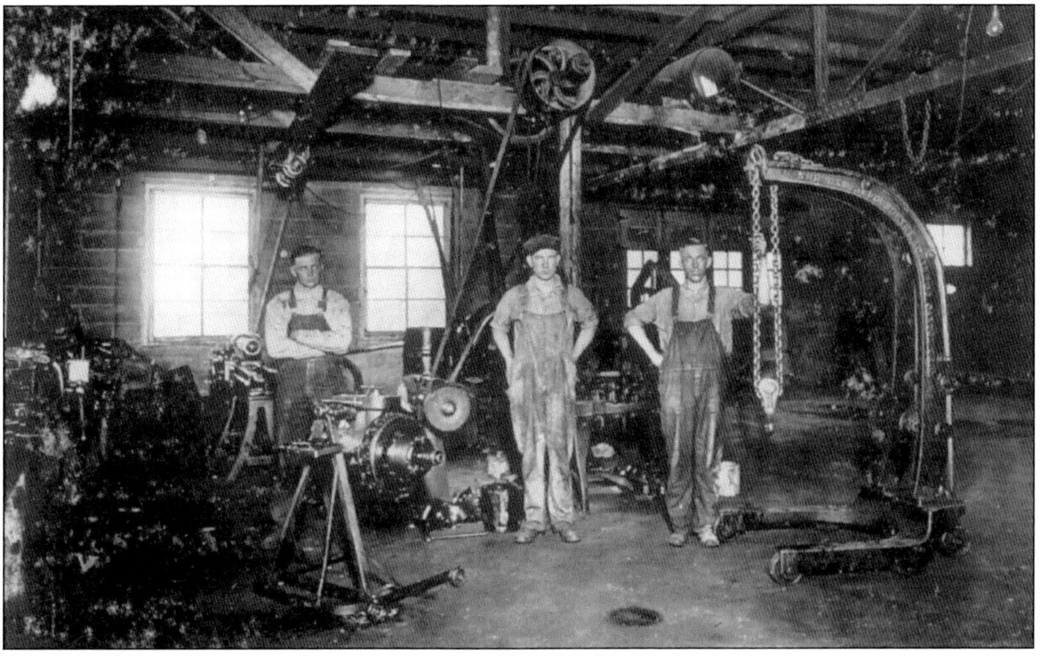

The E.L. Rogness blacksmith is pictured here. Leonard Rogness (right) also ran a corn-shelling and hay-baling business, started the Kenneth band, and was choir director for over 50 years at the Kenneth Lutheran Church. Leonard was instrumental in bringing movies to Kenneth during the 1940s and 1950s.

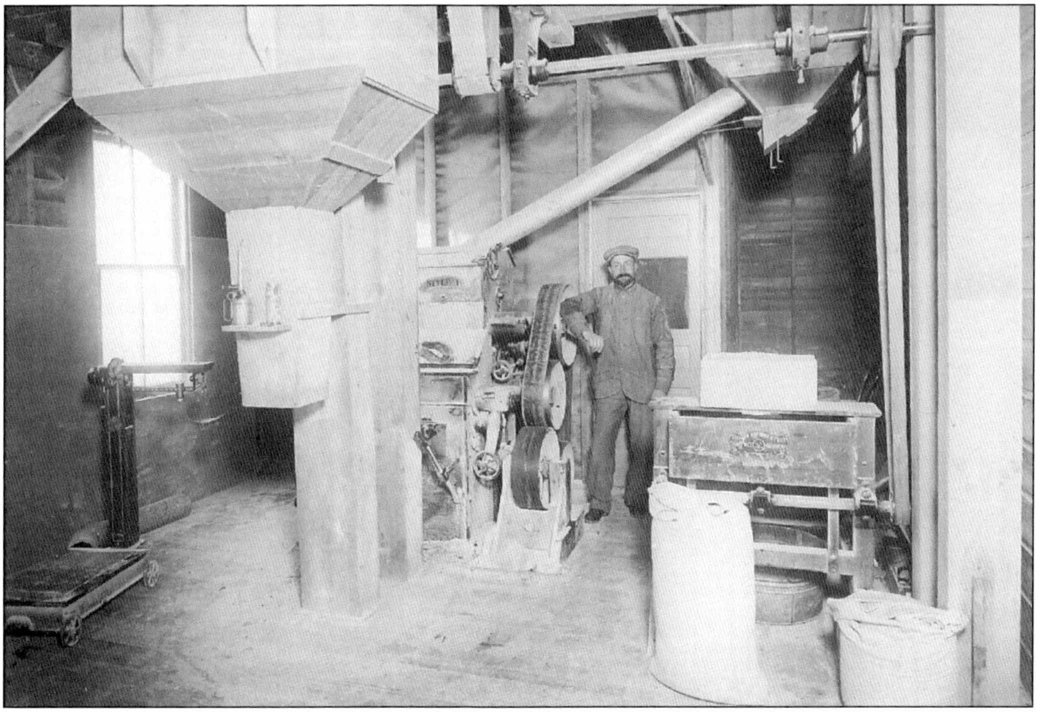

The Norby feed mill was one of the earliest businesses in Hills. Like other communities in Rock County, the local flour mill was a very important business for the grinding of feed and flour.

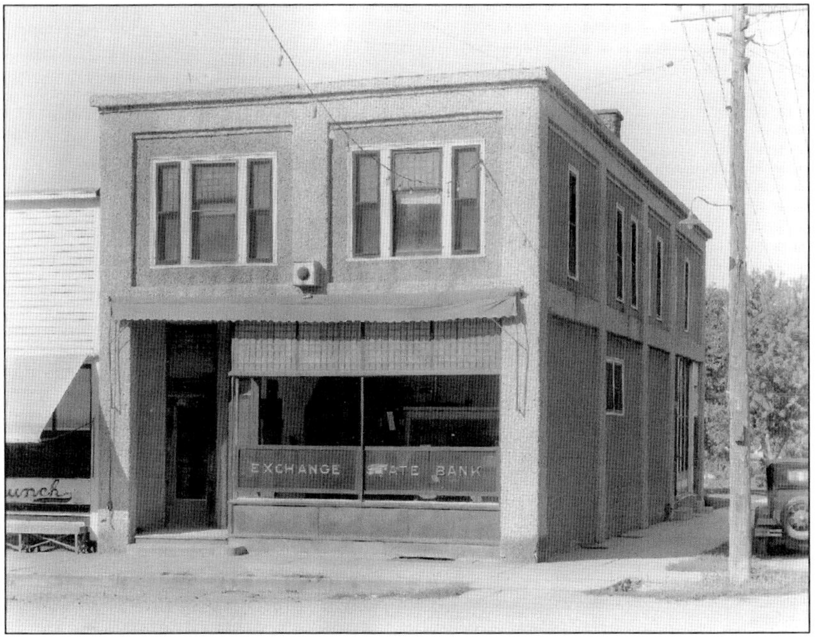

The Exchange State Bank of Hills erected this frame-and-stucco building in the 1930s. Living quarters were above the bank, and there was also room for a smaller business in the rear of the building. Note the alarm that is on the front that could be set off in the event of a bank robbery.

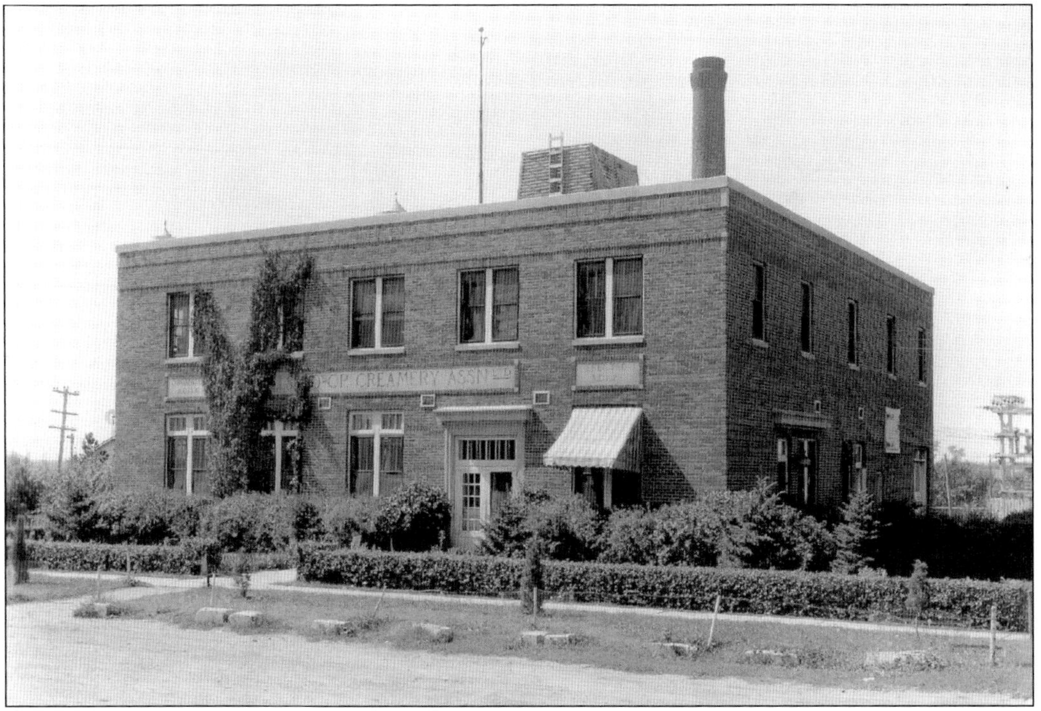

The Hills Co-op Creamery was constructed in 1927 and was one of the largest dairy-processing businesses in Rock County. The creamery took in raw milk from local farmers and processed it into pasteurized milk, cream, and butter available for sale. The association was made up of dairy producers in the Hills area.

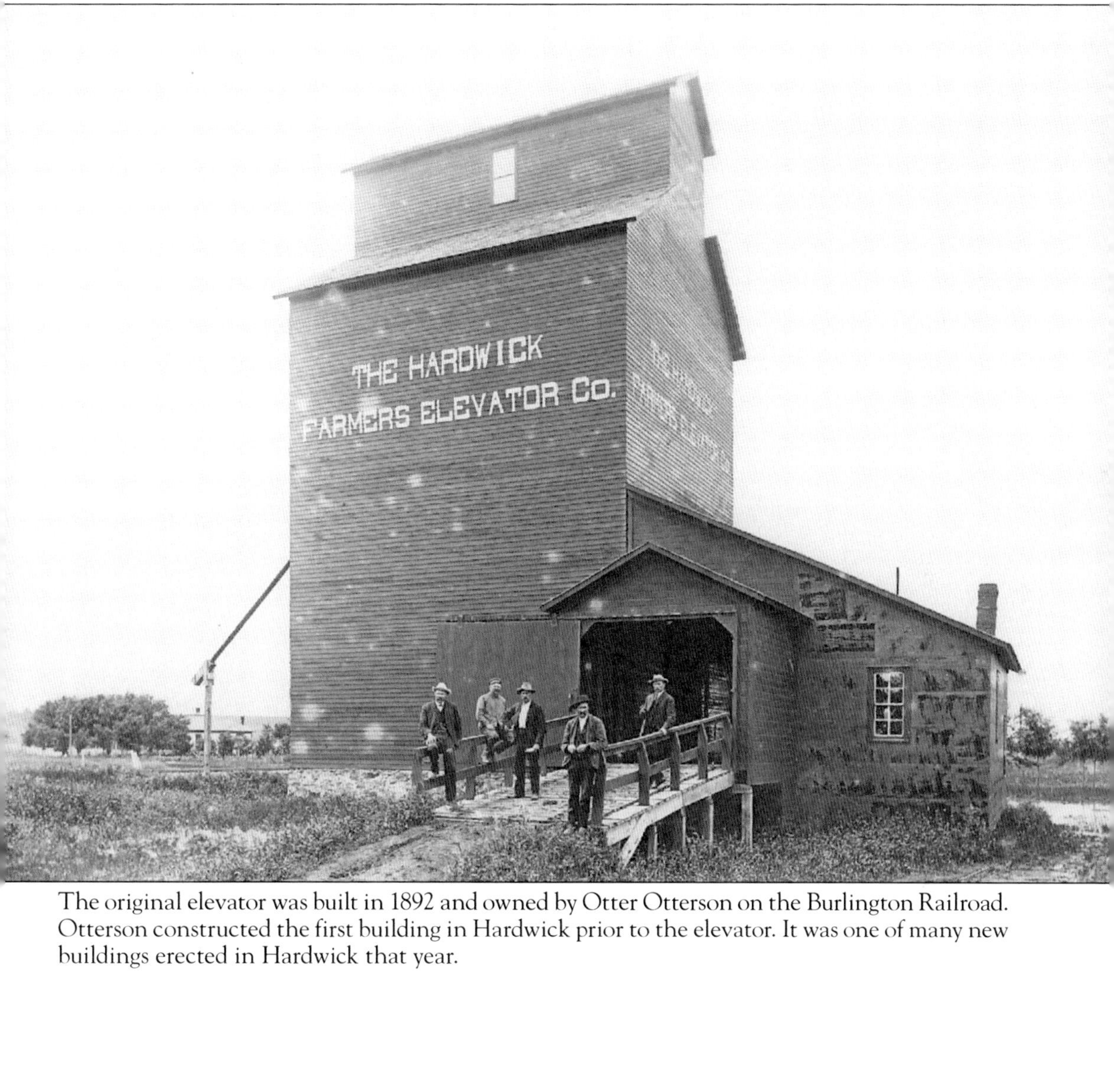

The original elevator was built in 1892 and owned by Otter Otterson on the Burlington Railroad. Otterson constructed the first building in Hardwick prior to the elevator. It was one of many new buildings erected in Hardwick that year.

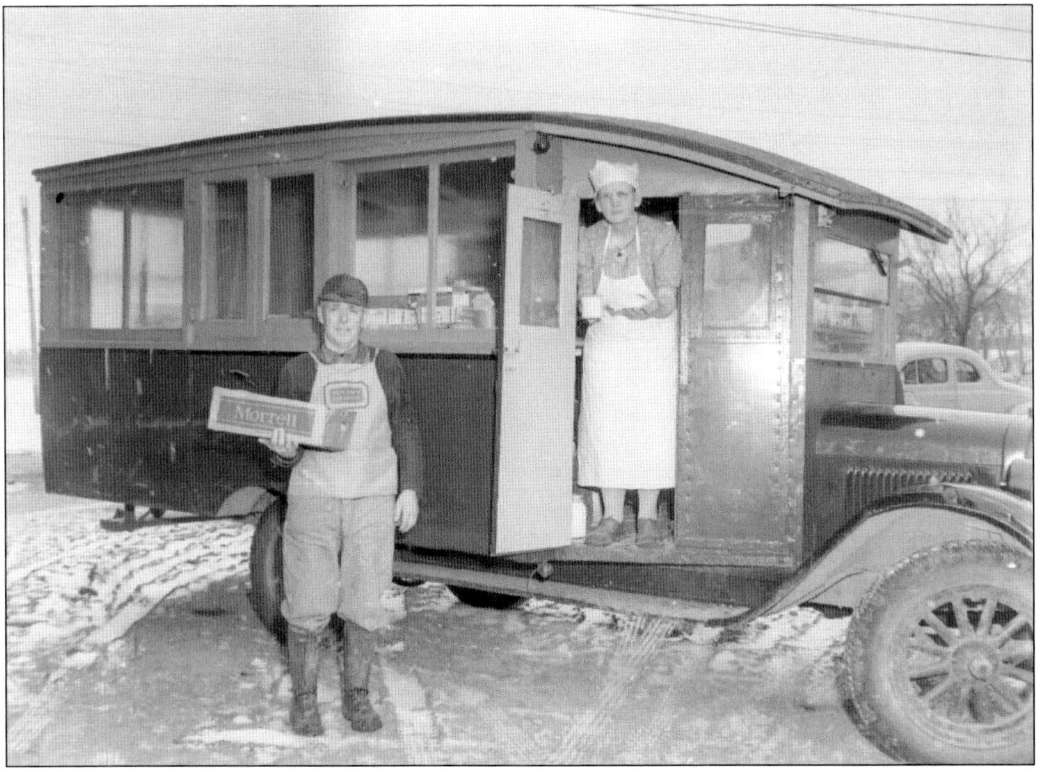

A unique business was the mobile lunch wagon. This wagon was used at farm sales and other community events. It was a forerunner to the present-day street vendors and mobile kitchens.

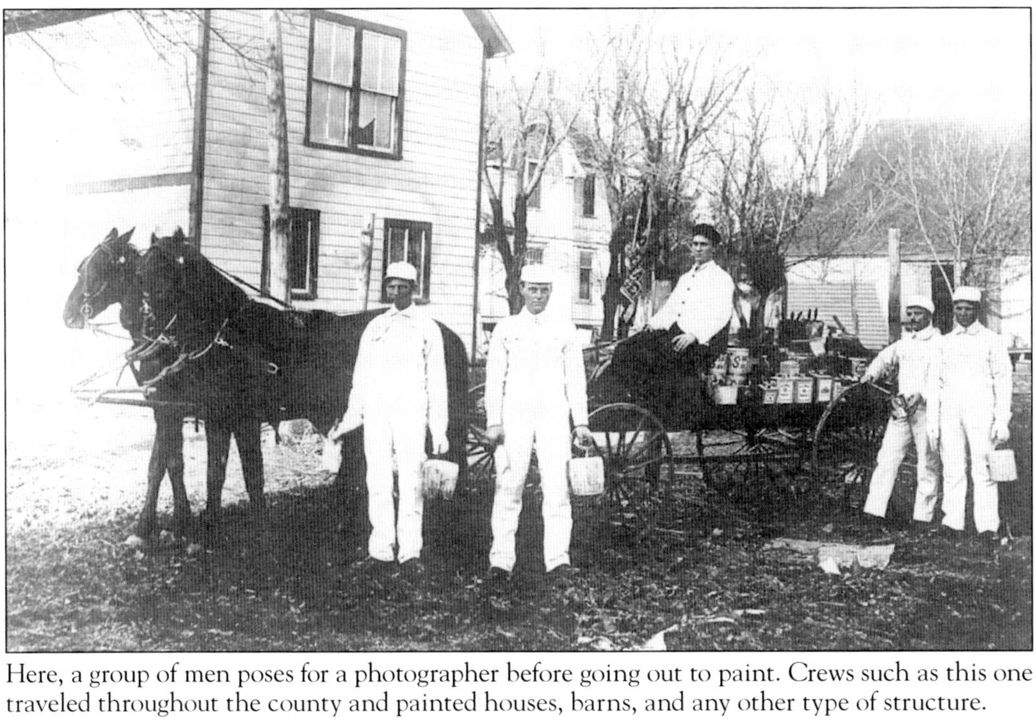

Here, a group of men poses for a photographer before going out to paint. Crews such as this one traveled throughout the county and painted houses, barns, and any other type of structure.

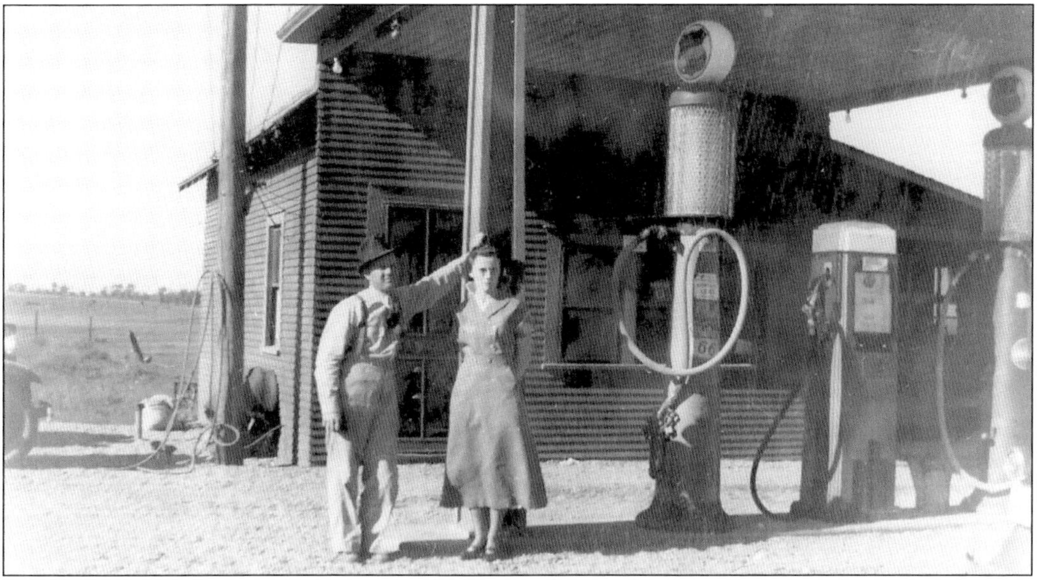

Beaver Creek gas station was located on the highway just off downtown Beaver Creek and became known as Arp's station. Pictured are Verlyn and Loretta Arp, who owned and ran the station for many years.

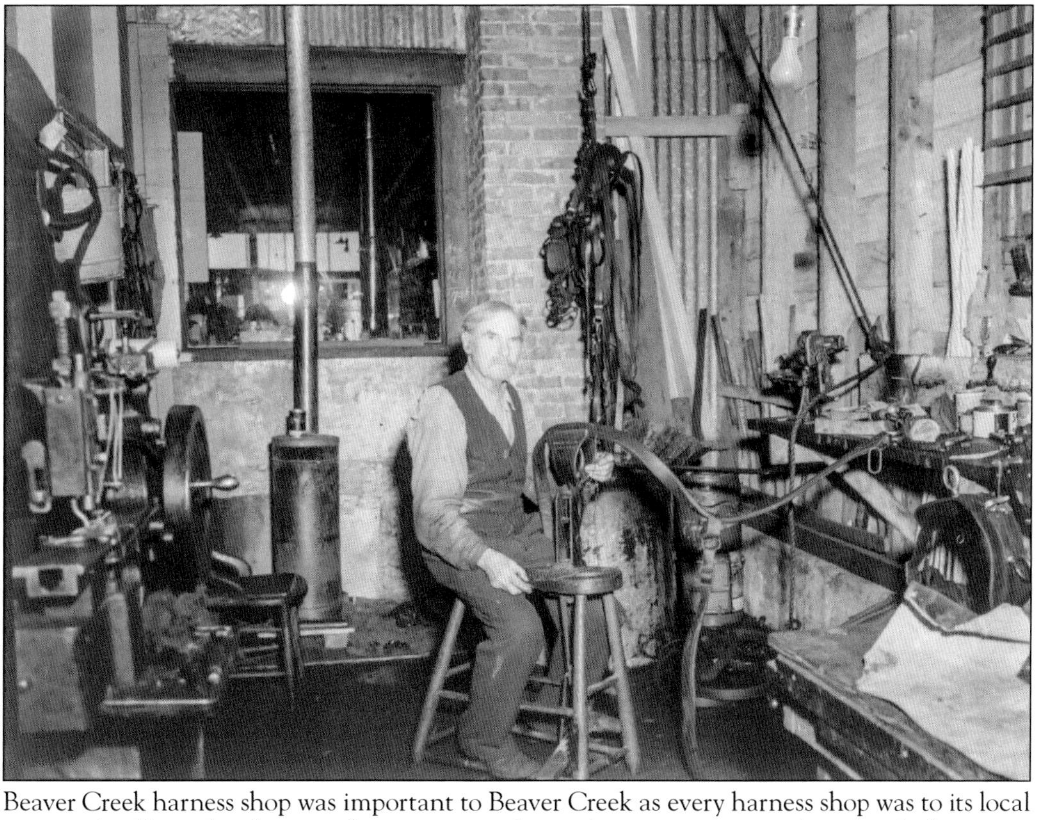

Beaver Creek harness shop was important to Beaver Creek as every harness shop was to its local community. From the photograph, one can see the equipment used to repair and make harnesses and other leather goods.

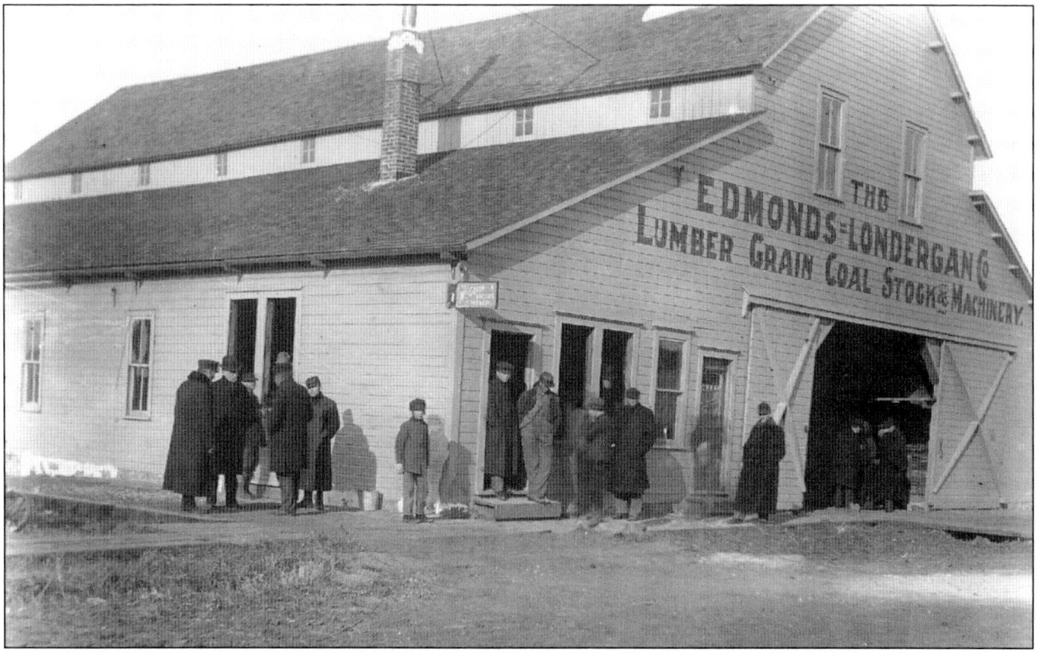

The Edmonds-Londergan Company was one of the major businesses in Steen. It was a lumberyard that also provided coal and machinery. The small sign above the door advertises McCormick mowers.

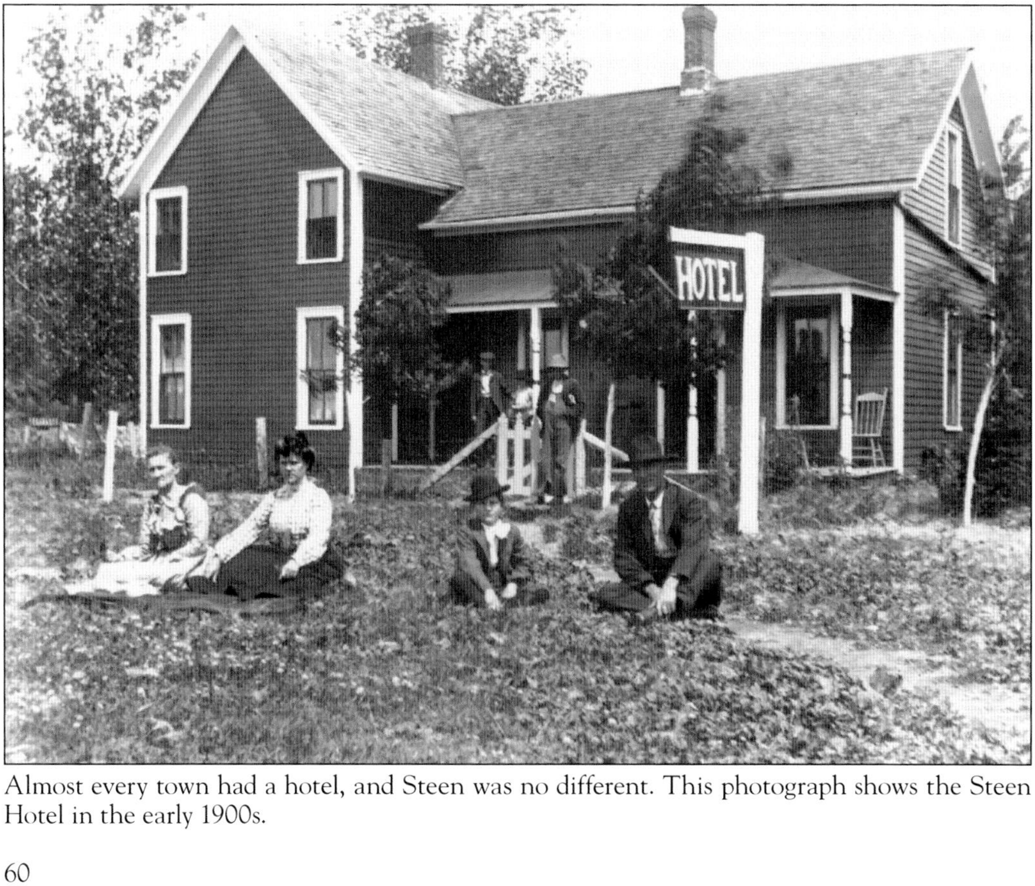

Almost every town had a hotel, and Steen was no different. This photograph shows the Steen Hotel in the early 1900s.

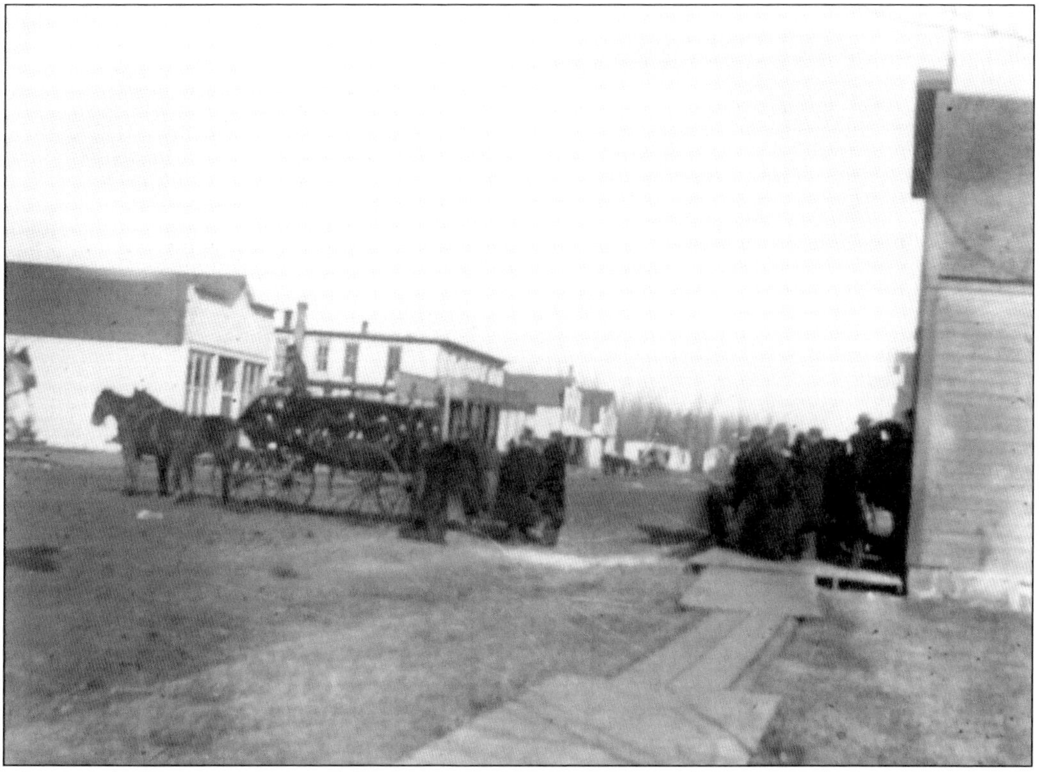

The town hall in Steen was used for a variety of purposes. Not only was it available for community meetings and events, but in this case it is being used for a funeral. The mourners are gathered outside the building, and the horse-drawn hearse can be seen on Main Street.

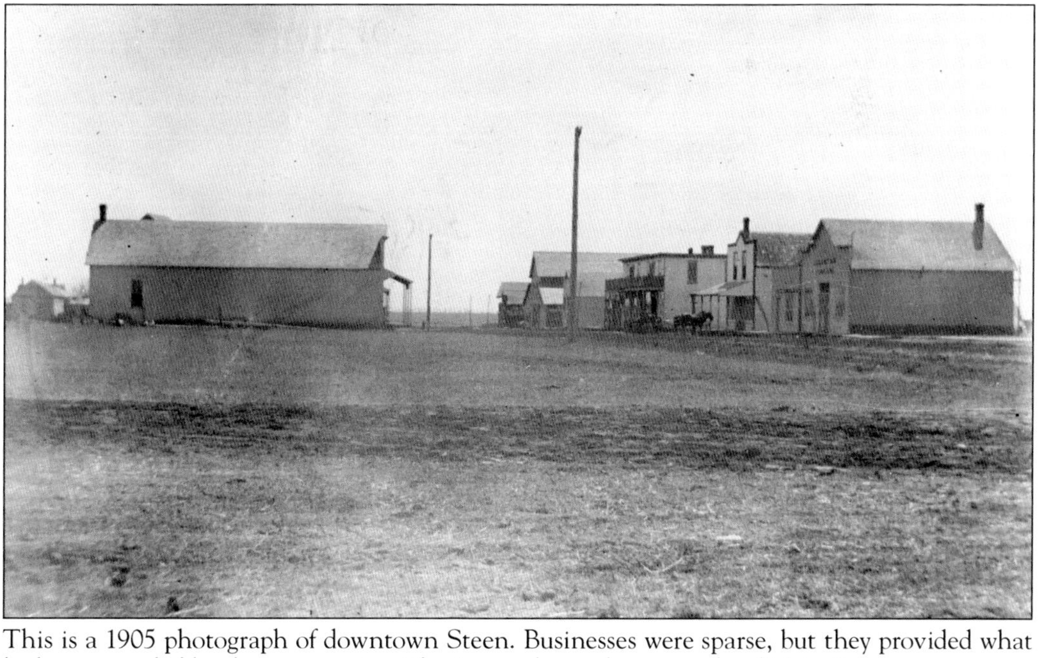

This is a 1905 photograph of downtown Steen. Businesses were sparse, but they provided what little was needed by the community. The image shows the west side of Main Street.

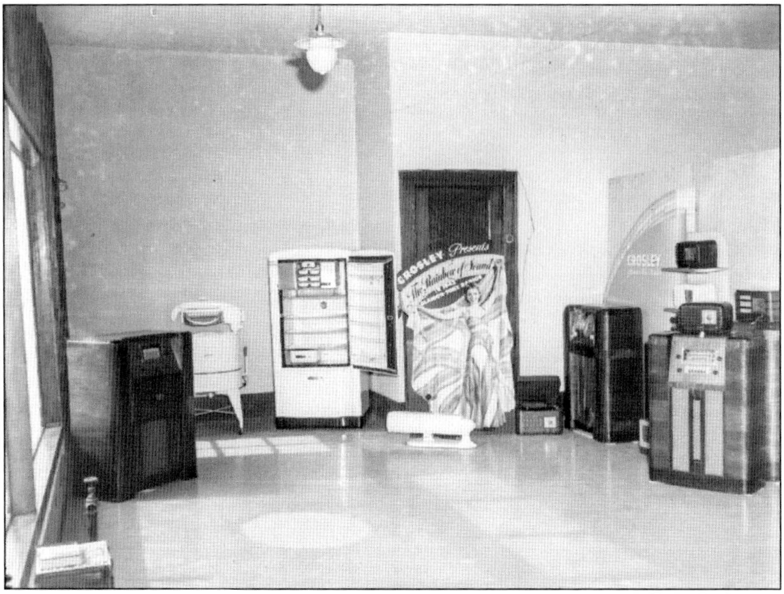

Here is a view of an early showroom of Crosley appliances in one of the stores in Luverne. Crosley appliances, which included a variety of radios, washing machines, refrigerators, and a mangle irons, were popular in the 1940s.

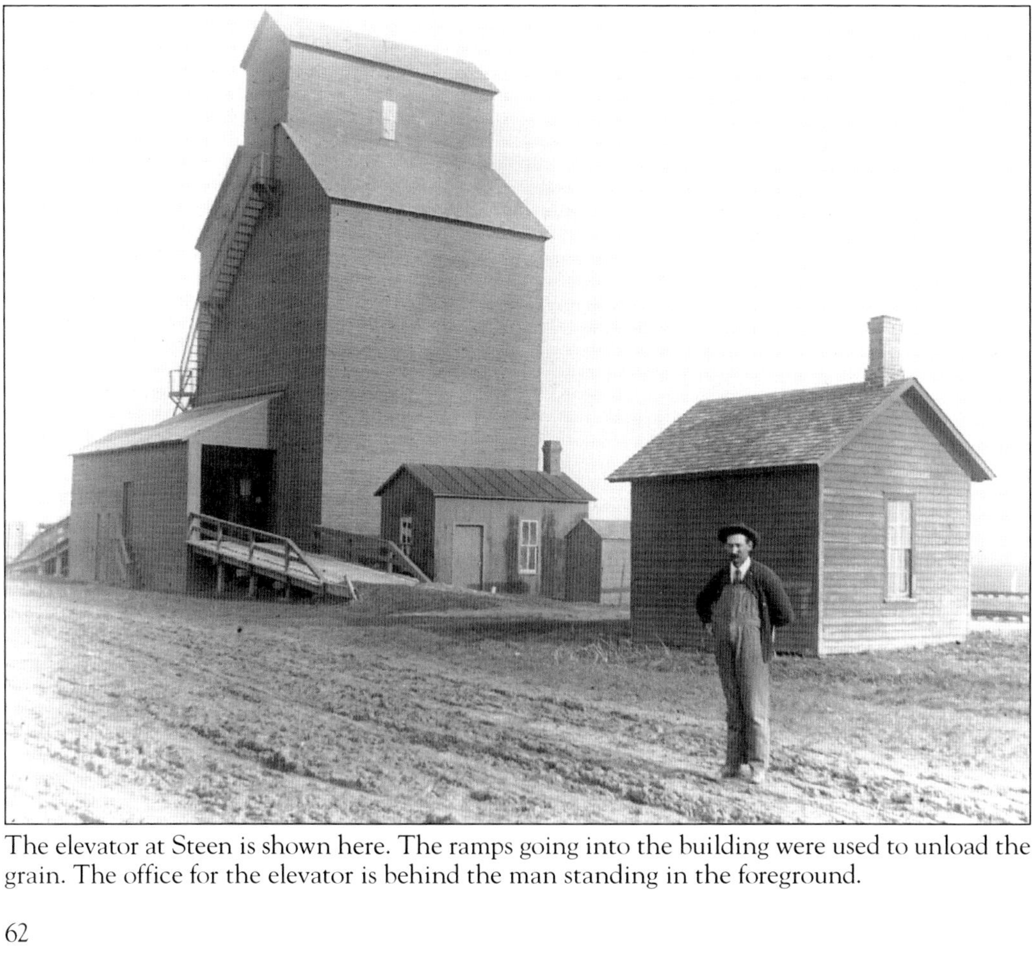

The elevator at Steen is shown here. The ramps going into the building were used to unload the grain. The office for the elevator is behind the man standing in the foreground.

Four

It Was Not All Work

During the early years of Rock County, hard work seemed to be the norm for most of its citizens. Many of the women in the communities got together for quilting parties, church meetings, and other social events. In 1873, farmers and businesspeople formed the Rock County Agricultural Society, and the first county fair was held one year later.

When rail transportation came to Rock County, new kinds of entertainment became available. Traveling shows and Chautauqua events began to arrive in cities throughout the county. Entertainment meant "big money," and in 1915 Herman Jochims built a brand-new theater, the Palace, to provide a venue for vaudeville and special featured shows.

By 1918, rural county youth joined to form 4-H clubs. These clubs provided both entertainment and education to children as well as adults.

Rail transportation was a quicker alternative than horse and buggies or oxen and carts. Soon, families traveled from one town to another aboard trains to visit relatives and take part in special events. Traveling on trains became entertainment itself and was an important social meeting place.

Many communities recognized the importance of establishing parks for picnics and sporting and social events. Families and friends gathered in city and county parks to enjoy afternoon and evening reprieve from the workday world.

Blue Mounds State Park was established by the State of Minnesota in 1934. By 1937, through efforts of the federal government's Works Progress Administration (WPA), two dams were constructed on Mounds Creek, which established the county's first fishing and swimming lake.

In the mid-1930s, the City of Luverne followed suit with other progressive cities by constructing a state-of-the-art swimming pool. It was located south of the Rock River Bridge on the west side of the Rock River.

Many local clubs and organizations grew at this time, providing not only social gatherings for members but also support for the community.

From the early days, schools became the major factor in community activities and recreation. Sporting events, musical programs, theater, art, and many other avenues provided a rich cultural experience for Rock County citizens.

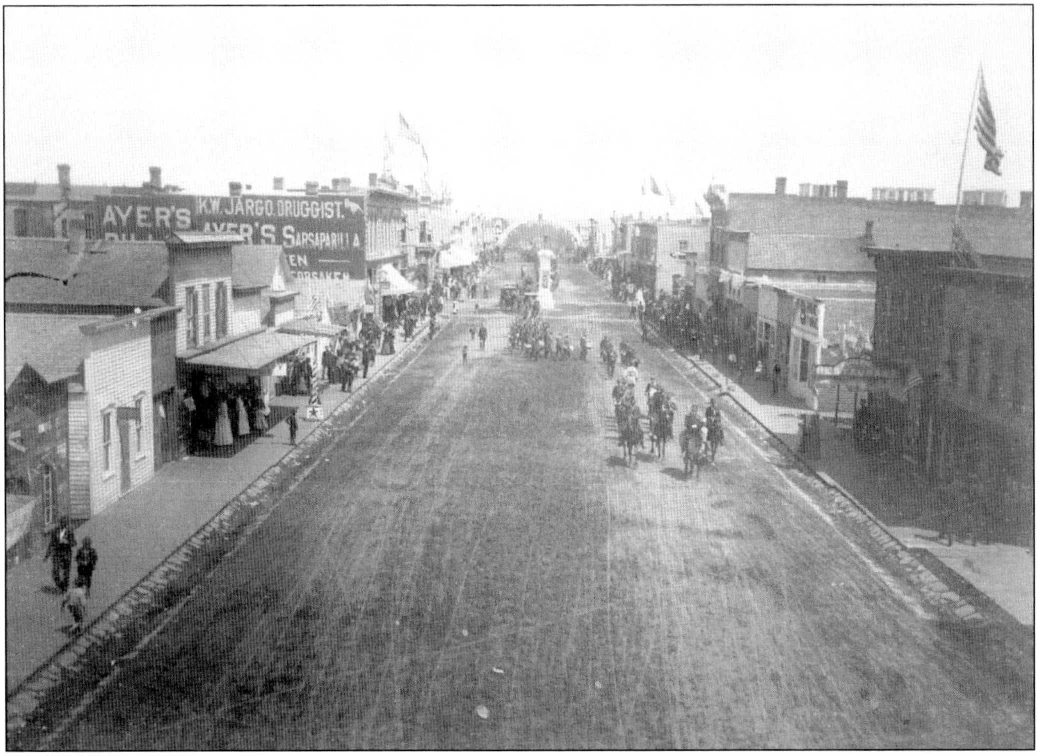

In 1897, Luverne citizens enthusiastically welcomed the parade of the Grand Army of the Republic. Here, Civil War veterans honor the anniversary of the end of the war. A grand arch, located on the east side of town on Main Street, marked the entrance to the parade route. Union flags flew over many of the buildings along the street.

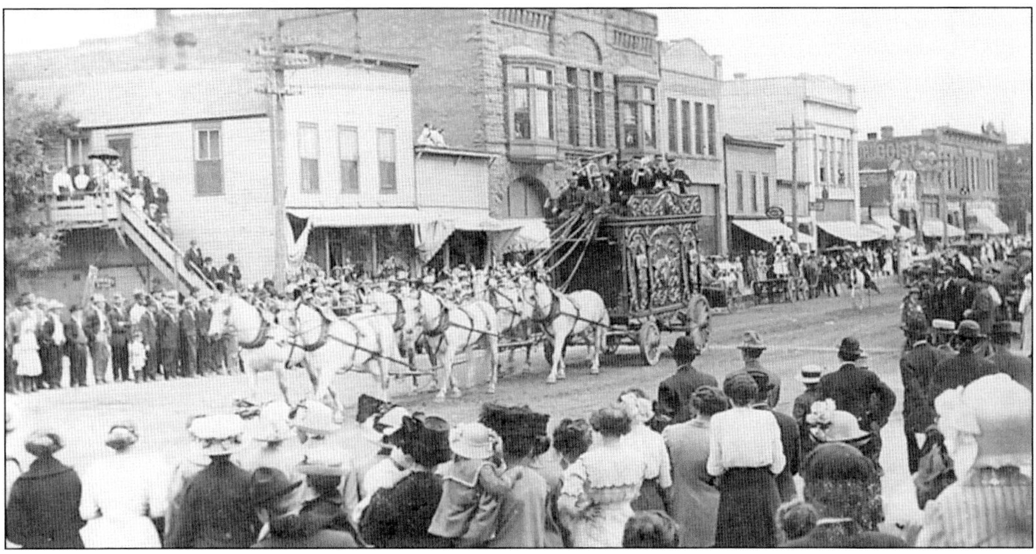

Live music was heard from this carriage on Main Street as a team of six white horses pulled a band down the street. The band was followed by a parade of horses and people, drawing parade watchers to Chautauqua tents in Luverne. People came from miles around to attend these traveling celebrations.

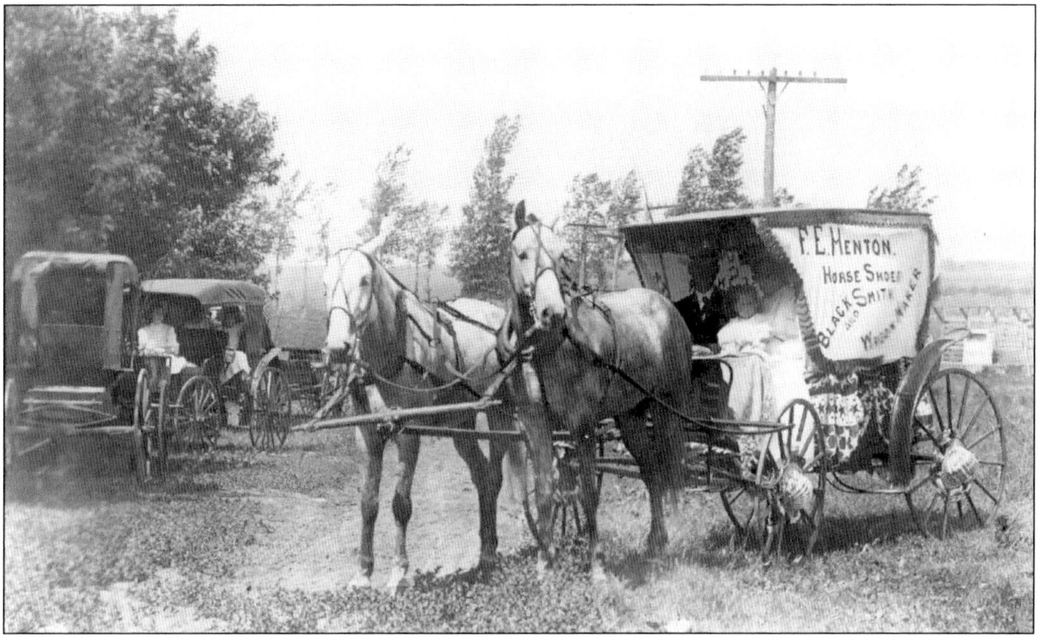

This photograph shows F.E. Henton's blacksmith carriage decorated for a Fourth of July celebration in Beaver Creek. Local businesspeople regularly rode in the parade, advertising their businesses. Horses were groomed, buggies cleaned, and metal polished as people put their best foot forward during these community celebrations.

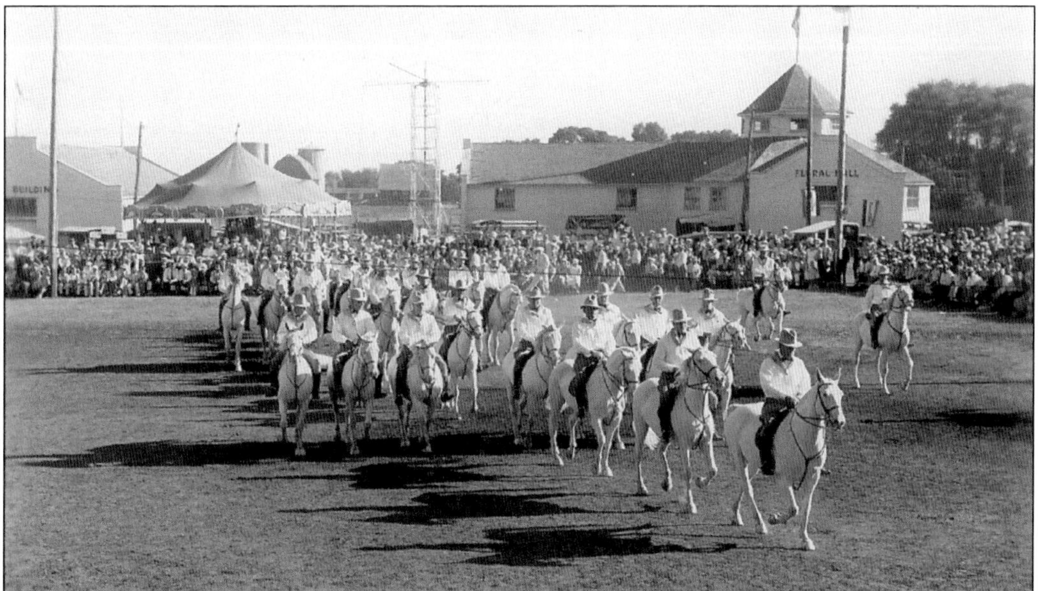

Pictured is the arrival of the horse patrol from Sioux City, Iowa, at the Rock County Fair. Fairgoers were thrilled to witness the precision riding and demonstrations of this team of talented riders. In the background is the fair's Floral Hall. The hall, built in 1915, has been the home of open-class exhibits and remains in active use today. Today's fair, like those of the past, features plant and animals exhibits and judging, as well as fine arts and cooking. There is nothing like the Rock County Free Fair!

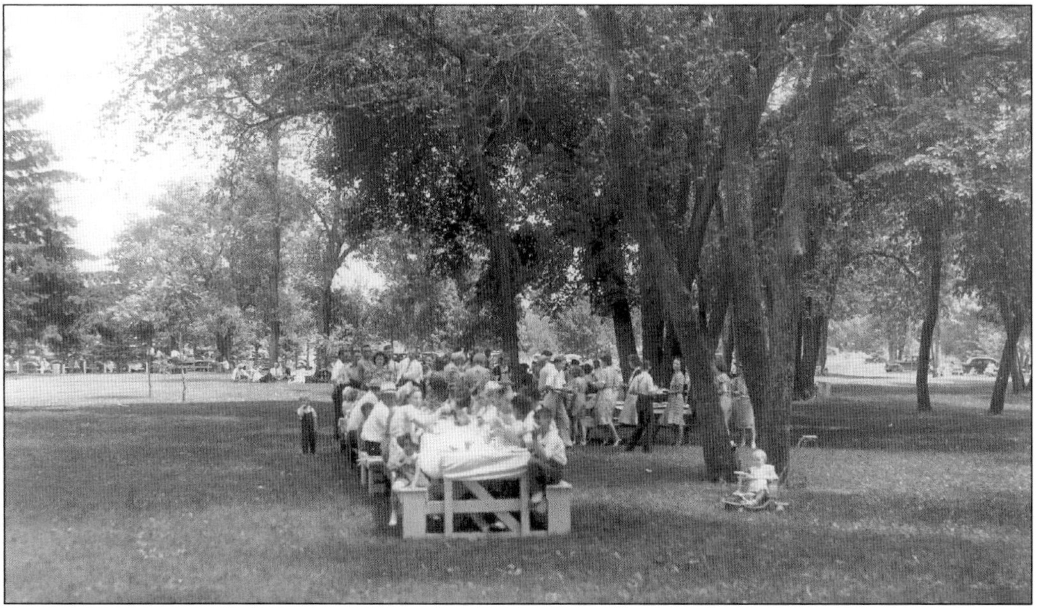

Family, neighborhood, church, school, and community picnics happened just about every weekend in the summer. The beautiful tree-lined Luverne City Park was often the home for these gatherings. Tables loaded with food and beverages of all kinds, children of all ages, a wide variety of games to play, and great conversation were the standard for every picnic.

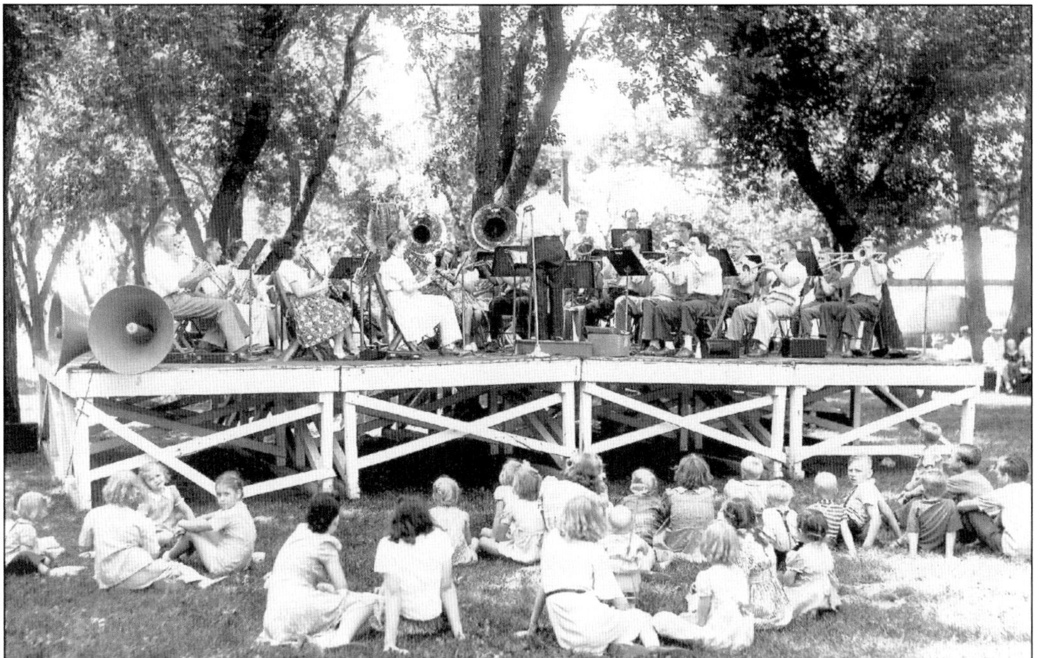

By the late 1940s and 1950s, the Luverne City Band made its mark as summer entertainment. People of all ages volunteered to play in the band. Members met for practice once a week to prepare for the Sunday afternoon concert at the Luverne City Park. Children eagerly sat in front of the bandstand, while parents and other adults relaxed on picnic tables under the shade trees.

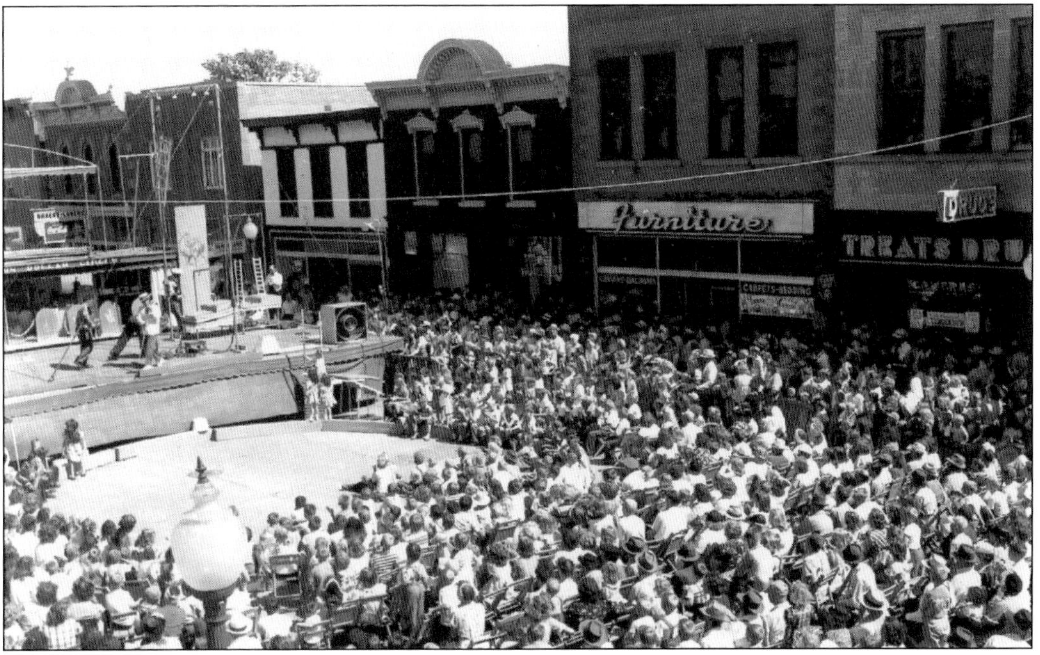

As the years went on, events tended to get larger and larger. This photograph, taken on Main Street in Luverne, shows a grand stage where a variety of acts performed live. Music, jugglers, acrobats, magicians, and other entertainment left the sell-out crowd spellbound.

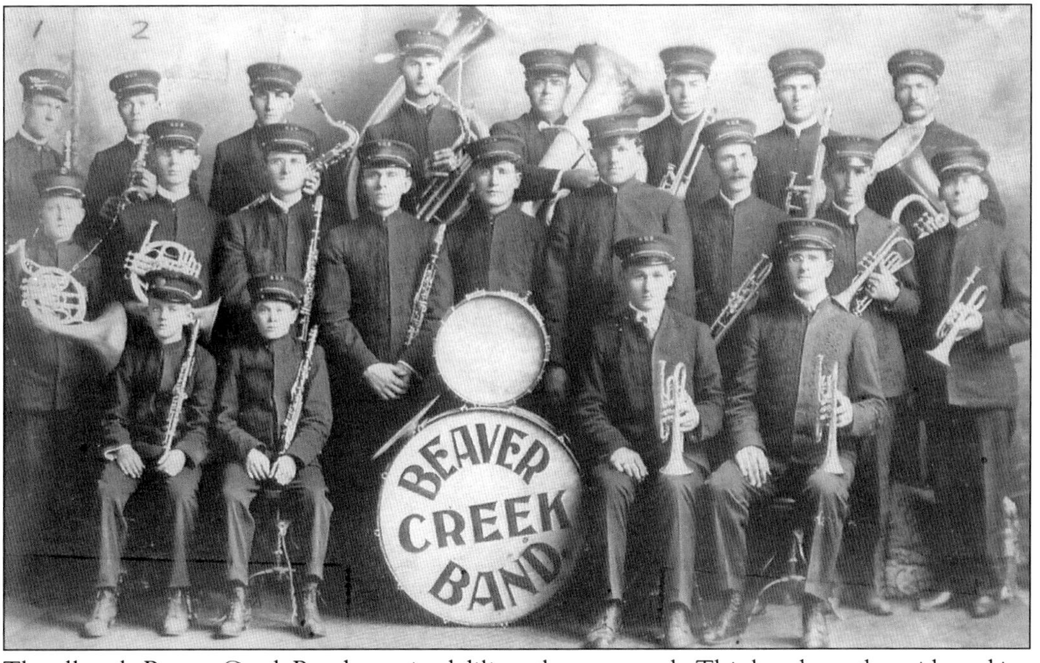

The all-male Beaver Creek Band practiced diligently every week. This band was the pride and joy of the community. There was never a parade or special community event that it did not perform in. The Beaver Creek Band was widely known in the region for its musical talent, and it regularly competed throughout the area. Residents and businesses joined to raise funds for uniforms, musical instruments, and travel expenses.

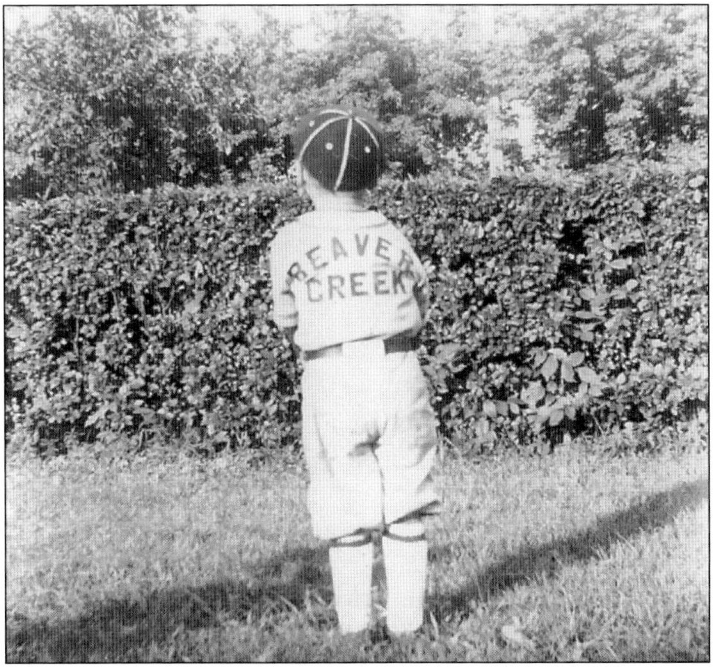

Baseball, kittenball (which used balls larger and softer than a softball), and softball teams were found in every Rock County community. Cities developed teams of different expertise. Ash Creek was the home of what was known as the best kittenball team in Rock County. Beaver Creek introduced one of the first youth baseball programs, and the community developed into a baseball powerhouse. Ball teams and fans traveled throughout the tri-state area for tournaments, games, and special competitions.

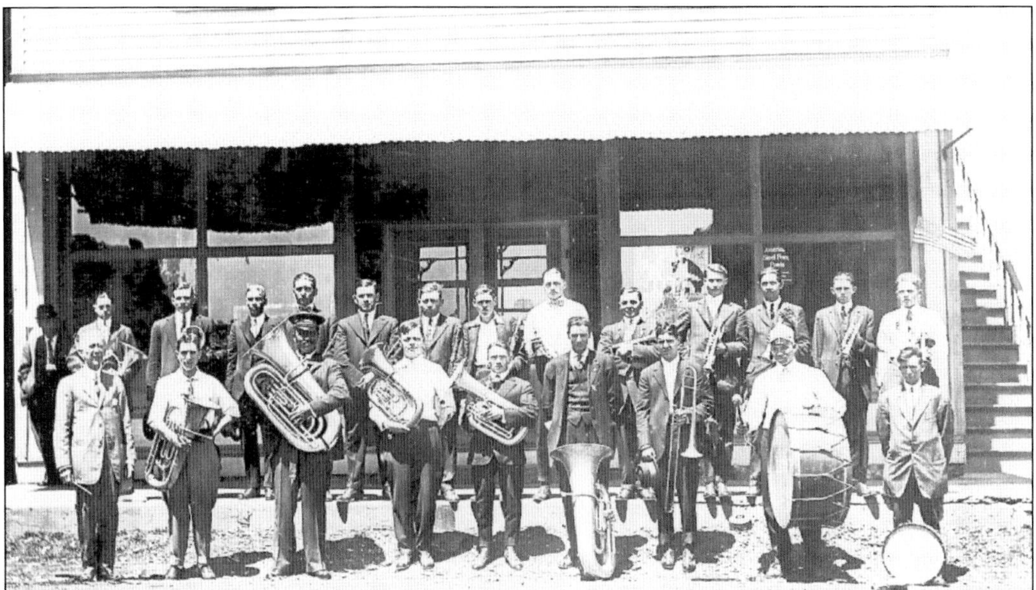

The unidentified Hardwick City Band director, located in the first row on the far left, developed this group of students, young men, and businessmen into one of the premier community bands of the region. The community enthusiastically supported the band.

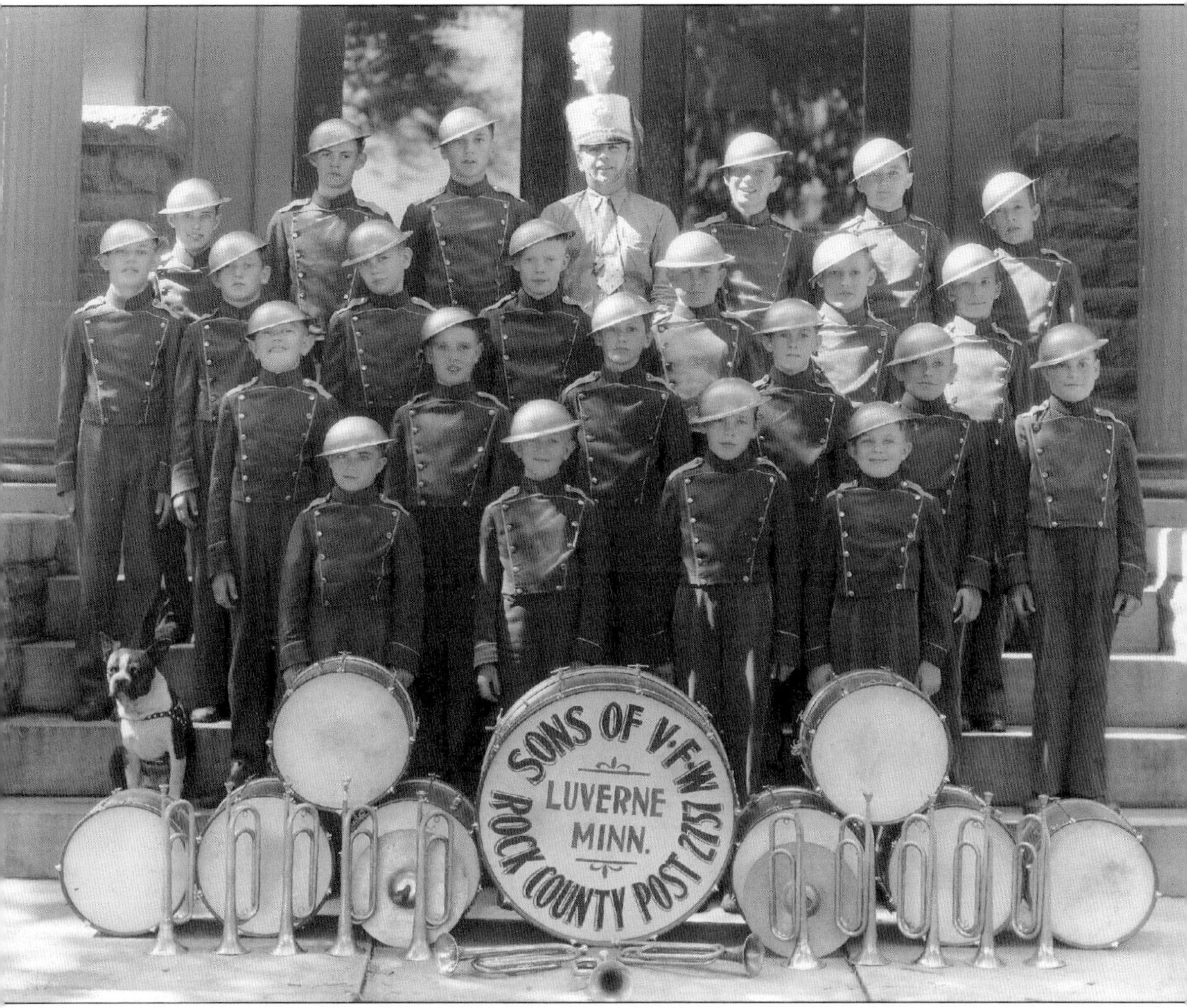

Rev. Augusta Carver of the First Presbyterian Church formed the Sons of the Veterans of Foreign Wars (VFW) Band. To be eligible for the band, boys had to be sons of World War I veterans. Boys both willingly and unwillingly marched in the band, playing their instruments as well as they could. Every young man was, however, proud to wear the uniform.

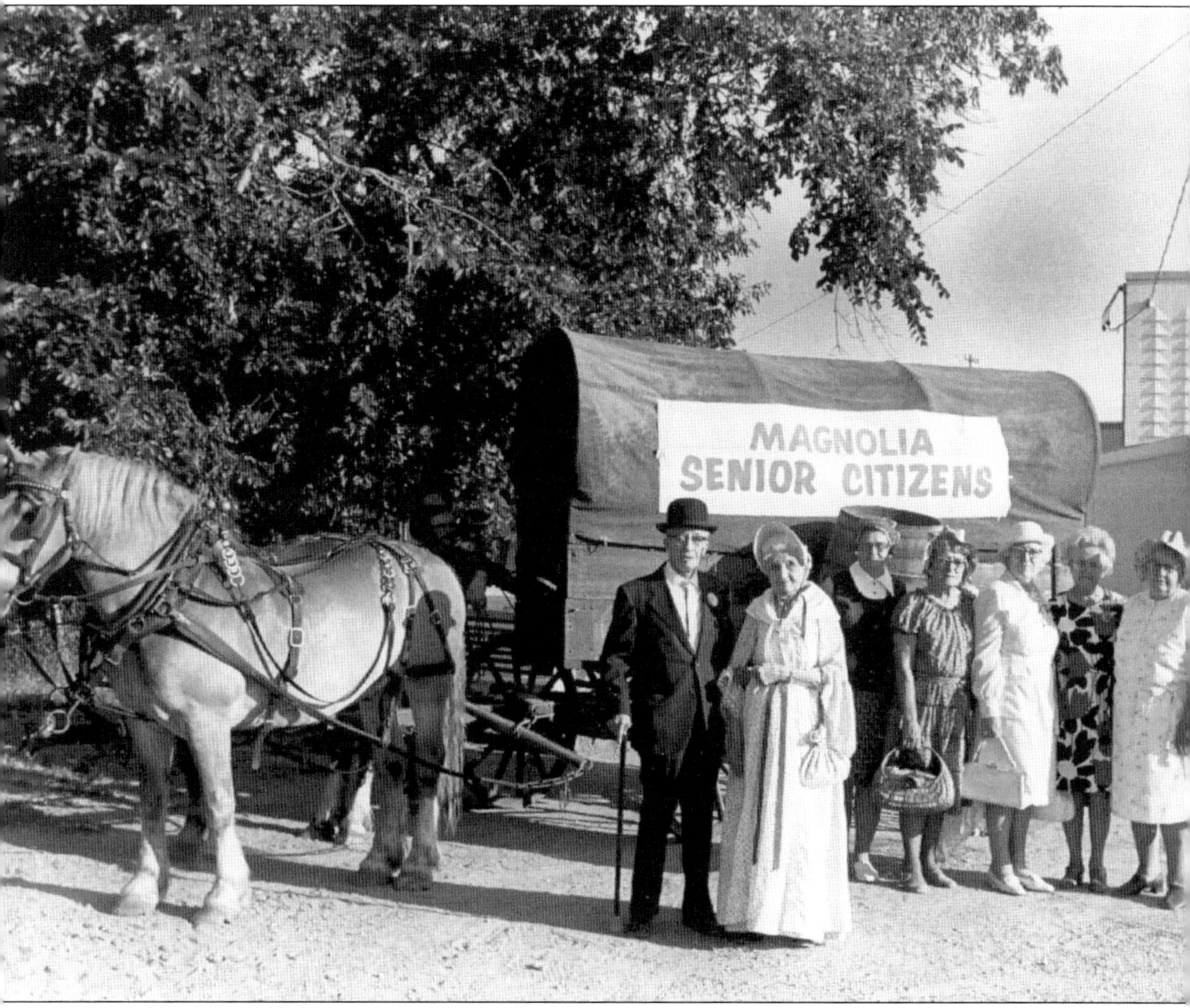

Standing in front of an authentic covered wagon from the late 1800s, these proud Magnolia senior citizens rode in the Luverne Centennial Parade in 1967. The man and woman in the foreground are wearing 1800s clothing. Every community organization worked to supply an entry in local parades.

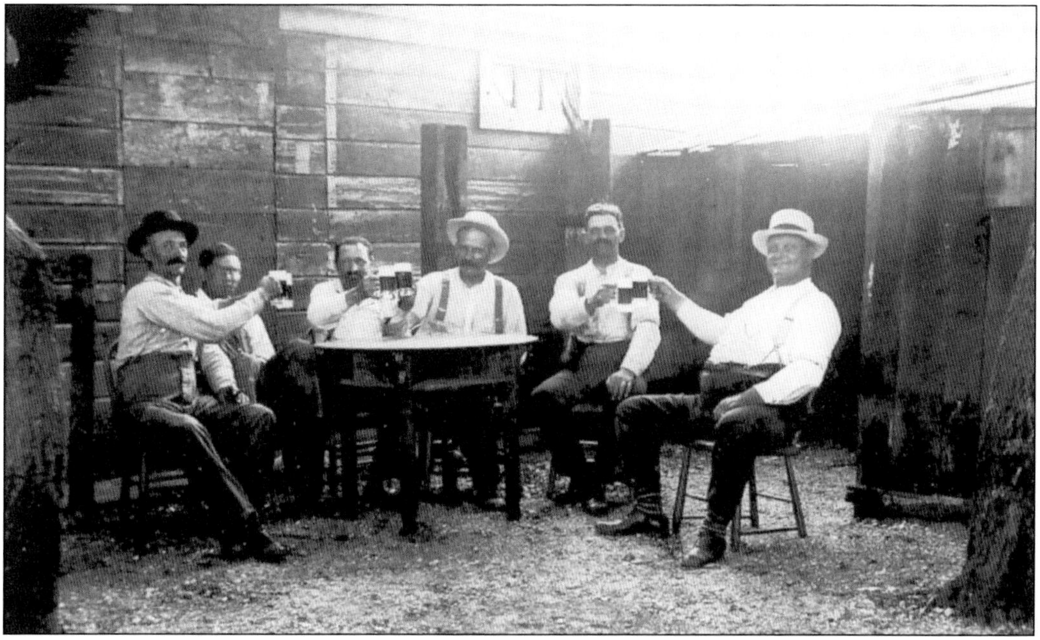

Nothing was more fun for the men of Magnolia than to get together at their local watering hole. This photograph, taken in the back room, showed a private meeting space for local businessmen to get together and discuss what was going on in the city. Private meeting spaces supported opportunities for games of cards or dice, hidden away from prying eyes.

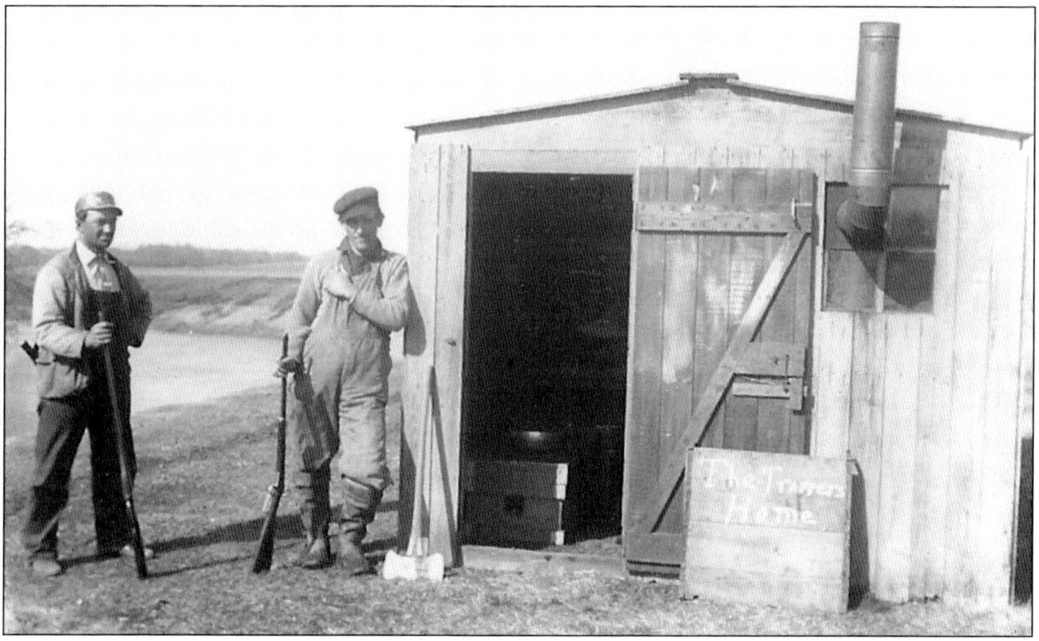

Hunting and trapping was an early way of life for many settlers in Rock County. The first white people who traveled through the county were trappers, harvesting the rich beaver population that lived in creeks. As the county was settled, trappers and hunters set up cabins that were simply built with nothing more than a wood-burning stove for heat. Pictured is a hunting cabin just outside of Magnolia.

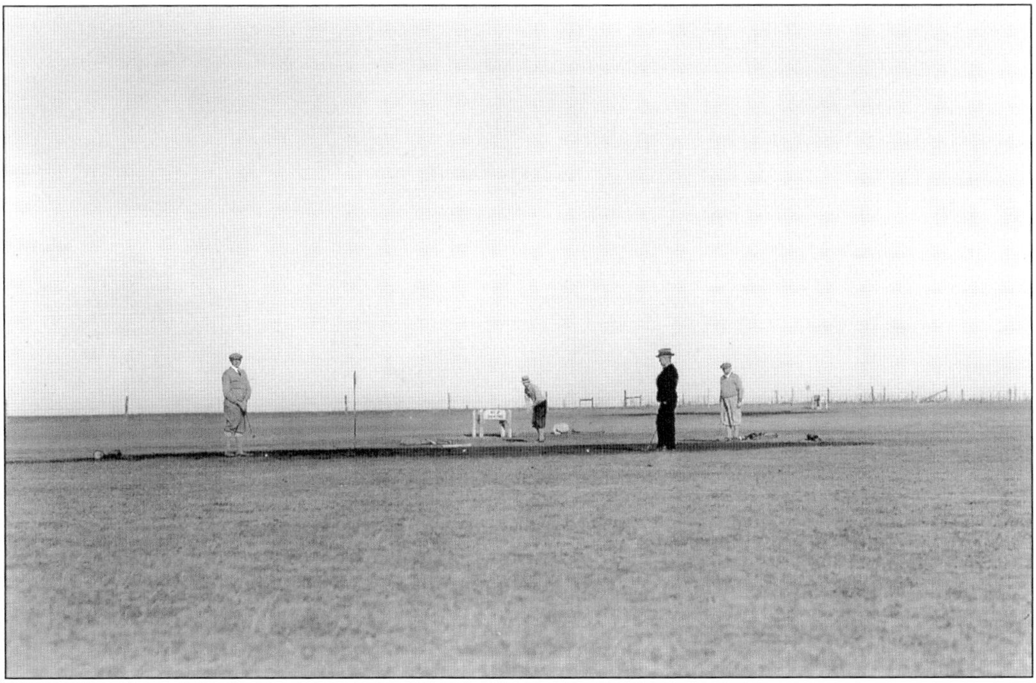

The plains of southwestern Minnesota provided wonderful opportunities for fairways and greens for golf. Luverne's first golf course was built west of town. The first greens were nothing more than sand, but men and women enjoyed the opportunity to golf nonetheless. In the early 1900s, when this photograph was taken, no one had to worry about trees or water hazards.

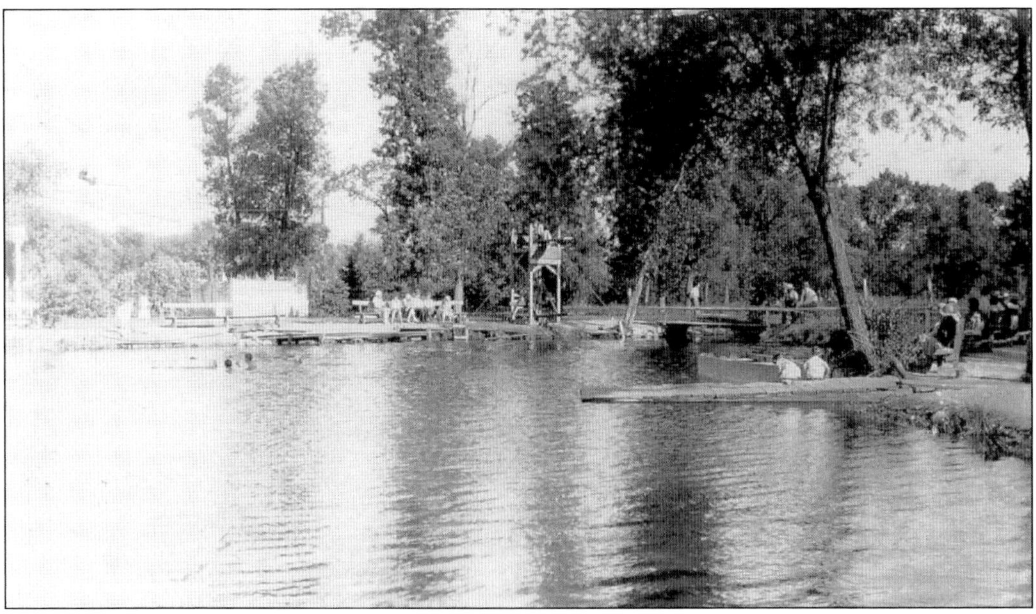

Nothing was more fun on a hot summer day than swimming. Creeks, rivers, and stock ponds provided swimming holes for adults and youth throughout the county. The first organized swimming area was established on the banks of the Rock River. The dock, diving platform, and floating pier offered great fun for everyone who loved the water.

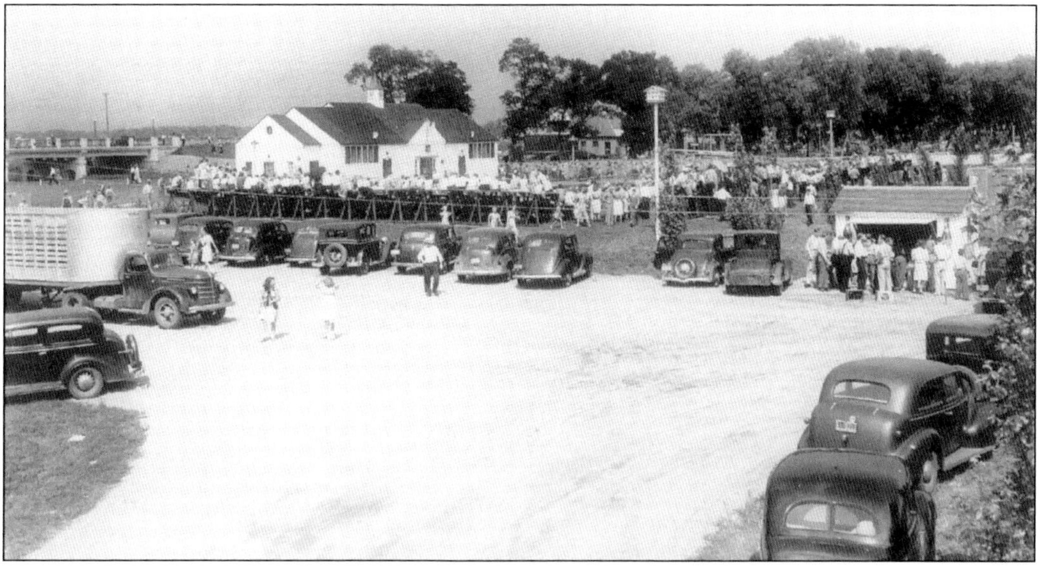

A new swimming pool was built in Luverne in the late 1930s south of the Rock River Bridge on the west side of the Rock River. The pool, with bathhouse, showers, diving boards, and wading pool, became one of the most popular summertime locations. This photograph shows a crowd of people enjoying swimming and diving demonstrations. A new indoor swimming pool was built in the 1980s, and this facility was closed and torn down.

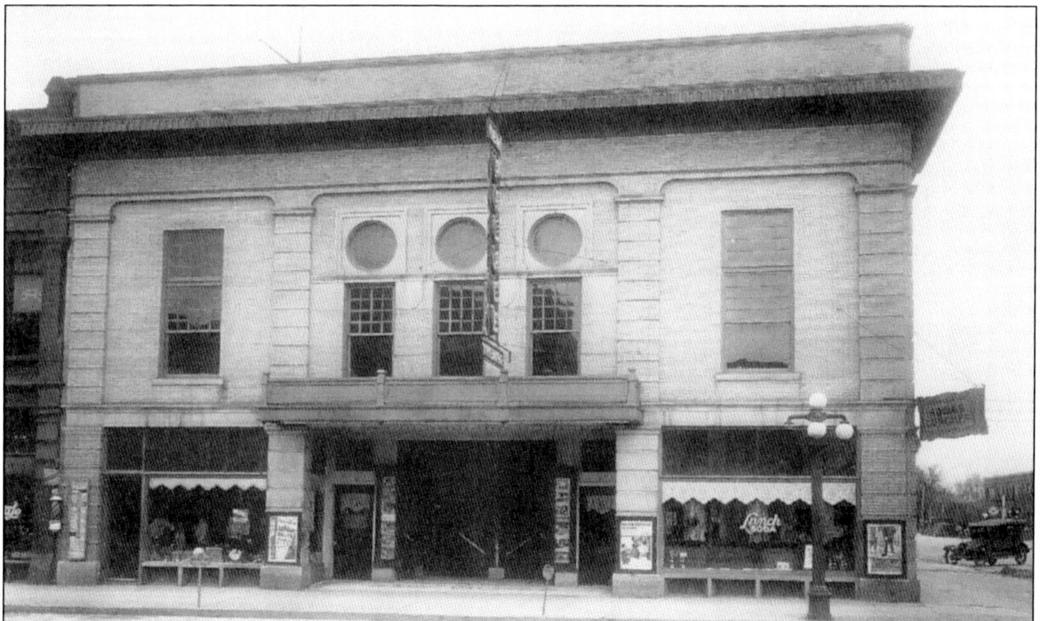

Herman and Maude Jochims built the elegant Palace Theatre in 1915. Vaudeville, live theater, musical performances, and silent and sound movies entertained people from the tri-state area. The second floor of the building housed a ballroom that was used for special events. It also had two rental properties on the first floor. A restaurant and soda shop were located on the right side of the building. The theater remains in use for live events and movies. A nonprofit board of dedicated volunteers continues to work diligently in the theater's renovation and operation.

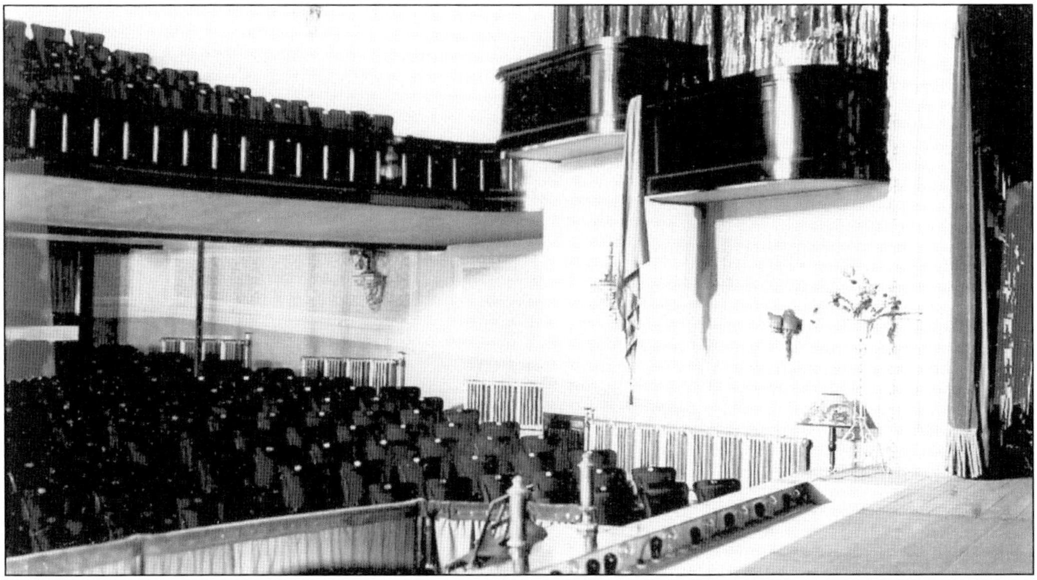

The interior of the Palace Theatre maintains its historic dignity in Art Deco design. The theater has a large stage and orchestra pit, featuring a Smith-Geneva pipe organ installed in 1926. This organ is still in working order and is played today for special occasions and performances. It is the only theater organ in the United States that remains in its original home. Pictured are the balconies and stage footlights. Beneath the stage is a series of dressing and prop rooms.

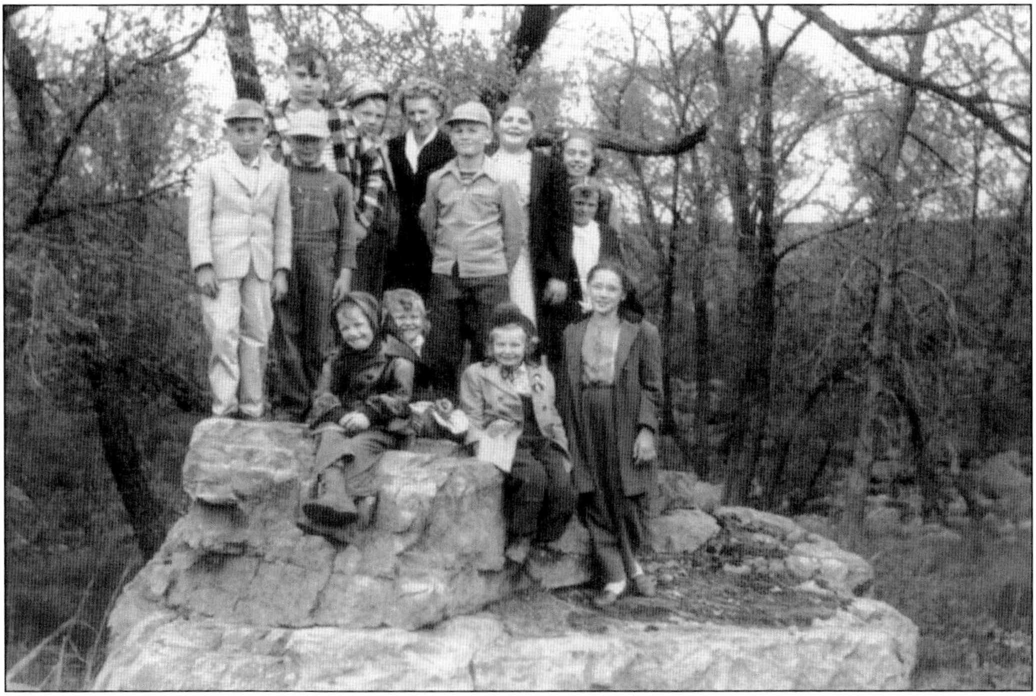

Decades of children have enjoyed school outings at Blue Mounds State Park, which has long been a popular spot for picnics, rock climbing, hiking, and swimming. Students are seen standing proudly on one of the large Sioux quartzite boulders that create the end of the large rock ridgeline, called Buffalo Ridge, running from eastern South Dakota into Minnesota.

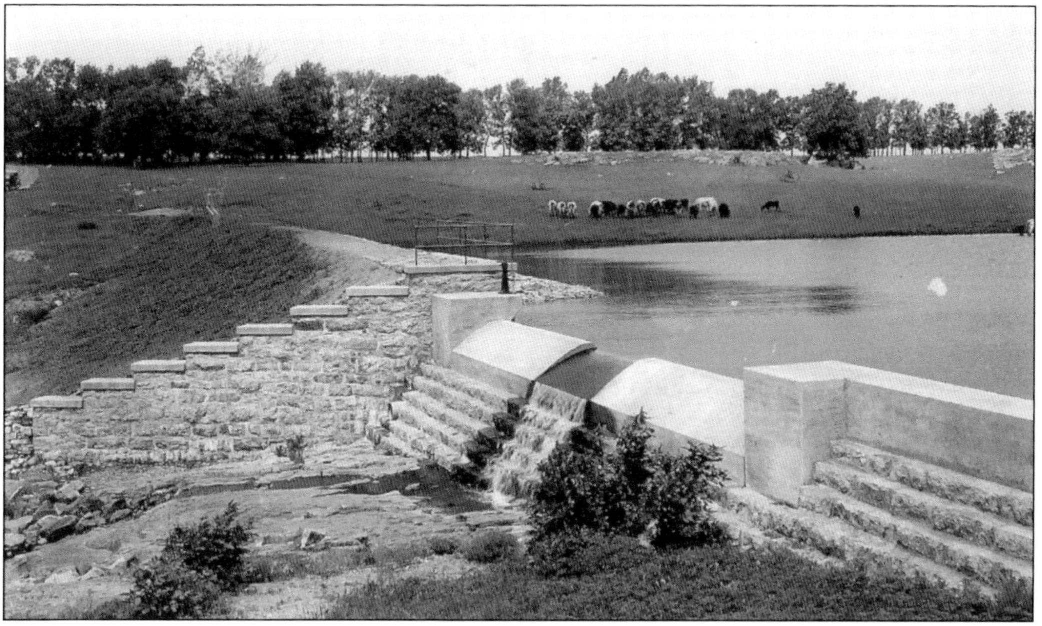

In the 1930s, the WPA constructed a dam on the west side of Blue Mounds State Park, which has become known as Upper Lake. The dam, built with the park's Sioux quartzite, provides a beautiful spot for picnics and special events. The farmland was eventually purchased, and a public campground was established.

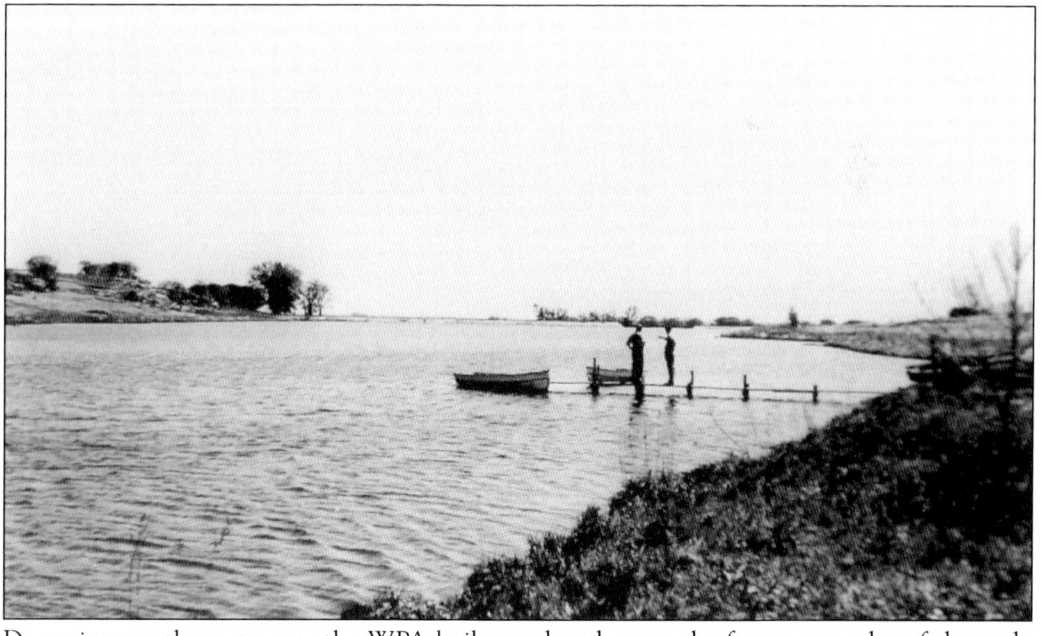

Downriver on the waterway, the WPA built another dam on the far eastern edge of the park, which created Lower Lake. This lake became popular with campers and swimmers, as it created the only constantly controlled water feature in Rock County. In later years, the State of Minnesota built a bathhouse and added a sand beach.

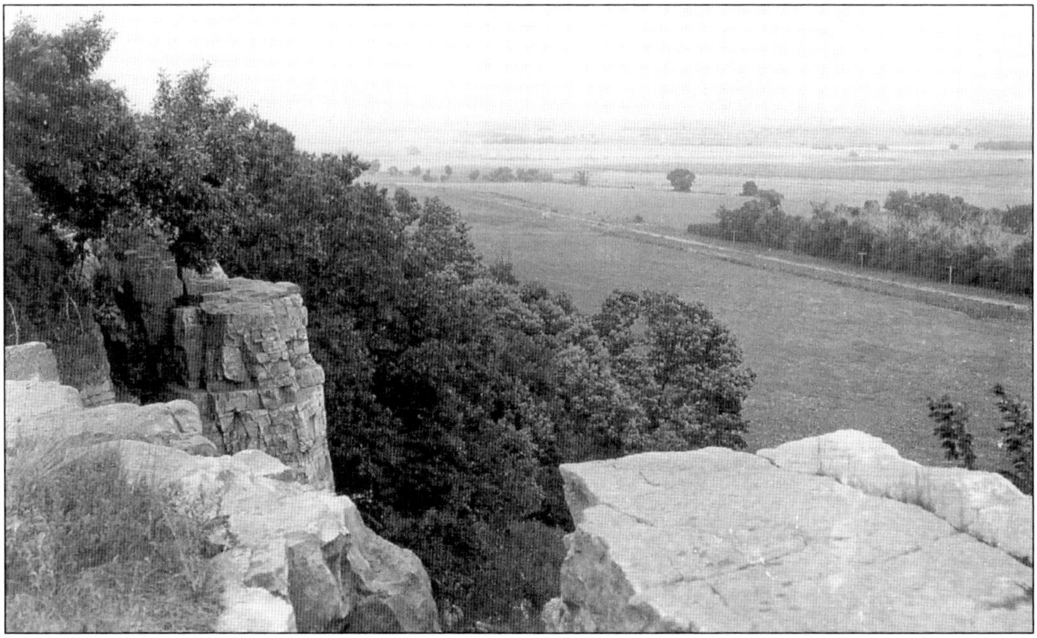

The Blue Mounds cliff line rises 120 feet from the prairie. When settlers first came across the prairie, there were essentially no trees. They saw this ridgeline that appeared to rise from the prairie, which made the topography look even more impressive. From the distance, the rock line looked "blue," thus the name Blue Mounds.

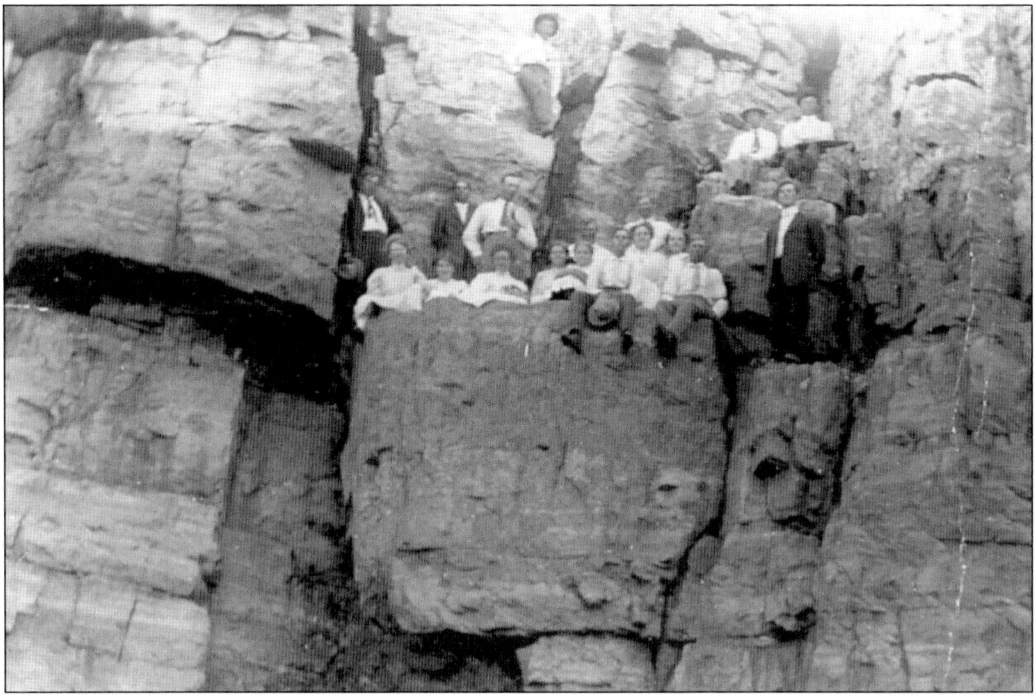

Rock climbing has always been a popular activity at the Blue Mounds. This photograph shows a group of people from Hardwick who climbed the rocks after a picnic despite wearing their Sunday best. This is hardly the gear rock climbers of today would use.

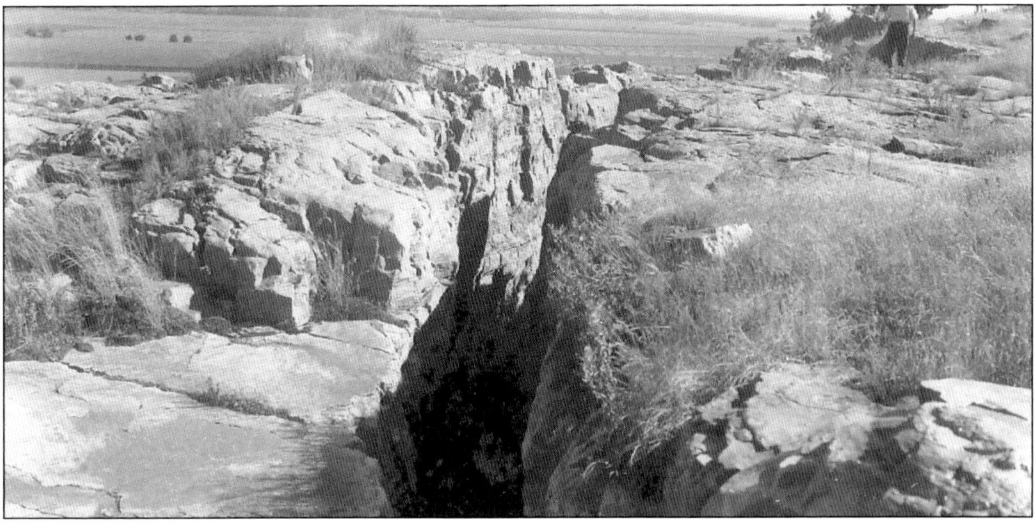

Among the rock formations at the park are unique natural crevices and caves that dot the cliff line. This particular formation was believed to be a hideout where the famed Jesse James stayed when he passed through the area after robbing a bank in Sioux Falls, South Dakota.

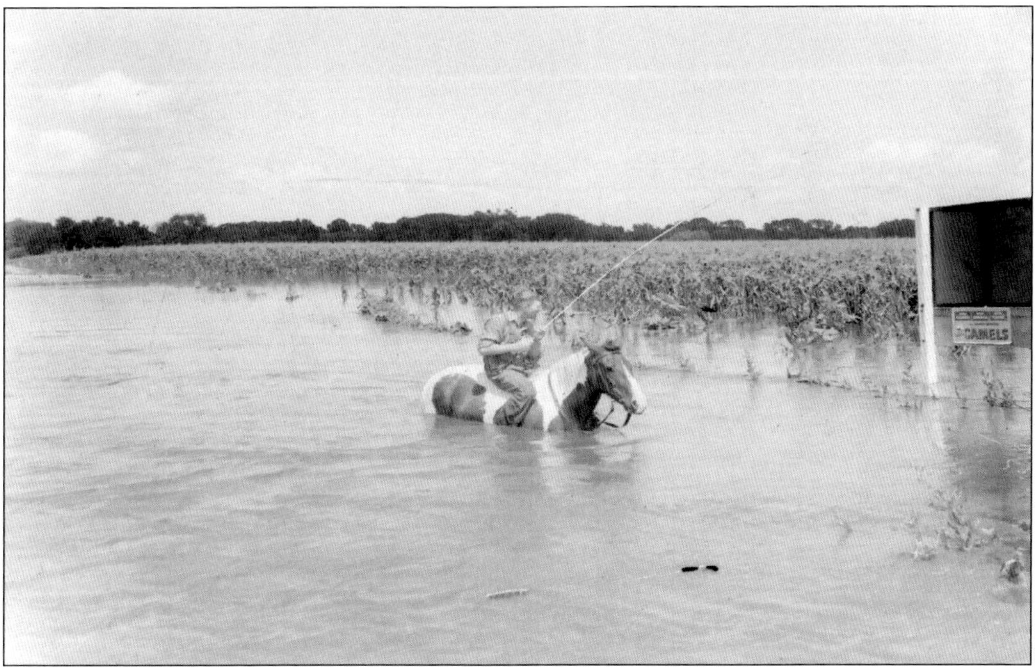

Farming along the creeks and rivers in Rock County had its difficulties. After heavy rains, fields would occasionally flood for hours, days, or even weeks. Sometimes, all a farmer could do was to make the best of a bad situation. In this photograph, a young farm boy has done just that. With rod and reel in hand on his trusted horse, he is fishing in his cornfield to see if he can catch his supper.

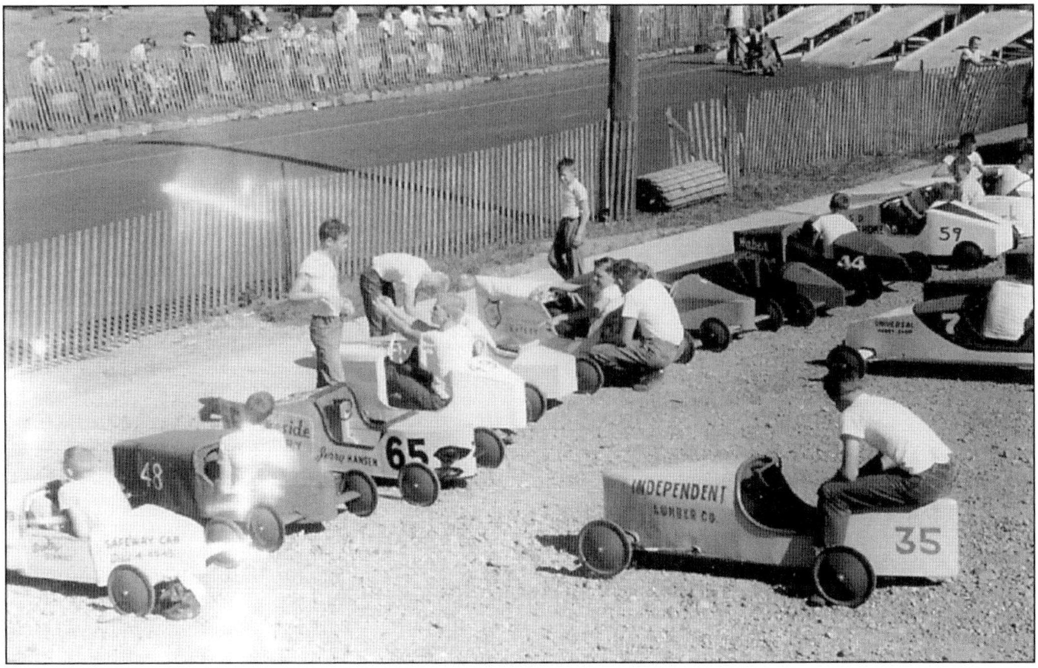

Fathers and mothers in the 1940s spent many hours helping their sons and daughters create the perfect age-appropriate driving machines. Soapbox derbies meant innovative designs and engineering. A photograph of a regional competition shows families and friends cheering on the racers.

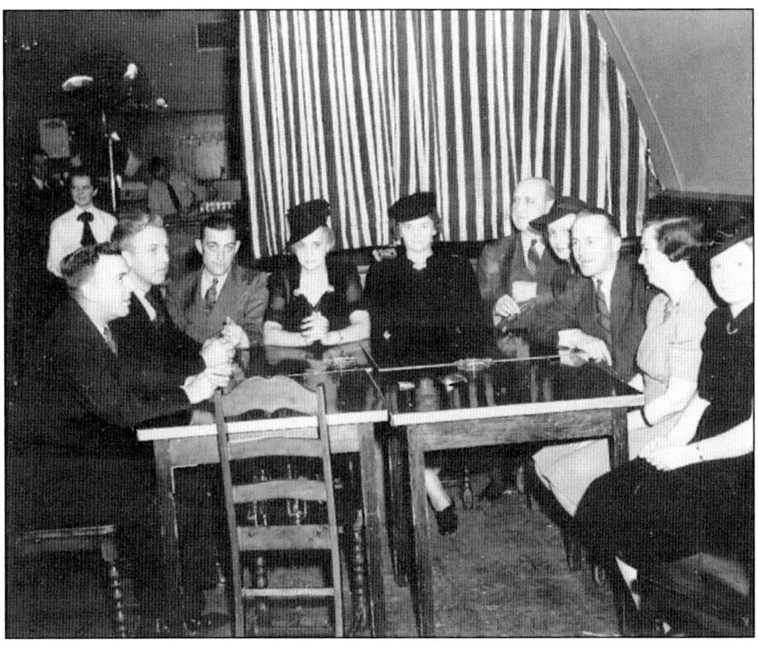

Dance halls, supper clubs, and bars were popular places for adults to gather after a hard day or week of work. Built on the northeast corner of Kniss Avenue and Hatting Street, the Chez Paree was an elegant establishment. Pictured here are five couples enjoying a night on the town in a portion of the club called "Kitty-Corner."

Five

LOCAL GOVERNMENT

As more and more people moved into the county, there was a need for a government to coordinate development, support local needs, and keep the peace. In its first years of settlement, Rock County was attached to Jackson County for civil and judicial purposes. The Act of 1857 formally established Rock County, but it was not until 1869 that citizens petitioned the Minnesota Legislature for formal organization. On March 5, 1870, the legislature authorized the formal government of Rock County. In August of that same year, Governor Austin appointed Rock County's first three commissioners.

These commissioners were formally charged with selecting the county seat and organizing a convention to elect men to serve as commissioners. Luverne was selected because it was in the center of the county, and it was the only city formally established. By September 24, 1870, Governor Austin issued a proclamation naming Luverne as the county seat.

From 1871 through 1878, twelve townships were formed within the county. Township officials were elected and installed to manage the affairs. As additional rail lines were established, more areas of the county were settled and organized. Cities and villages sprang up throughout the county to facilitate rail stops, support mail routes, and establish post offices.

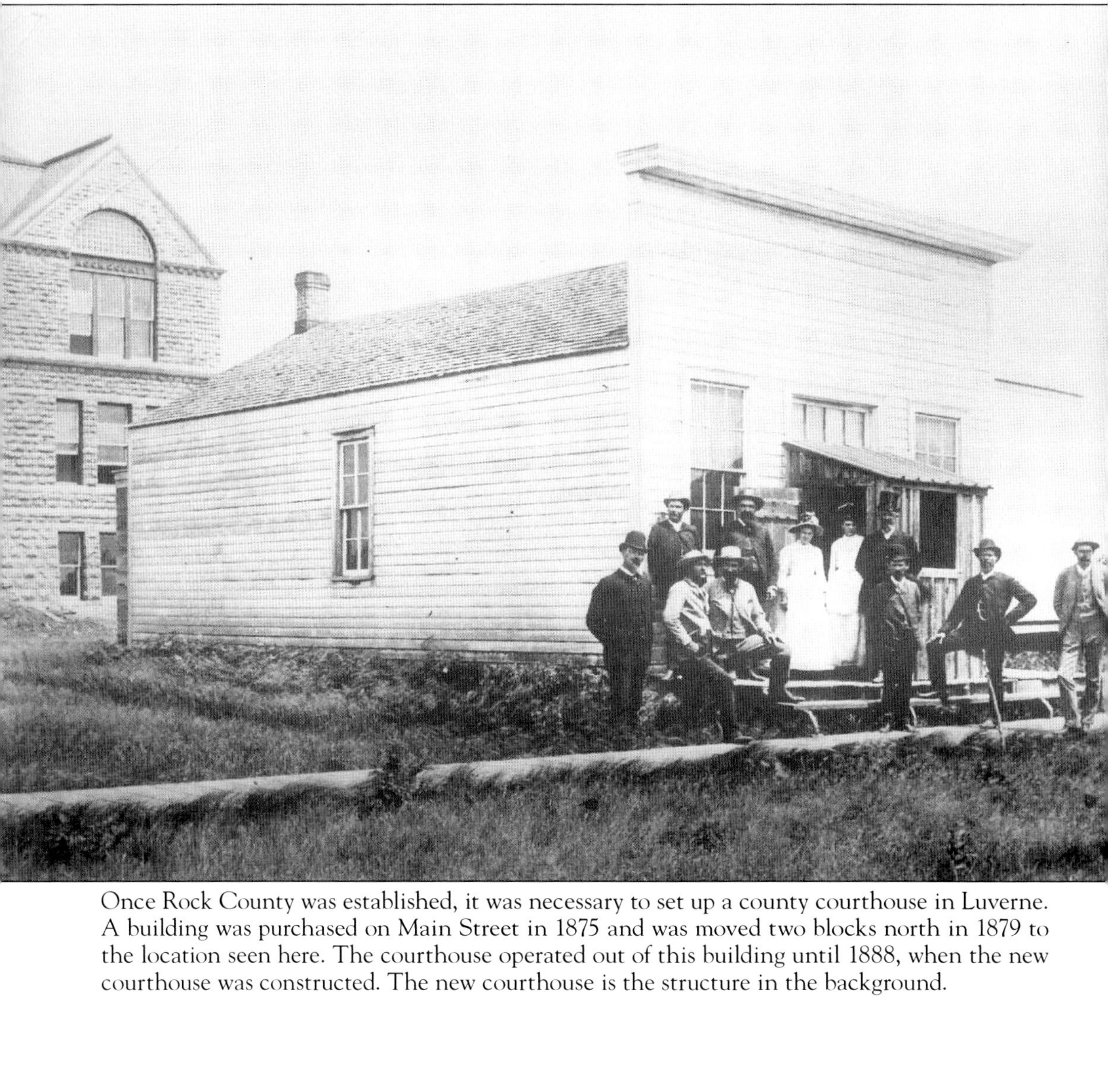

Once Rock County was established, it was necessary to set up a county courthouse in Luverne. A building was purchased on Main Street in 1875 and was moved two blocks north in 1879 to the location seen here. The courthouse operated out of this building until 1888, when the new courthouse was constructed. The new courthouse is the structure in the background.

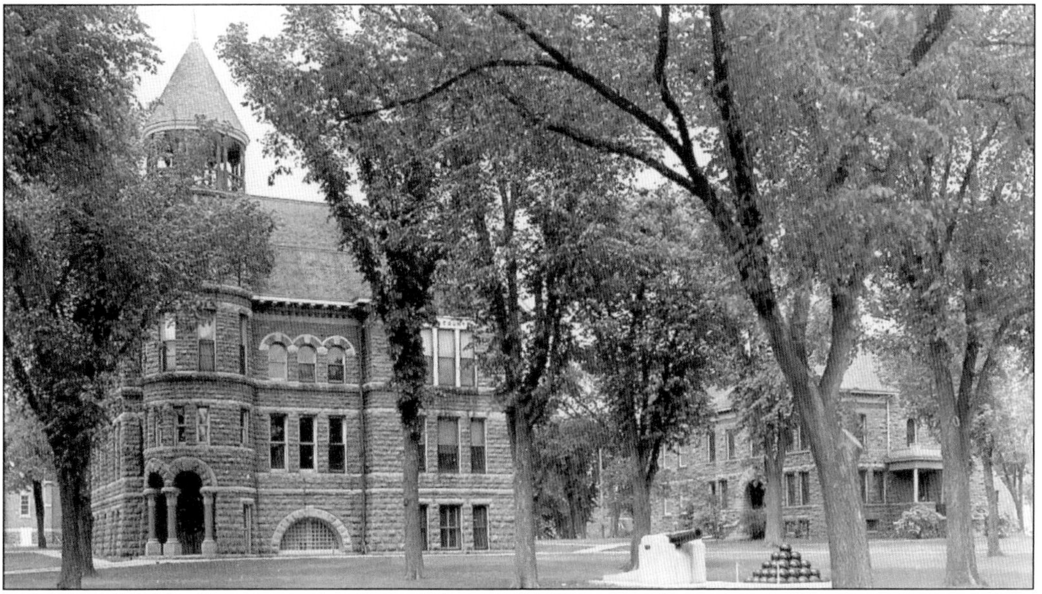

Here is the courthouse that was built in 1888. Upon its completion, all of the county offices were located within this structure, which was built of Sioux quartzite quarried just north of Luverne. To the right of the courthouse is the county jail, built in 1900. The jail also served as the residence, located in the front of the building, for the county sheriff.

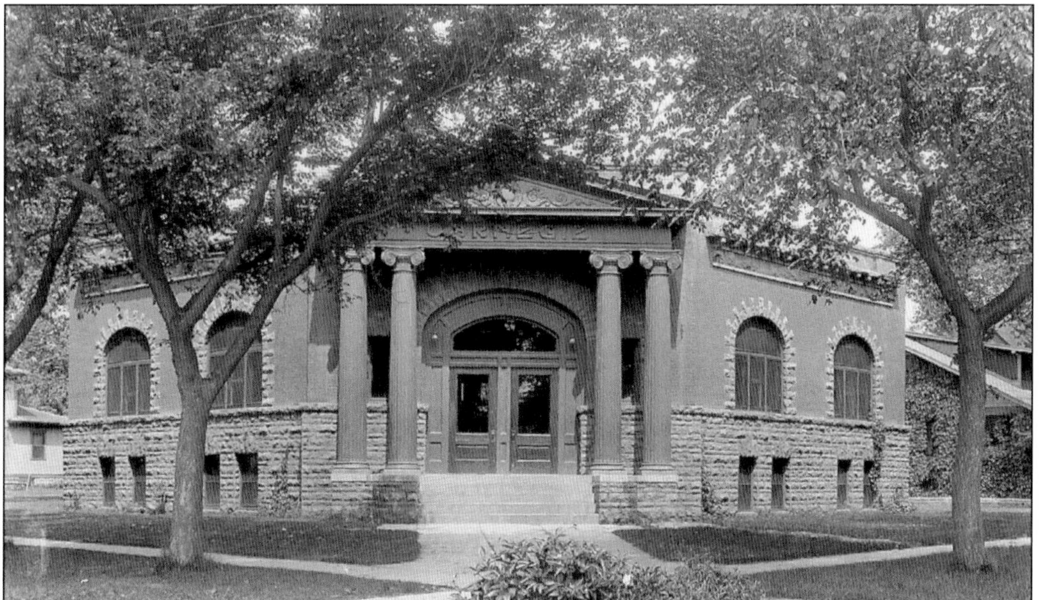

For many years, citizens of Luverne were interested in attaining a library. Pictured is the Carnegie library, built in 1904. Andrew Carnegie gave the community $10,000 for the construction of the building, and the city provided the site. The library, as were many local government buildings, was constructed of Sioux quartzite.

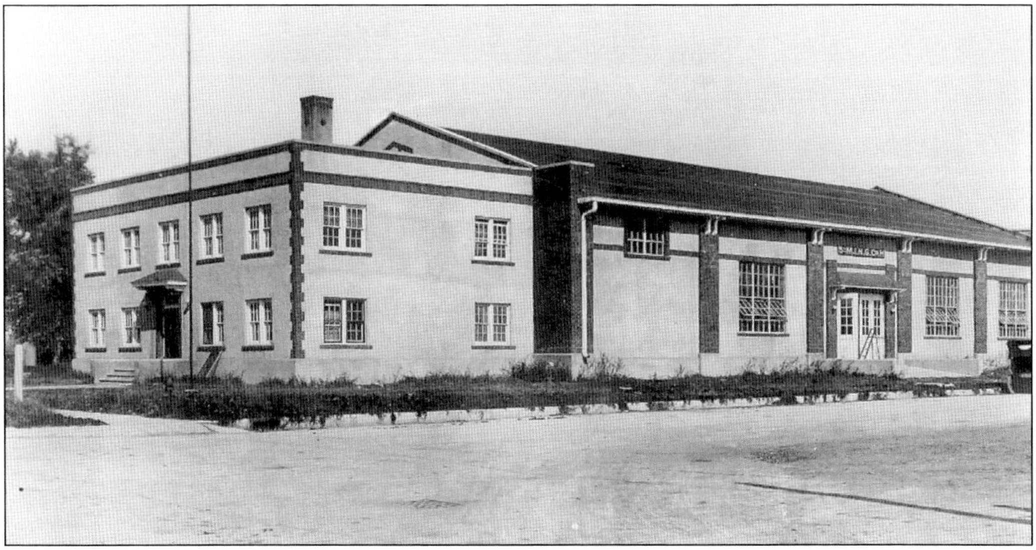

On March 17, 1919, a meeting was held for the purpose of building an armory in Luverne. After working with the state for months, construction of the National Guard armory began, and on October 6, 1922, the formal dedication of the armory was celebrated. There were hurdles to cross in its construction. When the city did not offer a site, a group of local citizens raised $3,400 to provide one.

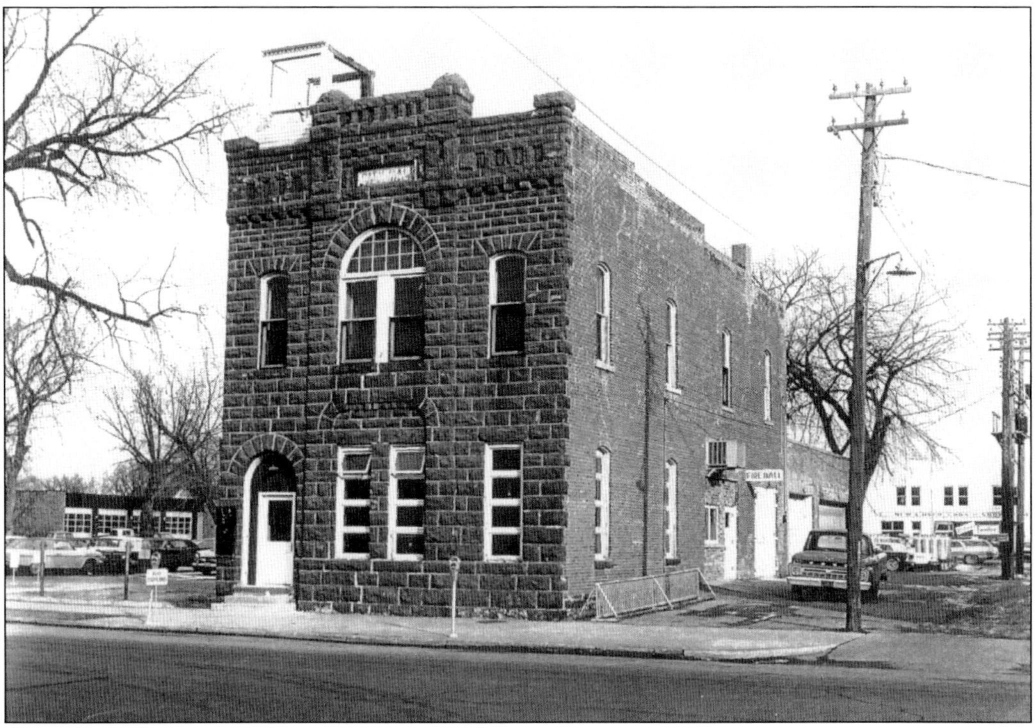

This building was used as city hall from the time of its construction in 1888 until 1968. Within it were city offices, a library, fire department, police department, and the municipal judge chamber. At the very top of the building is the bell tower that alerted volunteer firemen; a siren later replaced it.

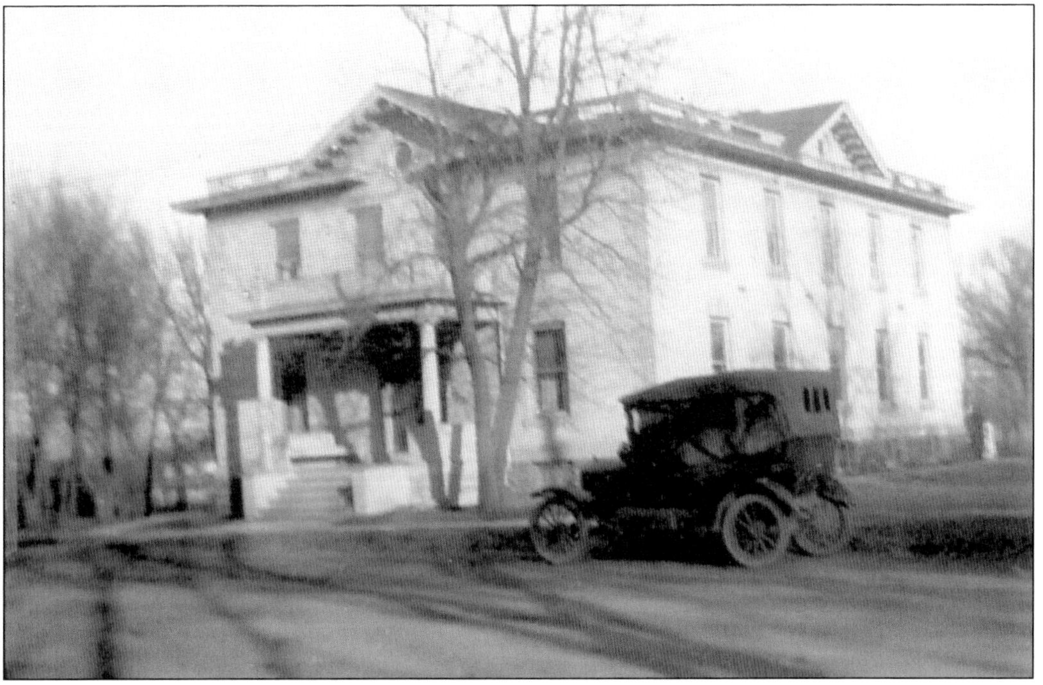

Luverne has always had a fine tradition of medical excellence. In 1878, Dr. A.E. Spaulding moved to Luverne and began his medical practice. In the 1890s, he opened a hospital in his home, and then in 1905 he constructed the hospital building pictured here. It was the center of medical services for all of Rock County. This building remained the city hospital until a newer, more modern structure was built in the mid-1950s.

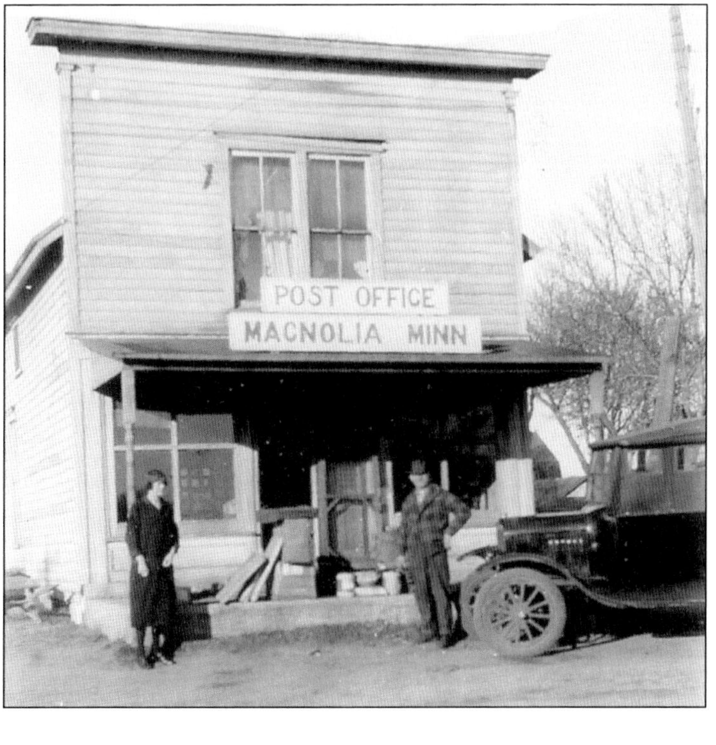

One of the first government buildings constructed in towns is the post office. Most of the post offices in Rock County were built along the railroad, which could provide postal service both in and out of the communities. The majority of post offices also housed local businesses similar to the one pictured here in Magnolia. The original post office was located one mile east of the site shown here.

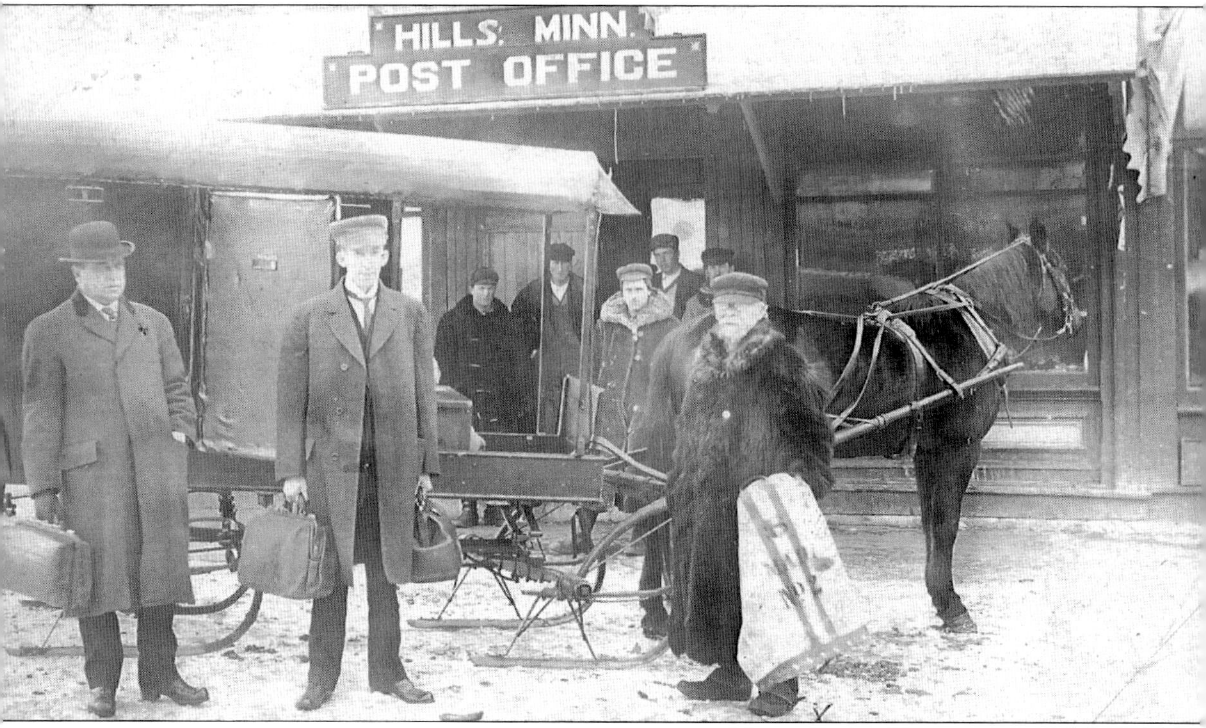

With almost every new postmaster, the Hills Post Office moved. There were six different locations before the post office settled in downtown Hills. Pictured here is the mail arriving at the post office from the depot by horse-drawn sled.

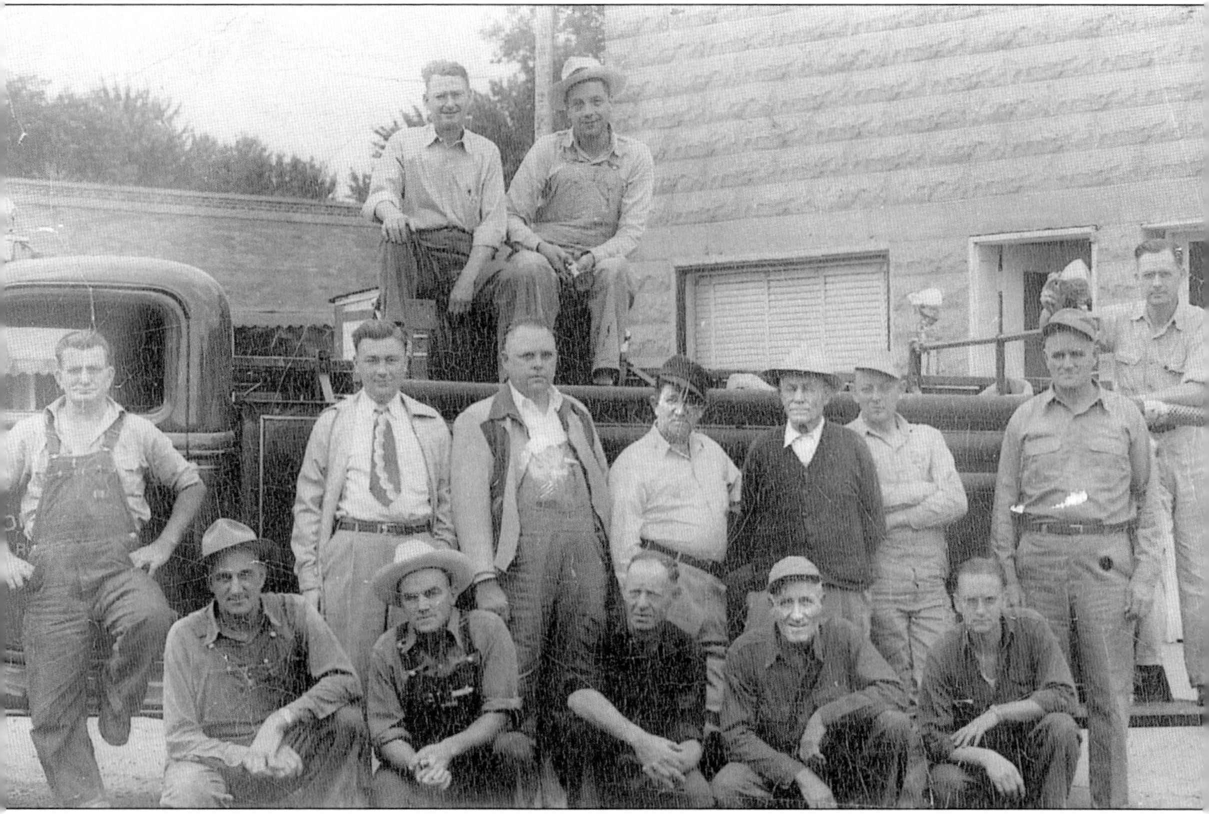

As communities became more established, local governments provided fire protection. Pictured here is the volunteer fire department from Hills, along with its 1948 Luverne fire engine. Since governments had limited funds, volunteers made up most fire departments.

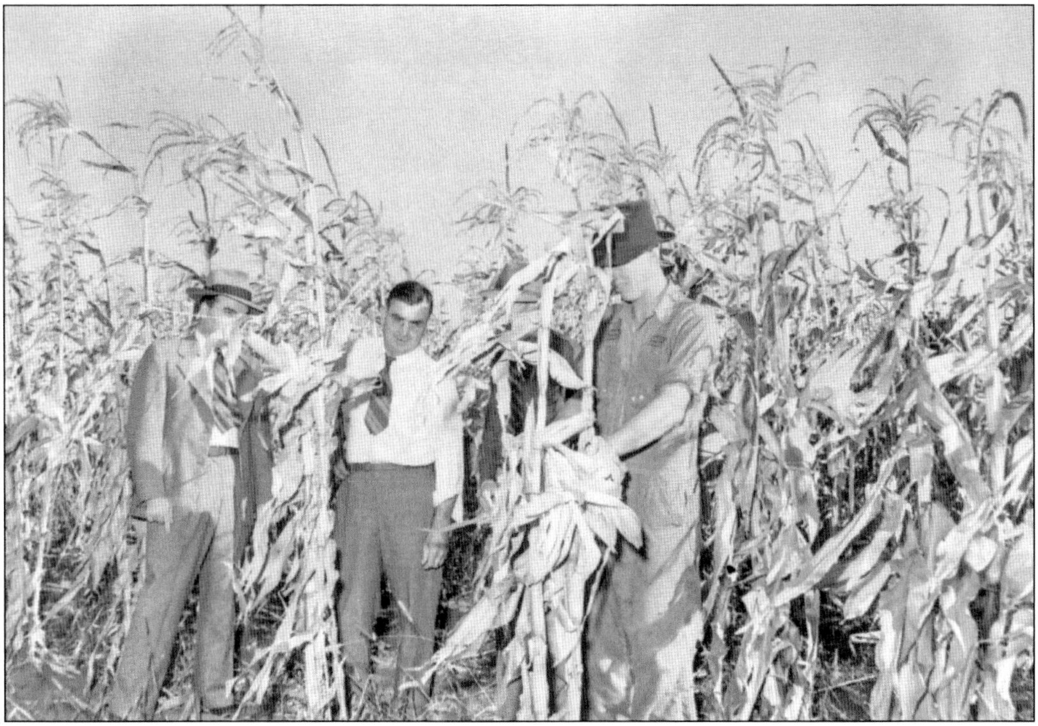

In the 1940s, the quality and quantity of the corn crop were of importance not just to farmers but also to others in the community. Local agricultural officials are checking out a portion of a cornfield with a local farmer. Agricultural officials and local bankers were always interested in the yields for the year.

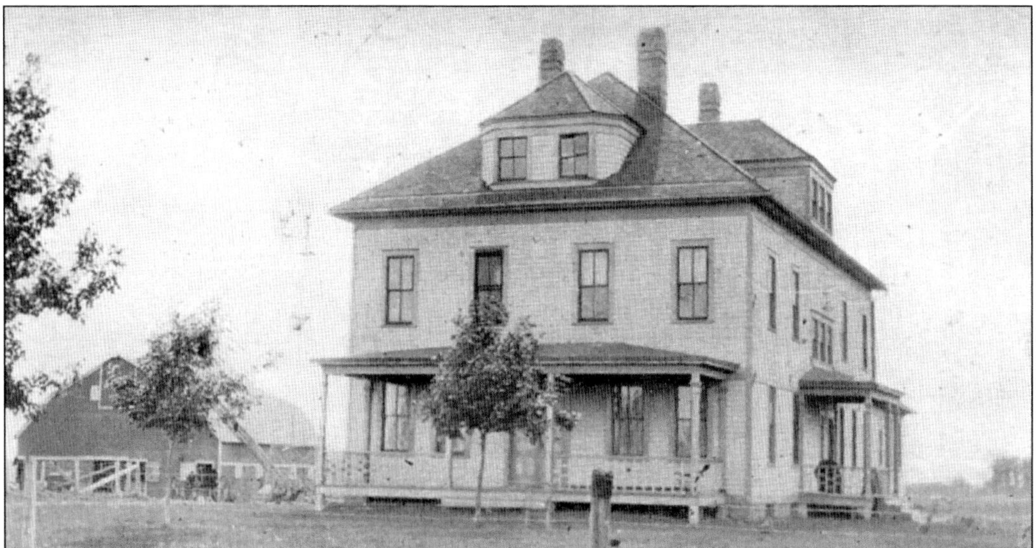

Another service provided by many counties was the county poor farm. For those who had fallen on hard times, the county poor farm provided a place to stay with regular meals and job opportunities. This photograph shows the Rock County poor farm, which remained in operation for many years. Those who were able to work helped with various chores around the farm.

Six

Rails and Roads

The first roads were established by wagons bringing settlers from the East to Rock County. Families and individuals laid their claims and established homesteads. As the years went by, township officials worked to grade the wagon trails. They set culverts to cross the creeks and built bridges to cross the larger bodies of water.

Township officials soon made use of the abundant natural gravel in the county. Large gravel pits were opened and mined to upgrade the roads so that they would remain passable in any kind of weather. Gravel was also used extensively to improve drainage and in manufacturing building materials.

Two major federal roadways intersected in Rock County. US Highway 75 (now named King of Trails Highway) went from the Gulf of Mexico to the Canadian border, passing through Rock County. US Highway 16 (now Interstate 90) passed through the county from the East Coast to the West Coast, intersecting US Highway 75 in Luverne. The federal government began to pave these roads in the 1930s, and that road system led the way to further business development within Rock County. With these major highways, Rock County became connected to the entire nation.

Trains brought development and settlers. By October 1876, the first train stopped in Luverne. Within a few months, more and more people and supplies were arriving in Rock County. Records show that on February 27, 1878, there were 80 people who arrived in Luverne, and on March 19, 1878, there were an additional 112 people. At approximately the same time (April 29 to May 17), over 500 covered wagons and prairie schooners arrived in the county.

By 1880, there were 3,036 people living in Rock County, only 13 years after the first city was established.

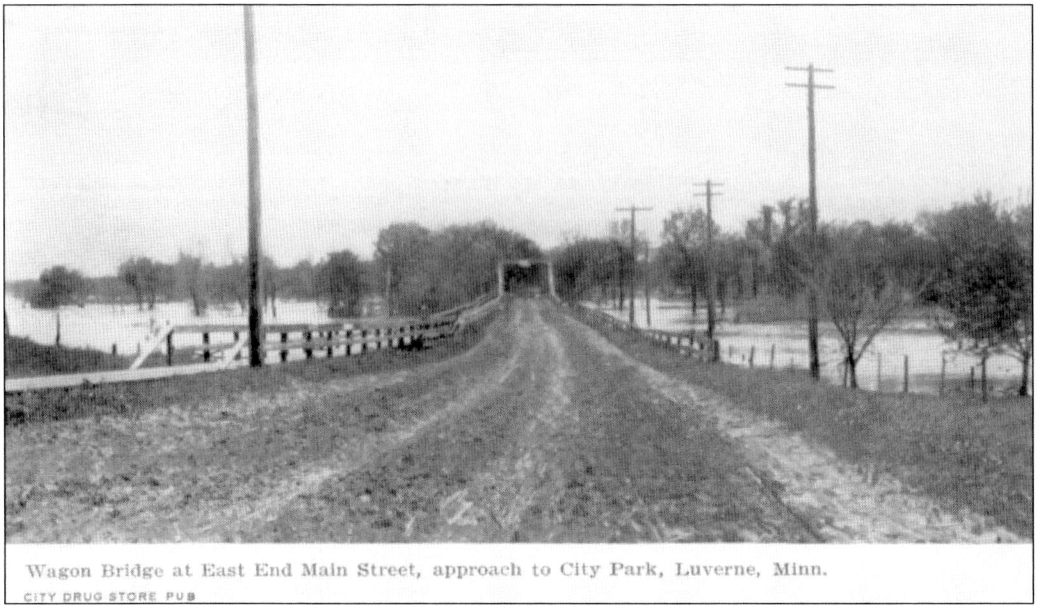

As early settler paths were expanded to roads, they became more user friendly. In this photograph, a dirt road leads from Luverne to the east across the Rock River and passes by the city park during a spring flood.

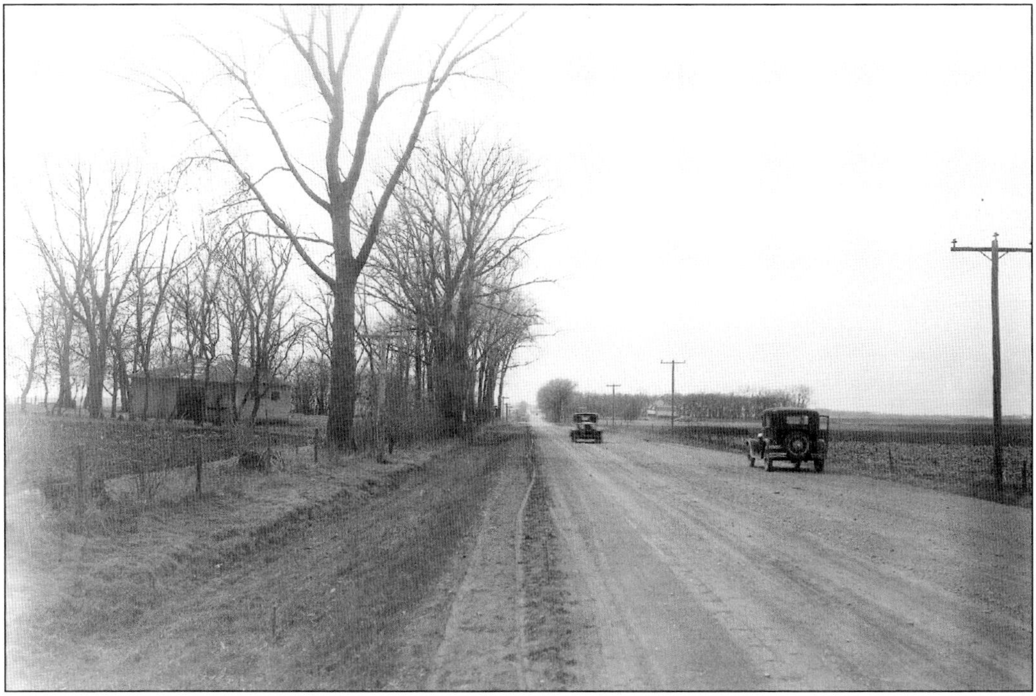

Pictured is one of the improved roads in Rock County. Because of the abundance of gravel within the county, many of the roads were improved when covered with it. This north-and-south highway became part of what was known as the King of Trails. Early roads in Rock County were merely extensions of the wagon-train trails from the Gulf of Mexico to the Canadian border. In the early 1920s, Luverne became part of the King of Trails, as designated by the Rock County commissioners.

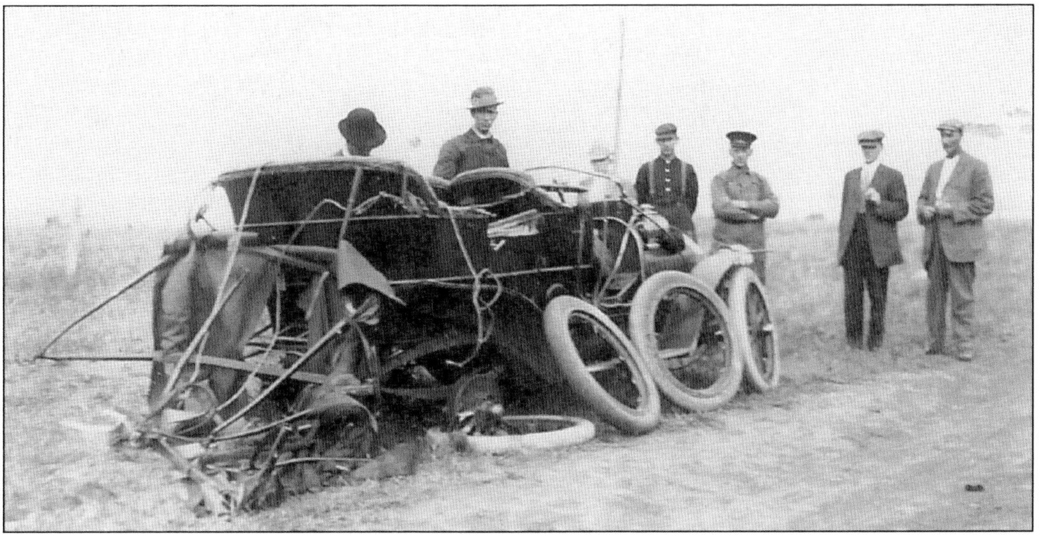

Not all of the roads in Rock County were in good repair, as can be seen here. Early automobiles were not engineered to handle the variety of perils that could be found on early roads. Three of the four tires on this vehicle appear to be damaged.

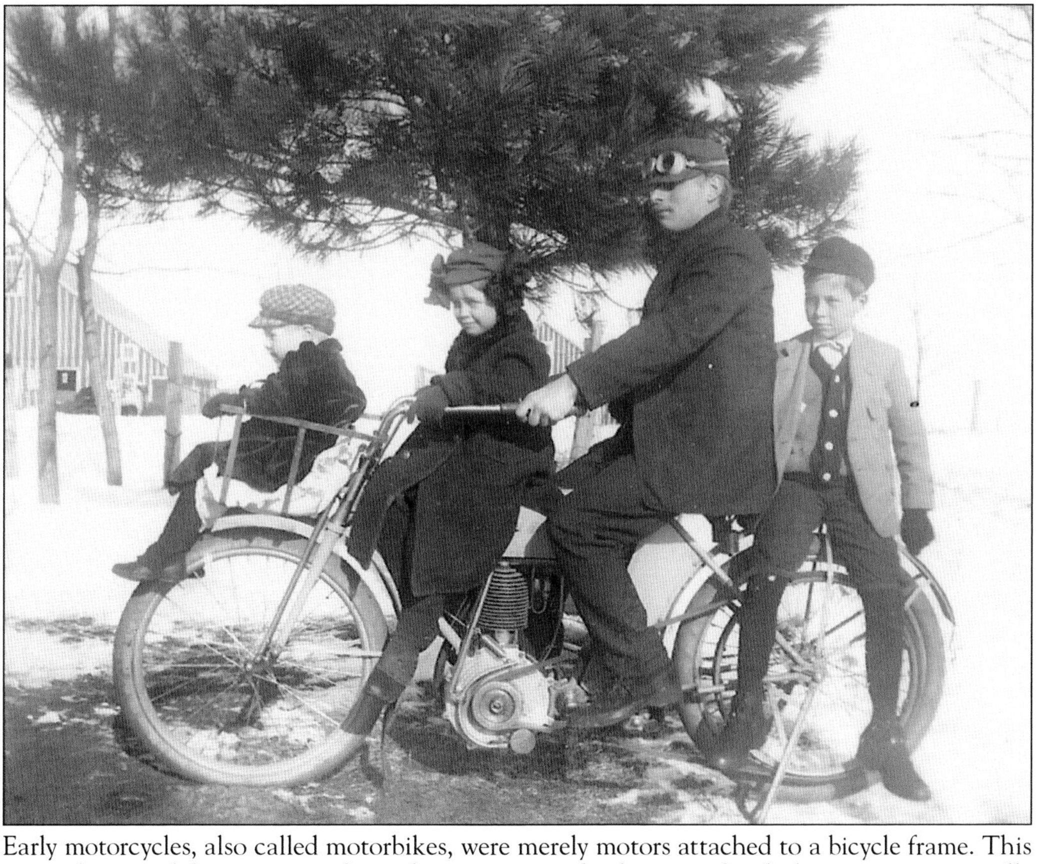

Early motorcycles, also called motorbikes, were merely motors attached to a bicycle frame. This particular motorbike was a great form of transportation for the entire family; however, it is especially precarious that this motorbike was usable in the winter with snow and ice.

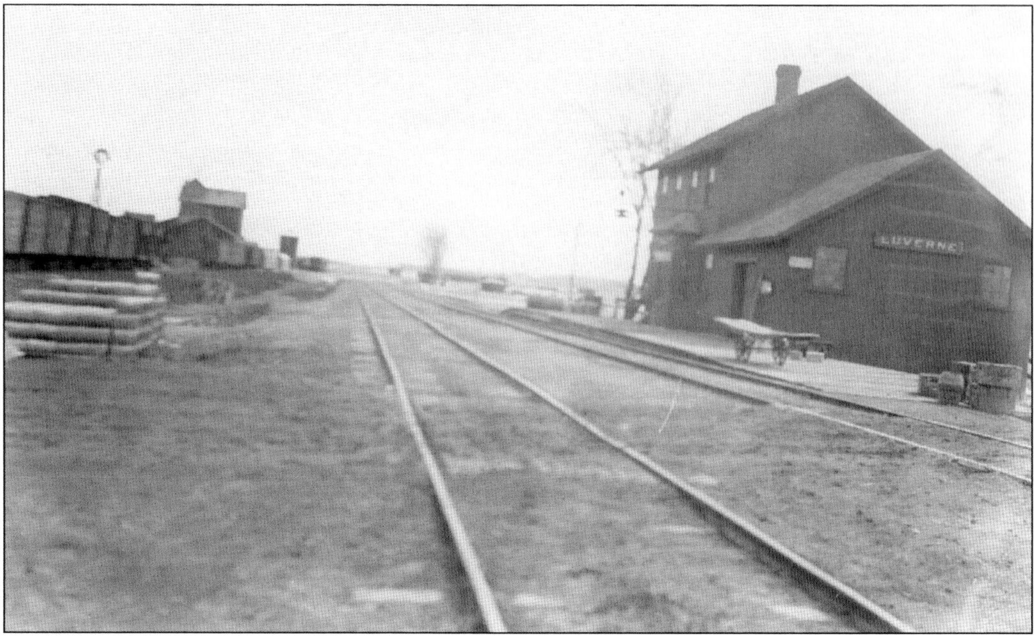

In 1876, the first depot was built in Luverne on what was called the Chicago, St. Paul, Minneapolis and Omaha Railway line. This track ran east and west and entered Luverne in 1876, traveling from Worthington. There are a number of tracks at this location, and additional cars could be brought in and left while they were filled with various materials for shipping in and out of Luverne.

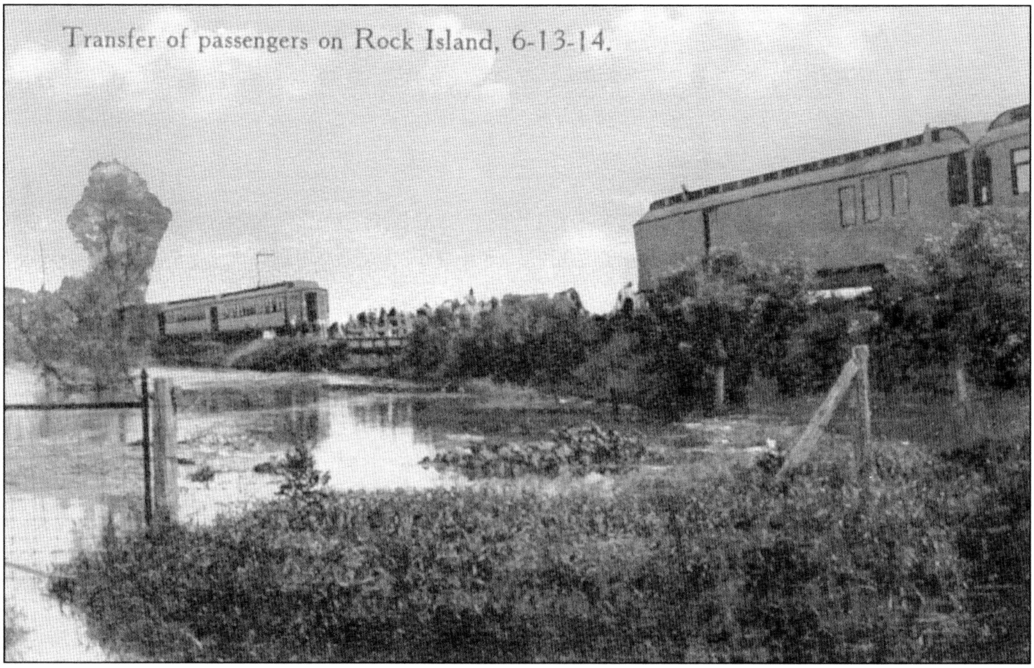

During the flood of 1914, the railroad bridge crossing the Rock River was in danger of collapsing. Trains were backed up to the railroad bridge, and passengers were unloaded and asked to walk across it. They were then loaded onto cars located on the other side of the flooded area.

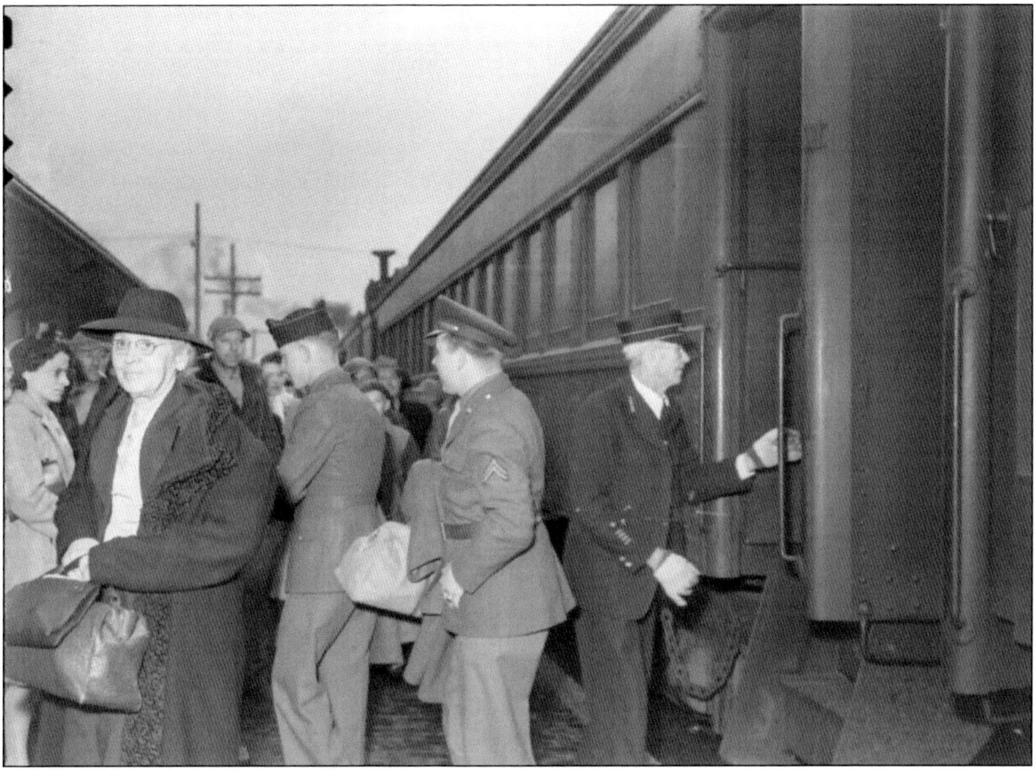

Shown here are troops returning from military duty for a leave or homecoming. A crowd of family and friends has gathered at the station for the reunion.

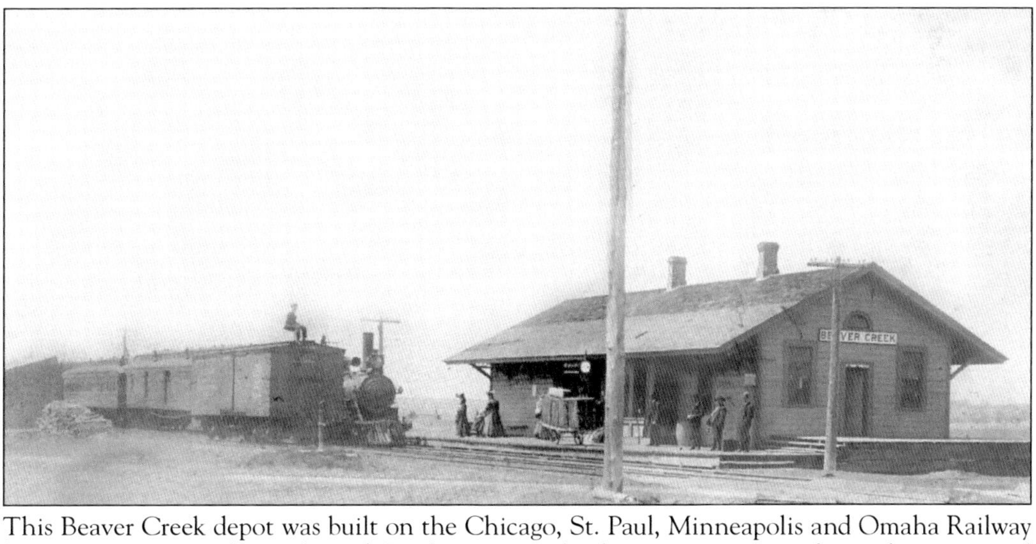

This Beaver Creek depot was built on the Chicago, St. Paul, Minneapolis and Omaha Railway line running east and west through Rock County. The depot site was part of an eight-acre parcel of land given to the railroad for a townsite, which eventually became the community of Beaver Creek. The side rails were used for cars to load and unload materials.

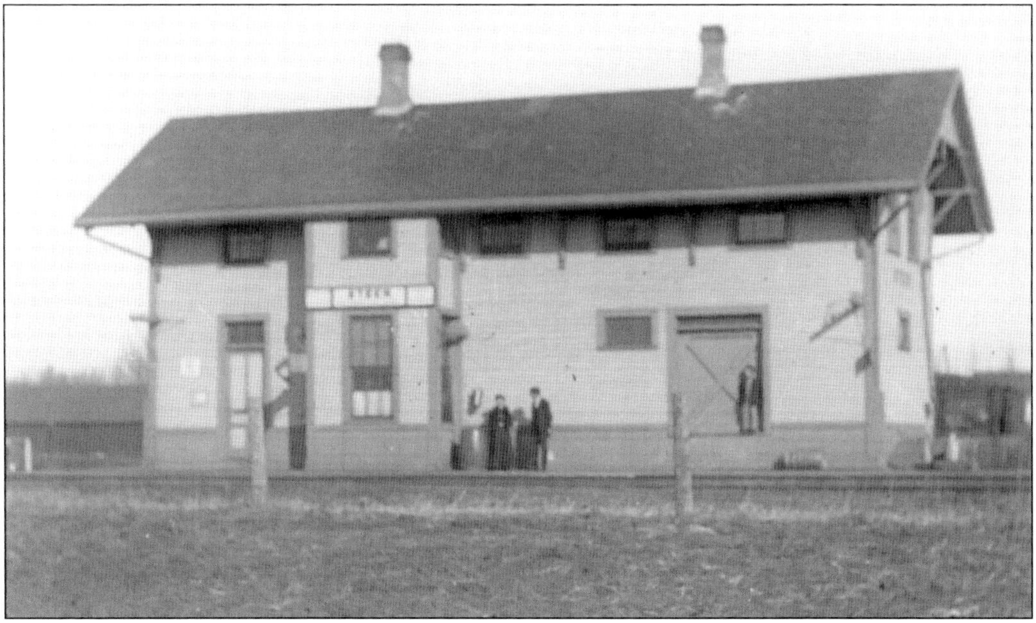

A family is shown waiting to be taken from the Steen depot to an unknown destination.

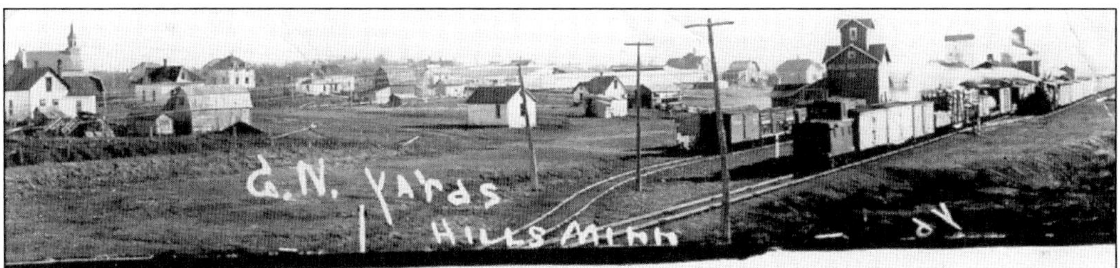

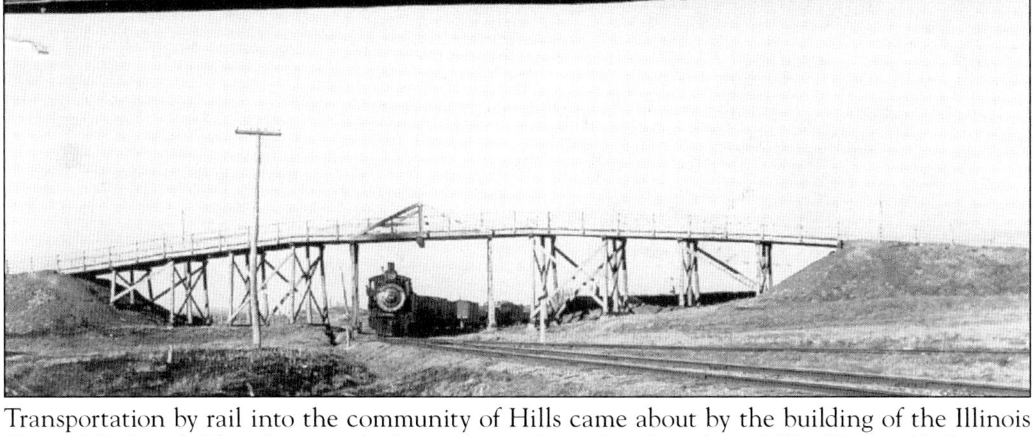

Transportation by rail into the community of Hills came about by the building of the Illinois Central Railroad. The photograph above shows the railroad yards in Hills. Pictured below is a train going under a wooden trestle.

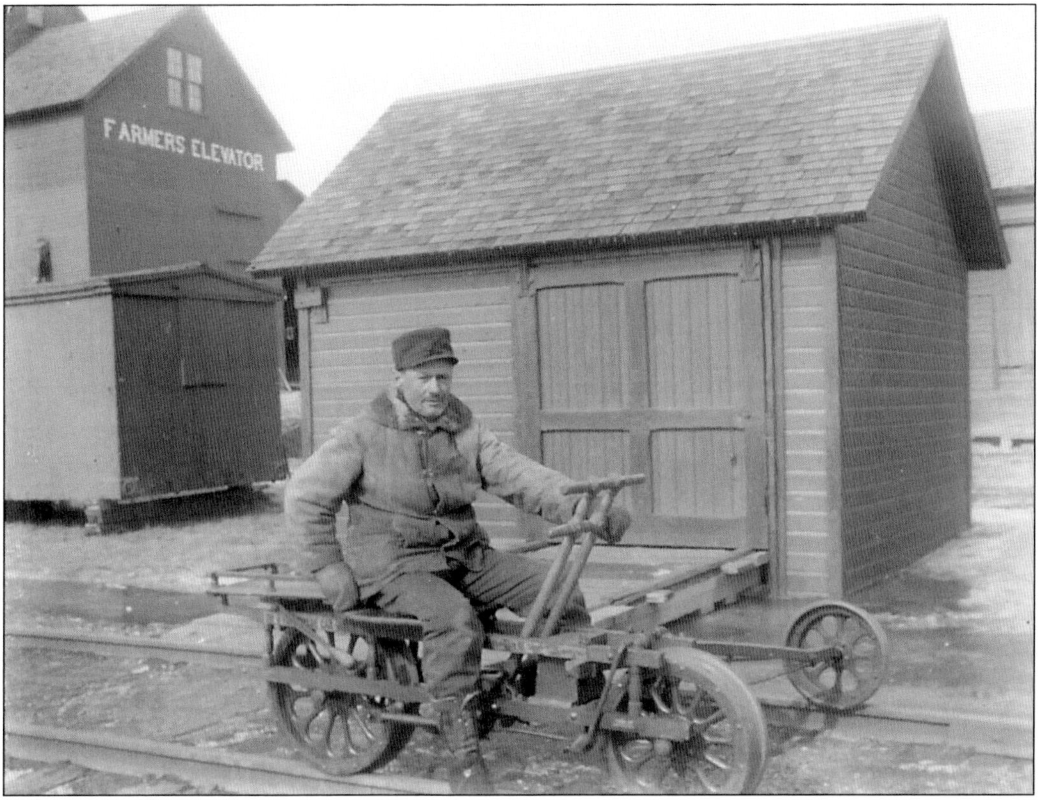

Individuals or crews driving handcars maintained of all of the railroads within Rock County.

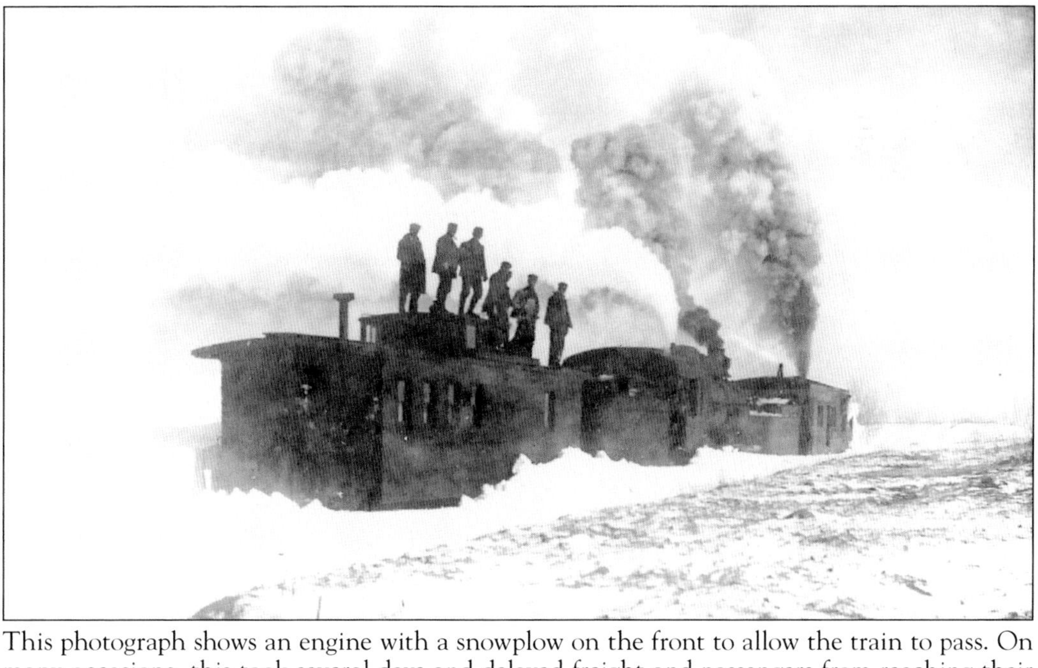

This photograph shows an engine with a snowplow on the front to allow the train to pass. On many occasions, this took several days and delayed freight and passengers from reaching their destinations. The men seen here kept the coal and wood stoked in the engine.

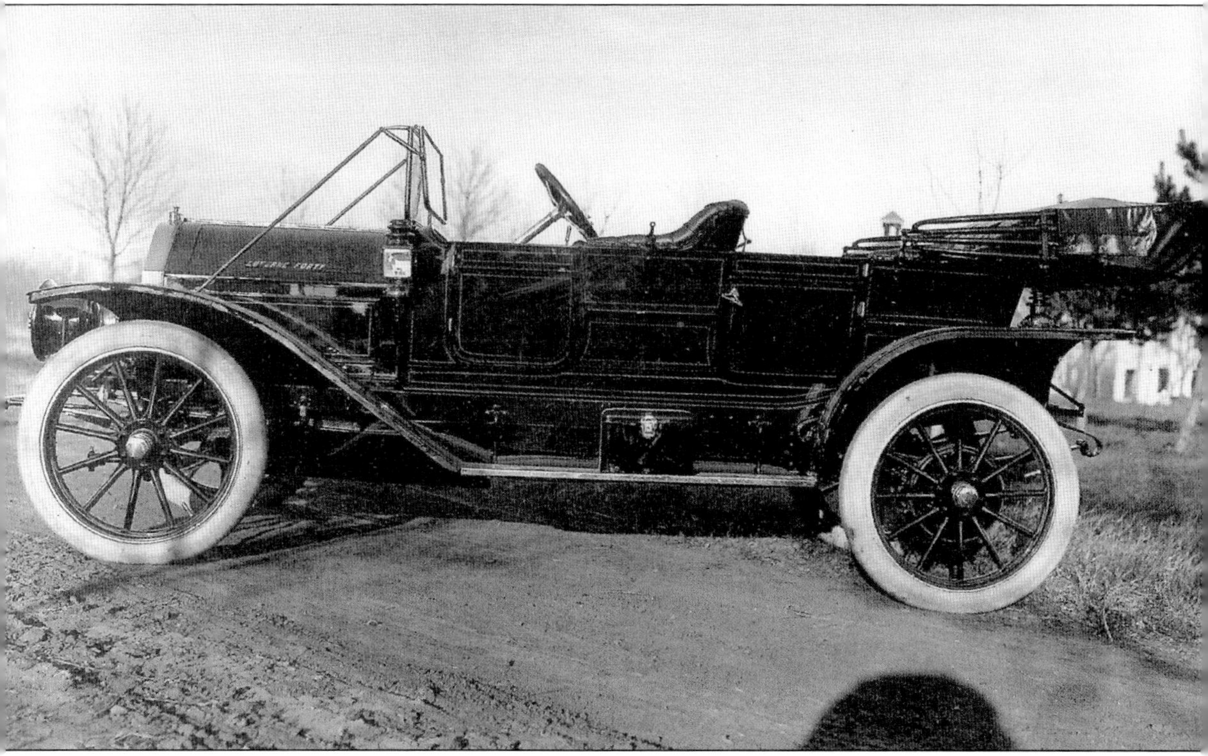

One of the early businesses in Luverne was the Luverne Automobile Company. It began manufacturing automobiles in 1909 and continued until 1919, when it changed over to trucks and eventually fire engines. The cars built here became very popular and were sold throughout the Midwest. The manufacturing of fire engines became a major product, and although some things have changed, the fire engines are still being produced under the Luverne name.

Seven

Mind and Soul

From its earliest days, education and religion were important aspects of life in Rock County. Pioneers came to this county deeply committed to their Christian faith. They settled the county, and as their families began to grow, they quickly needed churches and a good educational system. Every community that was established had a school and one or more churches. On county roads, country schools and churches sprang up to fill the needs of farming neighborhoods.

The Rock County superintendent of schools administered the robust country school system. Prior to World War II, Rock County had 74 country schools that dotted the landscaping, complying with the state law demanding that no student should travel more than three miles to his or her school. Each Rock County city established a school to fit the needs of community growth. Luverne established its school in 1870; Beaver Creek in 1877; Hills, Magnolia, and Hardwick in 1893; Kanaranzi in 1899; Kenneth in 1901; Ash Creek in 1903; and Steen in 1905. These schools became the centers of growth and vitality in the communities. High standards of education developed enterprising students who used their skills to establish and grow the local economy.

Establishing a life in a new frontier required strength of character, body, and mind. The men, women, and children who settled Rock County had strong religious convictions. Their faith gave them the strength to settle this land, not knowing what they would have to face each day. Circuit preachers were the first religious men in Rock County; soon, all types of churches were founded to meet people's religious needs. Extended families met to worship together, and churches grew out of those relationships. Historians estimate there were at one time more than two dozen denominations and religious sects represented in Rock County. Two churches of original construction remain in use in Rock County and are pictured in this chapter.

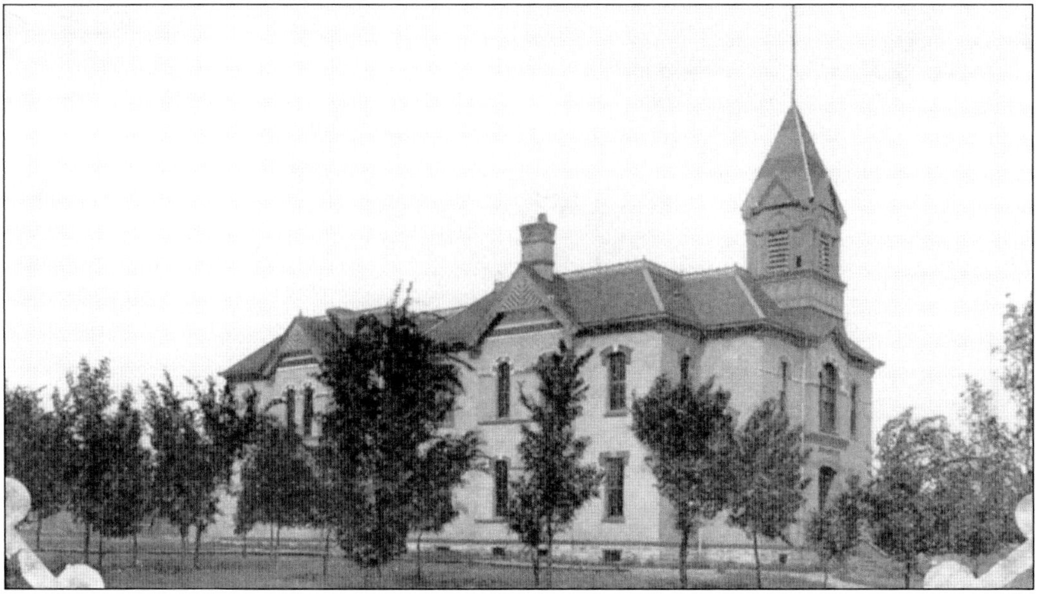

In 1882, residents of Luverne laid the cornerstone for their first school building. Completed in 1886, the school was located on Luverne Street between Freeman and Cedar Streets. It was used as the elementary school and aptly named Central School.

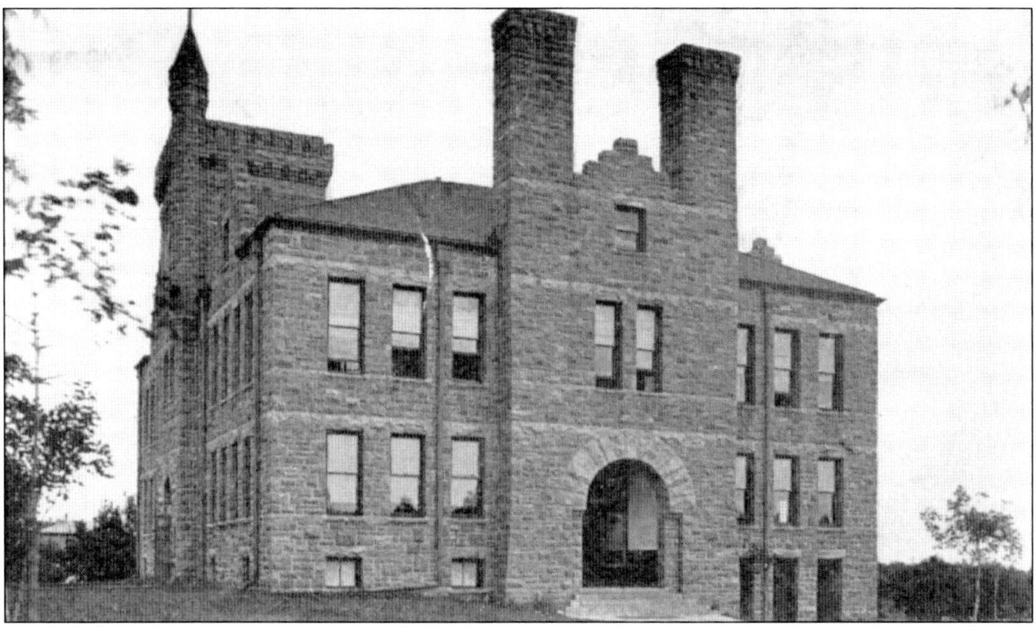

The first Luverne High School was on the 300 block of North Kniss Avenue. Constructed in 1895 of Sioux quartzite, the building operated as the high school until 1926, when a new high school was erected.

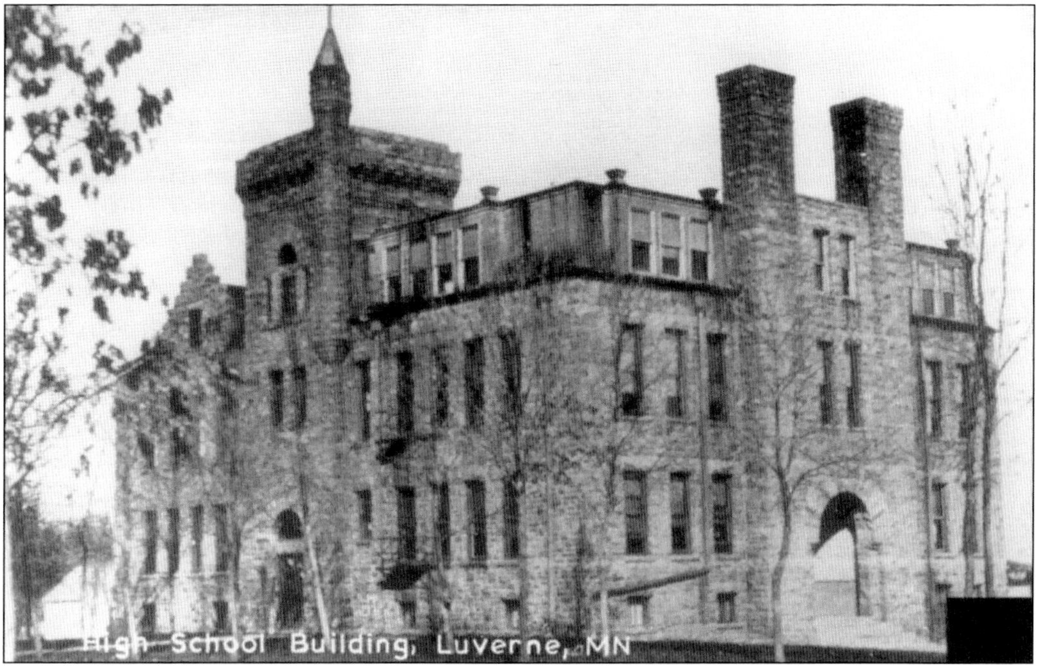

Within a few years of the high school's construction, the district responded to the need for additional room by adding a third floor to the building at 300 North Kniss Avenue. The third floor did not cover the entire structure, just the southeast and southwest portions. This floor contained the library and additional classrooms. A circular-tube fire escape was located on the east side of the building.

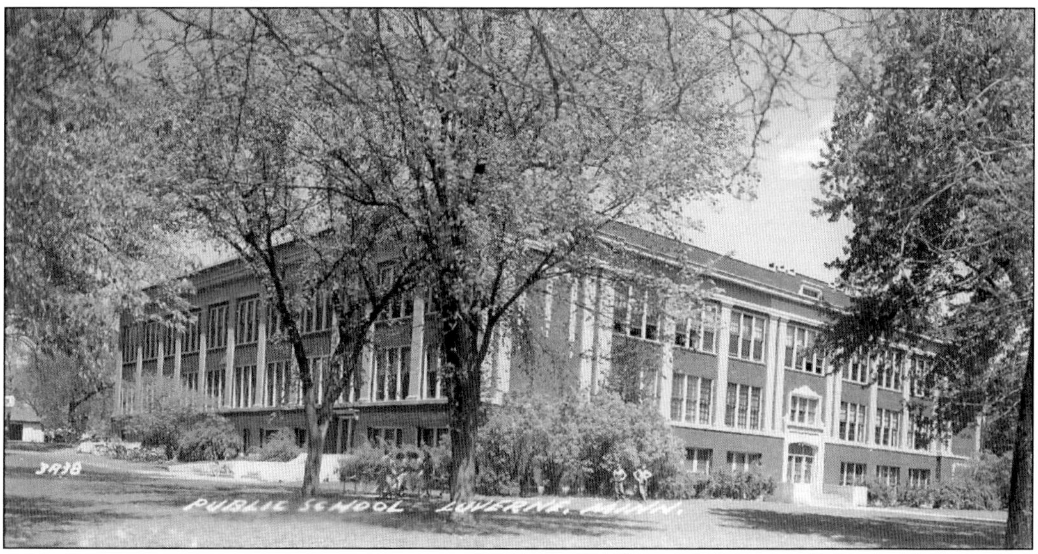

Growth of the Luverne School District resulted in the construction of a new high school in 1926. The new building was constructed on the site of the Central School, and the old high school on North Kniss Avenue became the elementary school. When the current high school was constructed in 1955, the elementary school abandoned the building on North Kniss Avenue and moved to this site. This building was the elementary school until 1990, when students were moved to a new building added to the high school at 700 North Kniss Avenue.

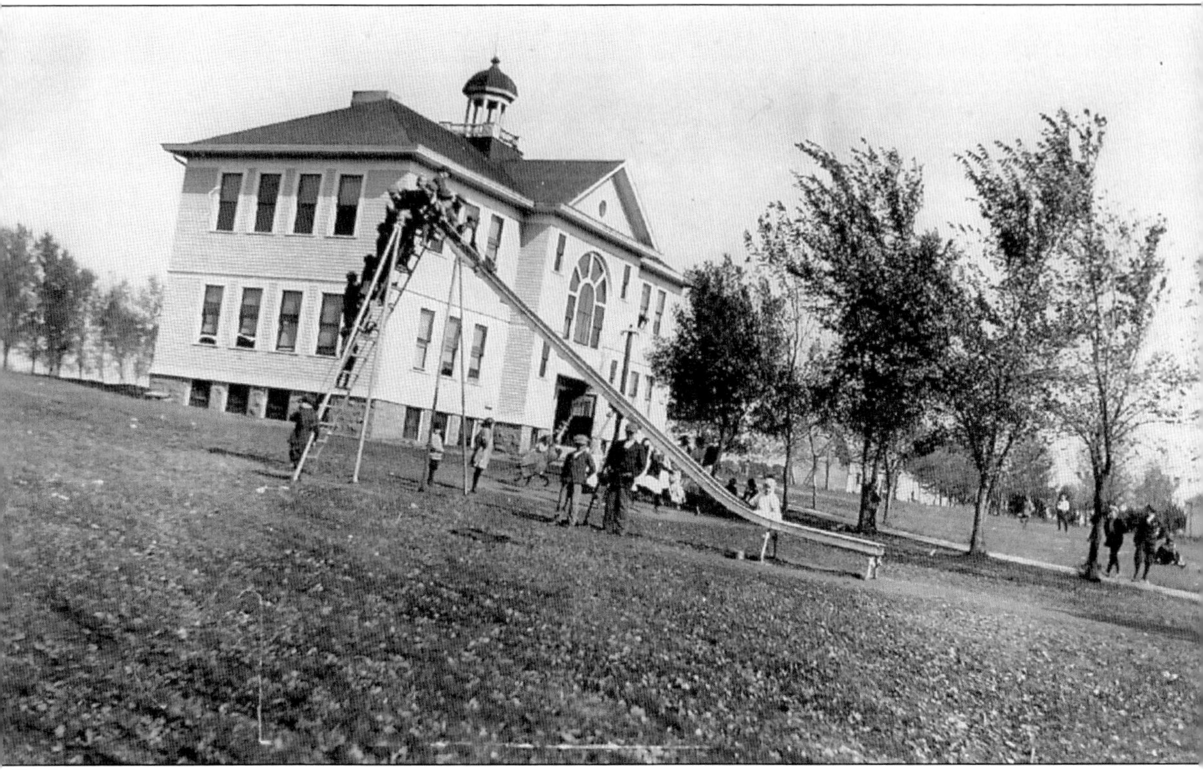

In 1894, the City of Hills responded to the influx of residents and growing families by constructing a three-story school building, anticipating the growth of the district. Multiple classrooms, a full basement, beautiful arched entrance window, and bell tower made an impressive sight on the prairie. The cost of the building was $5,000.

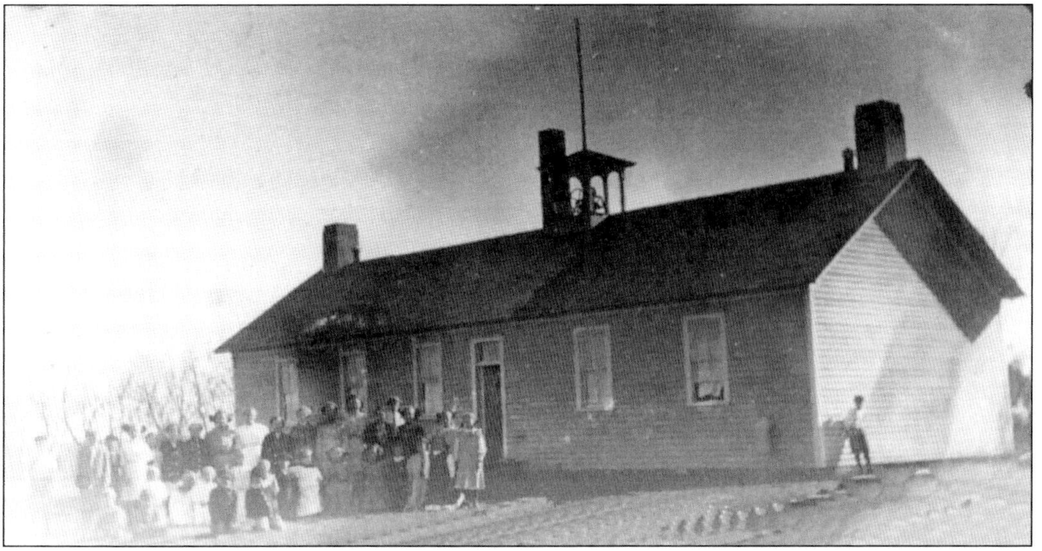

Ash Creek built its school in 1910. It had two classrooms for the two teachers in the district. One teacher on the south side of the building had grades one through four, while the other teacher had the rest of the grades on the other side. Located between the classrooms was a library. Each classroom had a cloakroom and entrance. Students were educated in this building until the district merged. The school was closed in 1957.

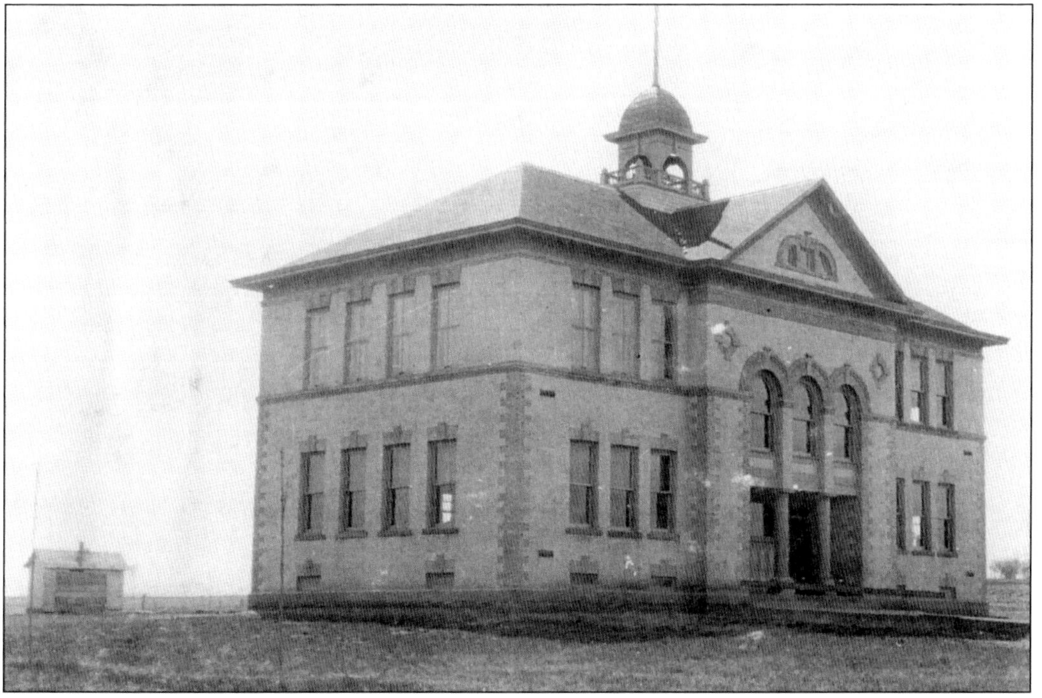

Beaver Creek built its first school in 1877 about a half mile west of the city. The following year, the building was sold, and Beaver Creek constructed a one-room building within city limits. By 1904, the needs of the district had changed, and a two-story, four-room brick building was constructed. The $10,000 building was dedicated in 1905. In the summer of 1920, lightning struck the school, and it was destroyed by fire. A new school was built on the same site.

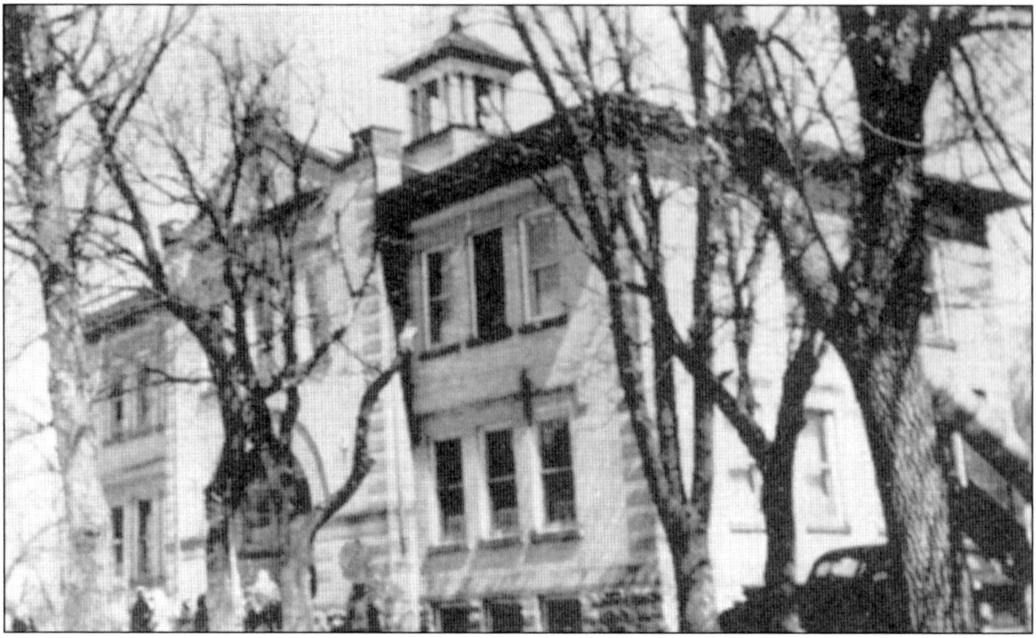

The first school in Hardwick was established in 1891. Student enrollment continued to grow, and by 1906 the district constructed a new school of sand-lime brick from the Luverne Brick and Tile Company, owned by R.B. Hinkly. The district's choice of light-colored brick was revolutionary during the period. The school continued to be used until the Hardwick District merged with the Luverne School District.

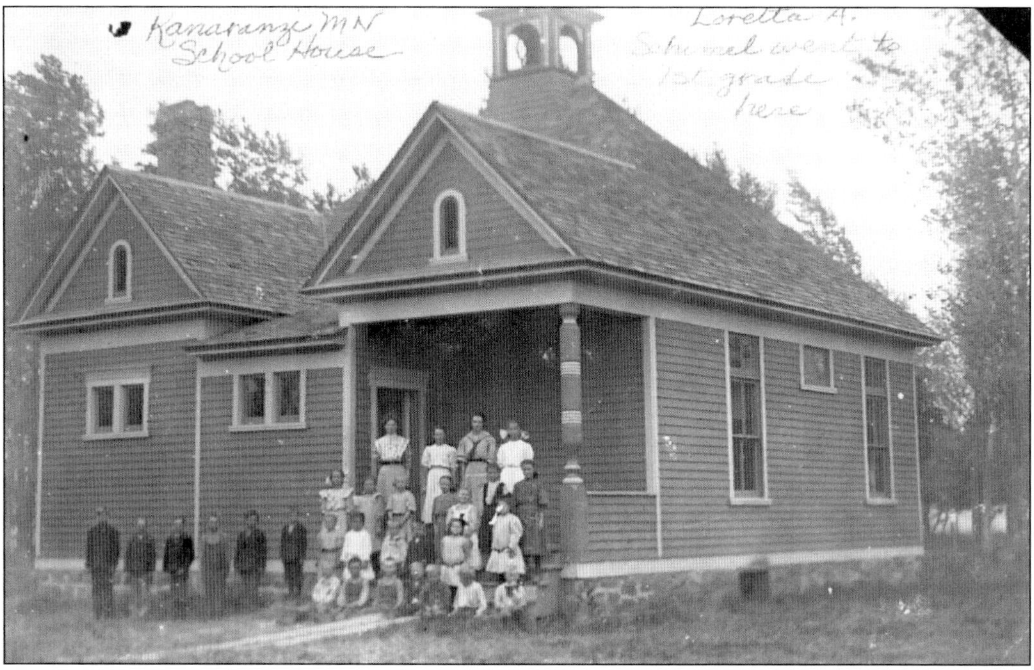

Kanaranzi responded to the needs of its residents and farm neighbors when it constructed this schoolhouse in 1886 north of the community. Myrtle Angell was one of the first teachers for District No. 23 in the early 1890s. Teachers instructed students of all grades and special needs.

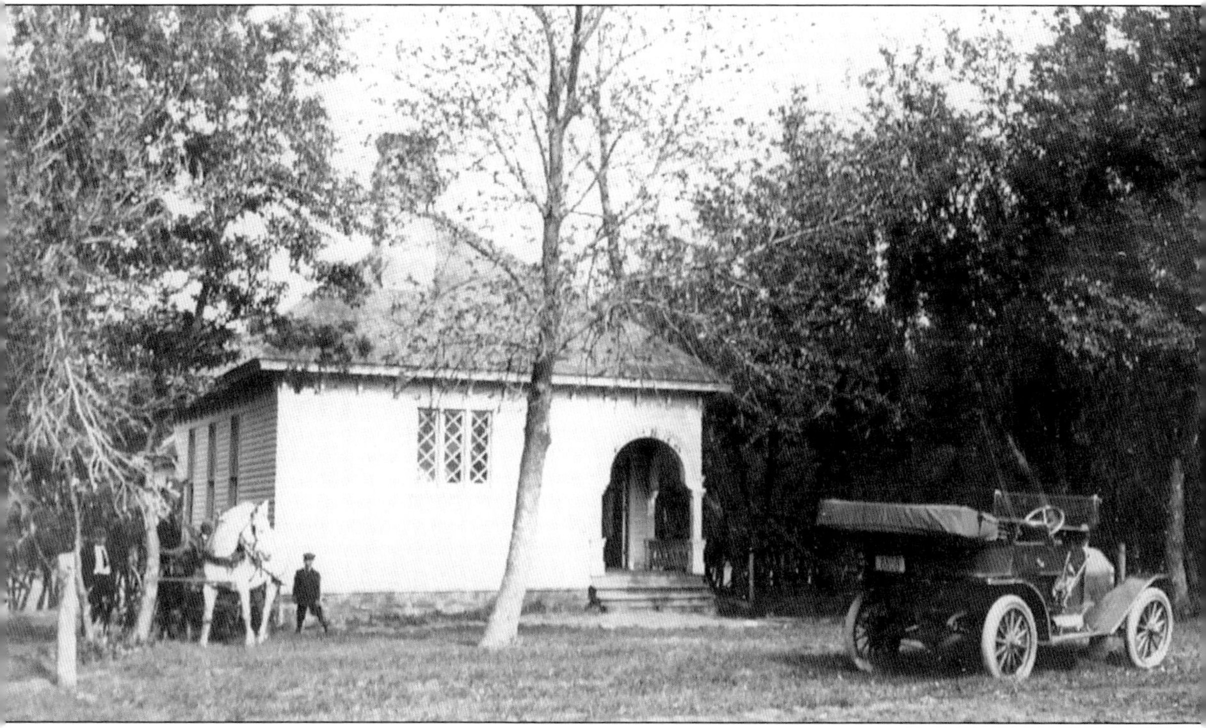

Located south of Ash Creek, District No. 1 was the first country school in the county. It was established in 1871, only a few years after Rock County was first settled. By the late 1930s, Rock County's 74 country schools educated many students in the county.

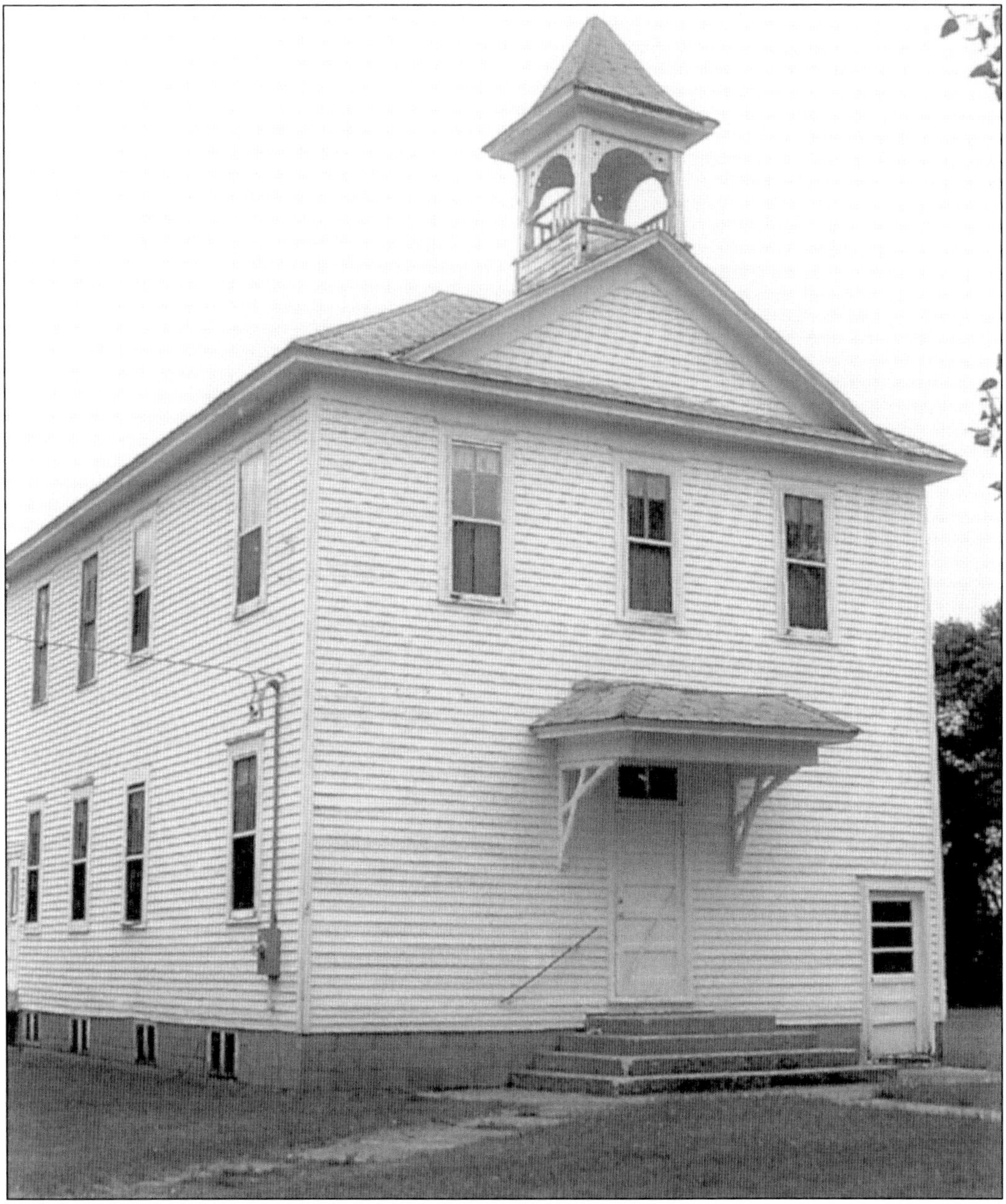

Kenneth was a bustling community, and in 1901 the community built this school at a cost of $2,500. Nellie Morse was the first teacher, and the schoolhouse was filled with 32 pupils. The two-story building offered classrooms for older children on the second floor and younger children on the first floor. The building still stands and is the only two-story, two-room schoolhouse left in the state of Minnesota.

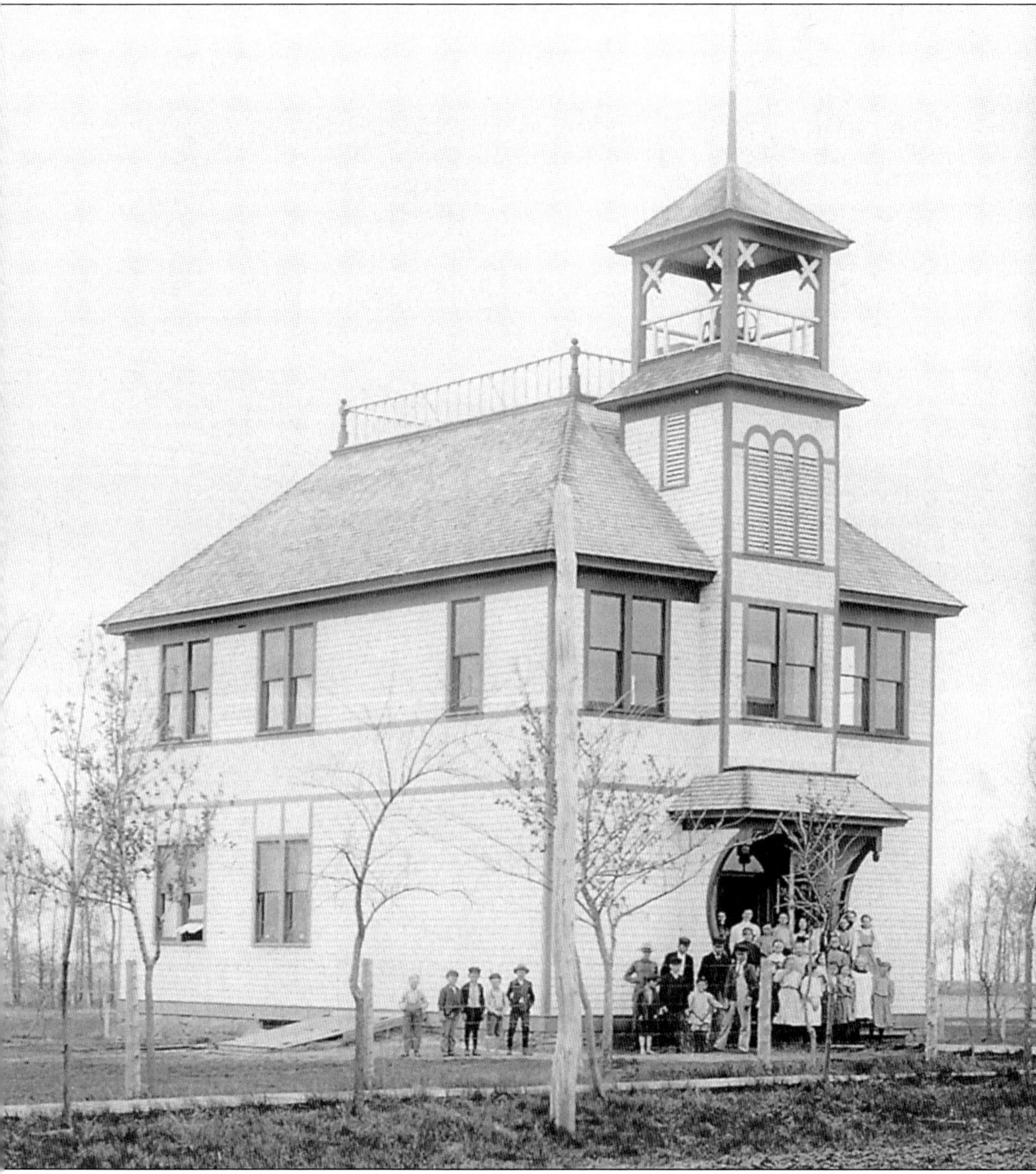

By 1919, Magnolia recognized the need to expand its school and constructed this building for the astronomical cost of $45,000. The school housed elementary students on the first floor and high school students on the second floor. Magnolia School consolidated with country school districts Nos. 5, 8, and 30 to become the Magnolia School District, the first consolidated district in the county.

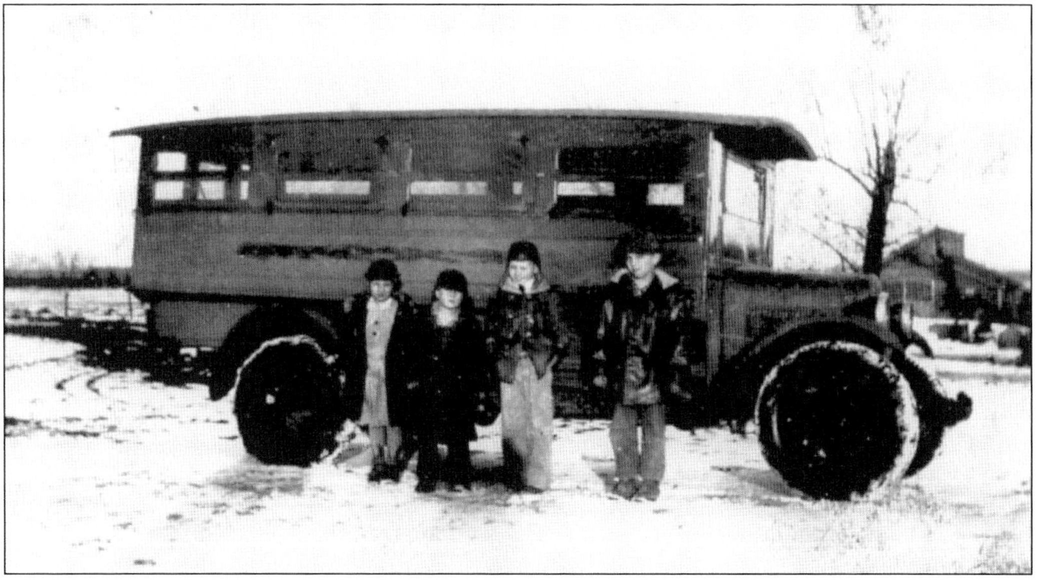

Consolidation brought a whole new series of challenges to school districts. One of the major issues was district transportation. Most students walked to school, and in complying with Minnesota state law, the three-mile rule made education available to all; however, with consolidation, students had much farther to travel. The Magnolia School District was one of the first in the county to offer school bus transportation to rural students. Pictured is the Magnolia school bus in the early 1930s.

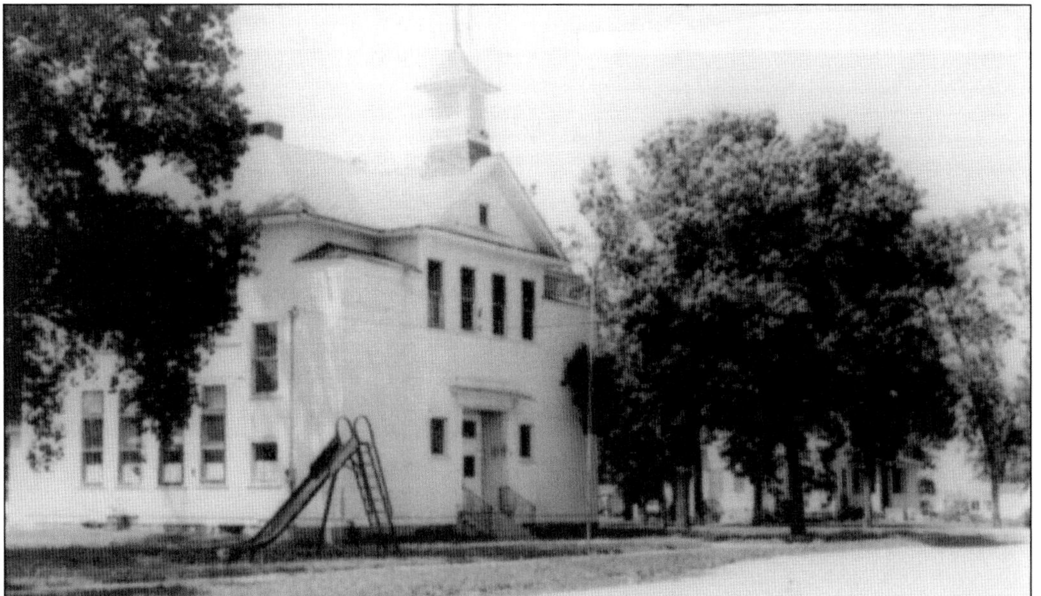

The city of Steen's new school was built around 1920. The two-story structure was used for the elementary and high school and continued to be used until the school closed and consolidated with the Hills district.

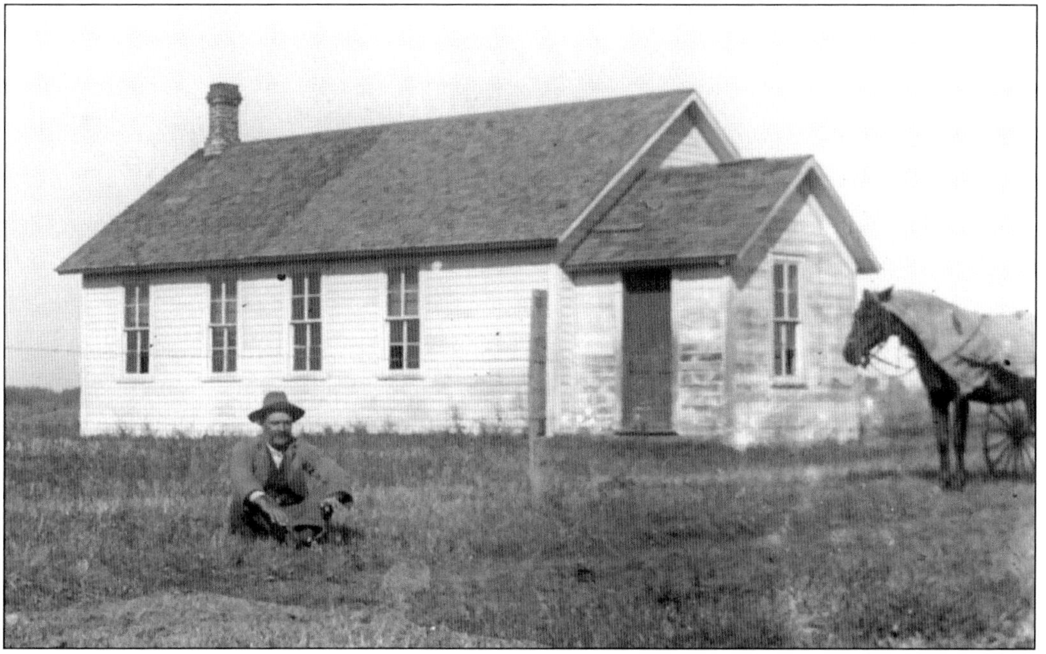

The area around Steen had a strong presence of country schools. This early-1900s photograph shows the one-room school where Rose McKeon taught. Otis Steen is laying a phone line from the school to the town of Steen.

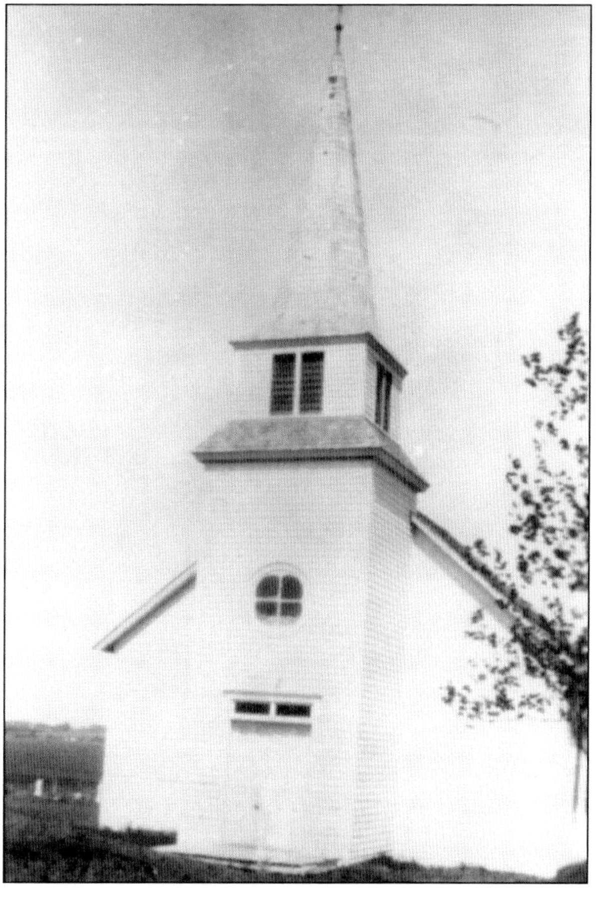

Norwegian immigrant families founded the Blue Mound Lutheran Church in 1872. The church was originally located one mile north and one mile west of its present location on County Road 19. In 1884, the church was moved by a tornado across the railroad tracks. No window was broken or door jammed in the event. The congregation moved the church to its present location and held weekly services until 1976.

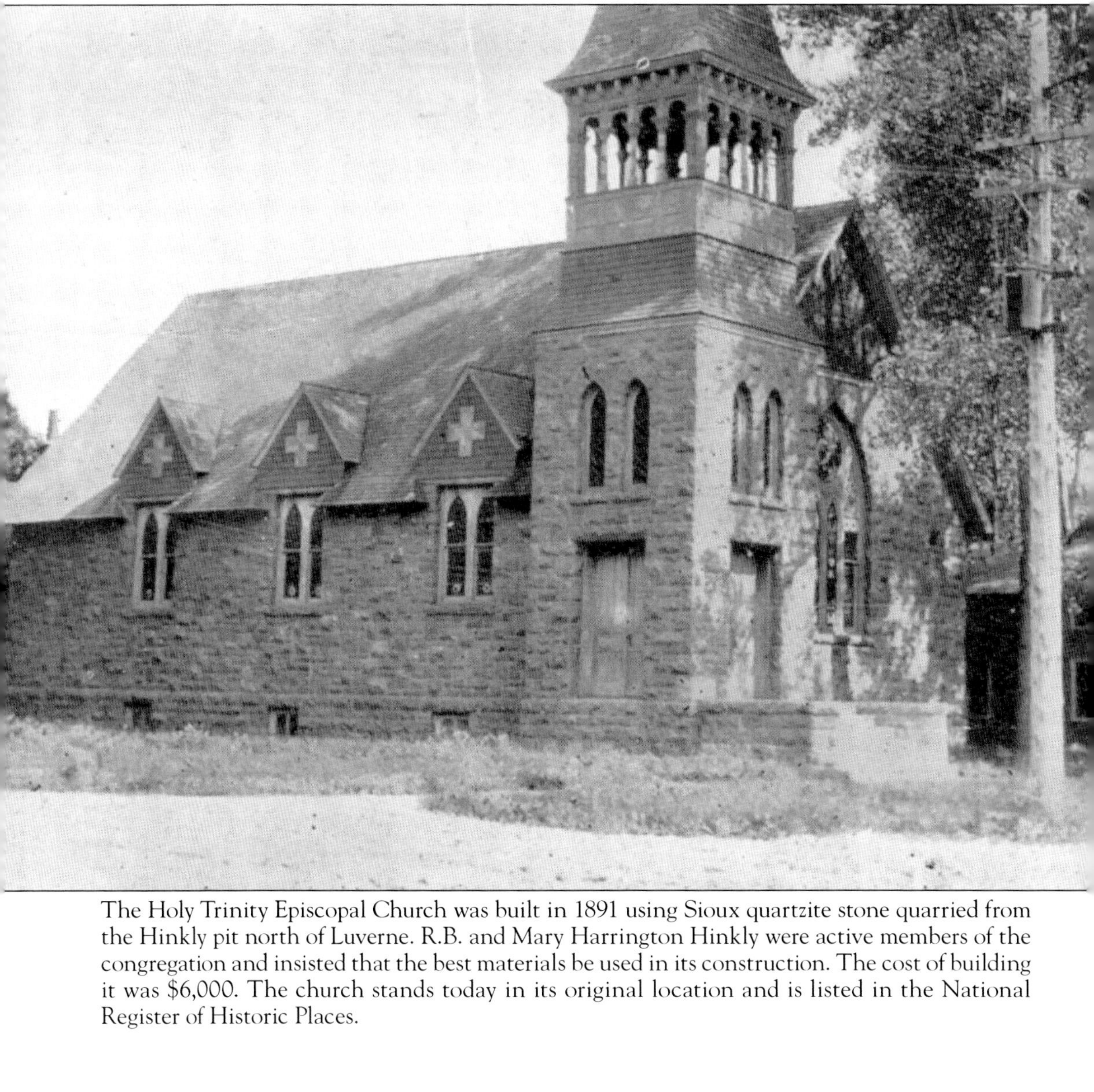

The Holy Trinity Episcopal Church was built in 1891 using Sioux quartzite stone quarried from the Hinkly pit north of Luverne. R.B. and Mary Harrington Hinkly were active members of the congregation and insisted that the best materials be used in its construction. The cost of building it was $6,000. The church stands today in its original location and is listed in the National Register of Historic Places.

Eight

Serving the Country

After the end of the Civil War, soldiers returned to their homes in the eastern and central parts of the United States to find that their jobs or families were no longer there, and so many veterans went west to find their fame and fortune. Rock County was untamed territory. There were no settlements of people, no rail service, and no form of government. There was nothing more than land, which is exactly what many Civil War veterans wanted.

Thousands of Rock County men and women have volunteered to serve their country, regardless if it was the Spanish-American War, World War I, World War II, the Korean War, the Vietnam War, the Cold War, or the Middle East conflicts—during war or peacetime, Rock County residents have answered the call.

Soldiers, sailors, Marines, Coast Guard, and airmen returned home to establish a strong network of service organizations. American Legions, the Grand Army of the Republic, Veterans of Foreign Wars, and other fraternal organizations offered opportunities for both veterans and communities.

No records of service were more documented than the stories of Rock County's World War II veterans. In doing research for his 14-hour PBS miniseries in 2007, documentarian and historian Ken Burns watched a two-part video series called *A Fighter Pilot's Story*, produced by Luverne native Quentin Aanenson about his service as a P-37 pilot in Europe in World War II. After viewing it, Burns contacted Aanenson, and a close relationship developed between the historian and the World War II ace pilot. That relationship became the reason why Burns chose Rock County as one of four communities to be featured in his miniseries. Ken Burns's *The War* was premiered in the Historic Palace Theatre in September 2007. The epic miniseries featured stories of service members as well as the stories of the people on the home front. After more than seven years of study and research, Burns's history of World War II was broadcast to millions of people throughout the world. Luverne and Rock County were in the hearts and on the minds of many all over the world.

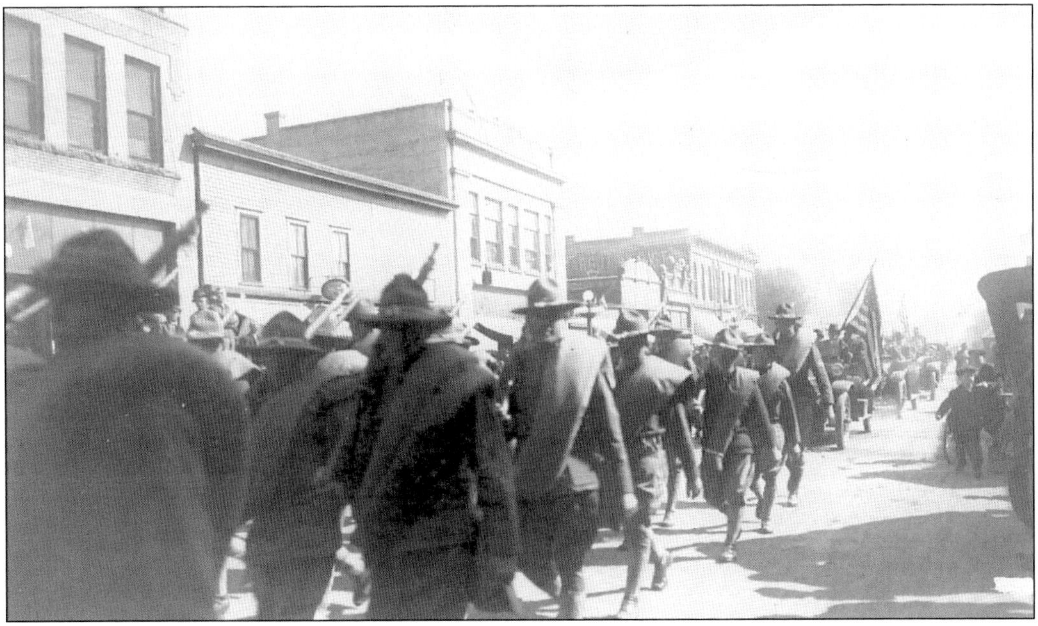

Marching down Main Street in Luverne in 1916, troops from Company A left their hometown to fight in the "war to end all wars." Fathers and mothers watched as their sons left to serve the United States. With packs on their backs and guns on one shoulder and bedrolls on the other, they marched in formation to board the train. Crowds of cheering people sent them on their way.

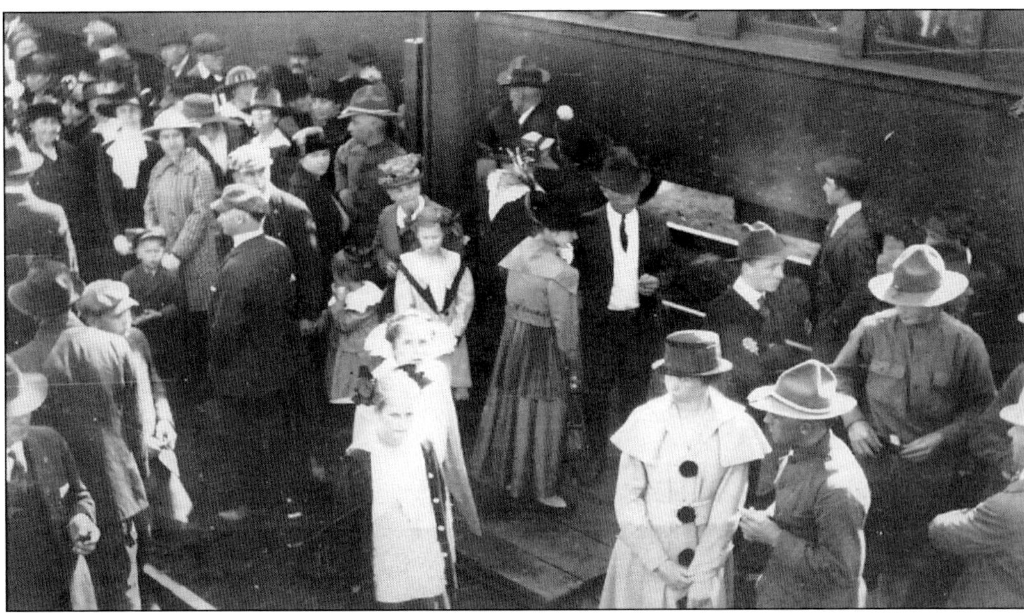

At the Chicago, St. Paul, Minneapolis and Omaha Railway train depot, soldiers and families say their final good-byes. Women, men, boys, and girls—all dressed in their Sunday best—shared those tearful final words not knowing if they would ever be able to speak to each other again.

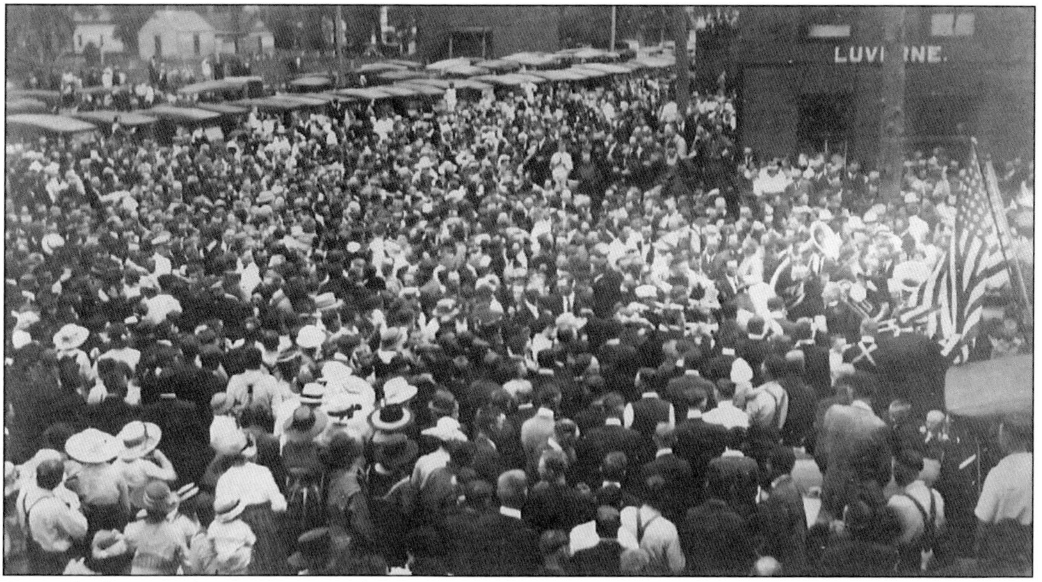

A total of 143 Rock County men shipped out from the train depot on September 28, 1917, to enter active-duty training at Camp Cody in New Mexico. The band played military and patriotic tunes, politicians delivered speeches, and the crowds waved good-bye. After a few months of training, on June 15, 1918, the men boarded ships on their way to France to fight in World War I.

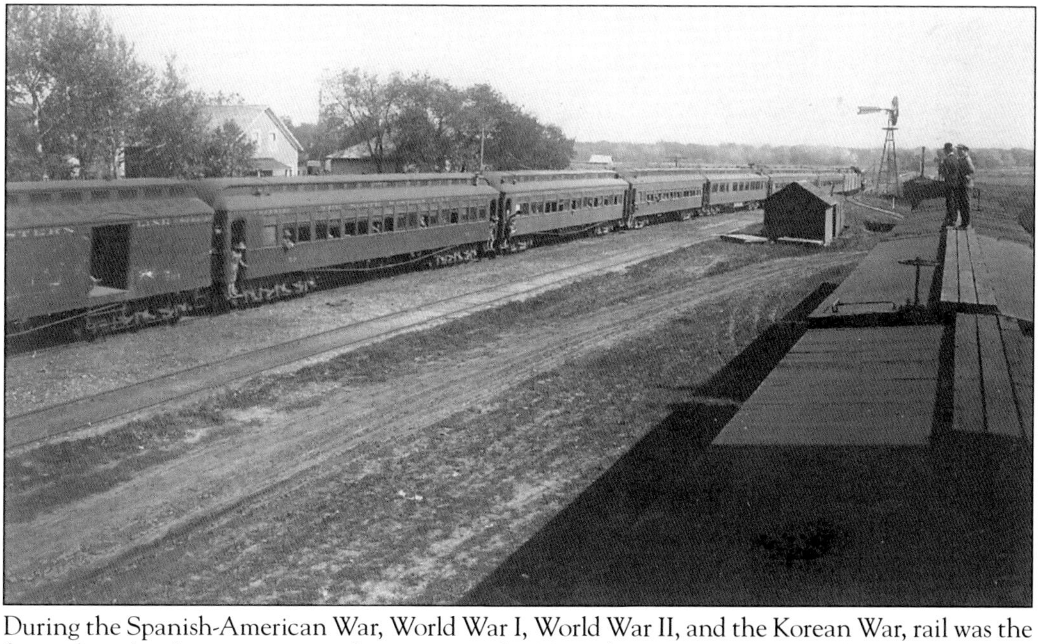

During the Spanish-American War, World War I, World War II, and the Korean War, rail was the favored mode of transportation for troops in the United States. At wartime, long lines of train cars carried troops from towns to bases for training and deployment. As they stopped at stations, people came to the tracks to hand soldiers baked goods, beverages, and newspapers.

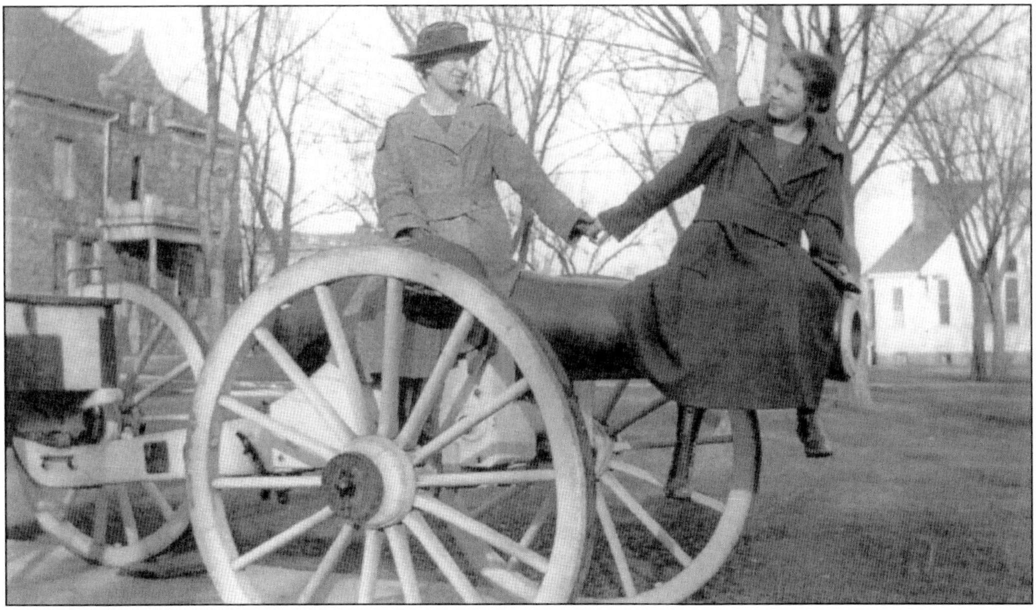

In 1896, Rock County accepted this Civil War siege cannon from members of the GAR's John A. Dix Post in New Jersey. The cannon, used on the USS *John Adams* in protecting Boston Harbor, provided a popular photo opportunity, as shown in this late 1920s image. The cannon still stands at the Rock County Courthouse Square as an integral part of the Rock County Veterans Memorial.

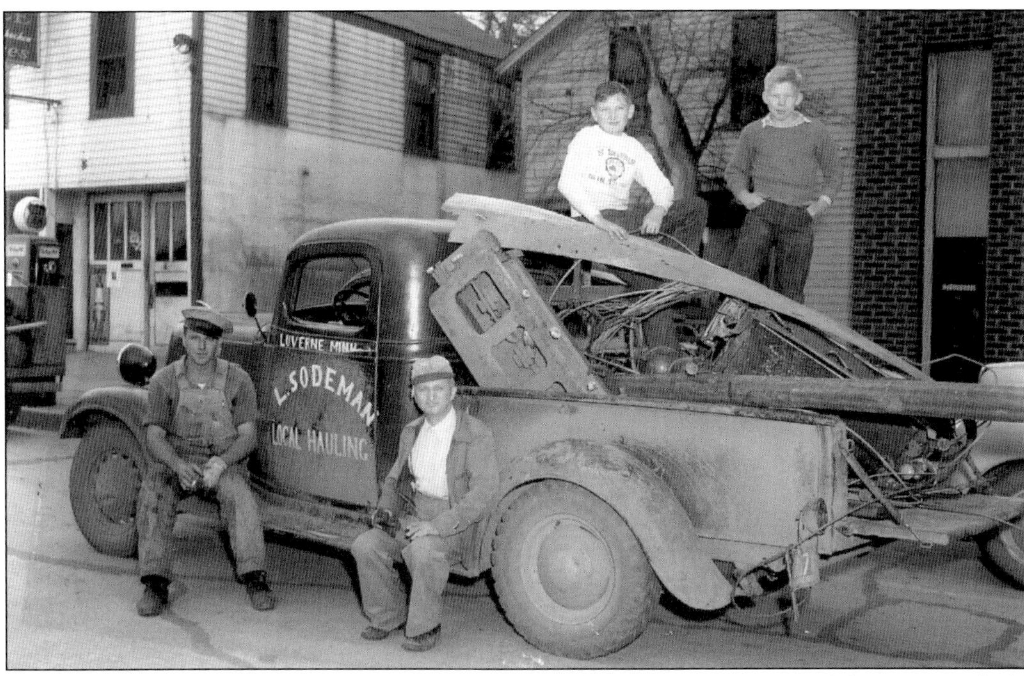

L. Sodeman recruited energetic young men during World War II for scrap-metal drives. Household, industrial, and agricultural scrap was collected in a massive effort to meet the demands of the US war machine during World War II. Scrap metal was turned into guns, cannons, airplanes, tanks, vehicles, ships, and many other types of military hardware.

Troop and soldier morale were always important. Boxes of goodies were regularly mailed to soldiers serving at home and all over the world. Before the outbreak of World War II, the Luverne National Guard was deployed to Alaska and stood watch against the predicted invasion. Hundreds of local citizens got together and wrote this "longest letter" to the deployed unit. Before the letter was mailed, businessmen rolled out the letter and stood proud as this photograph was taken.

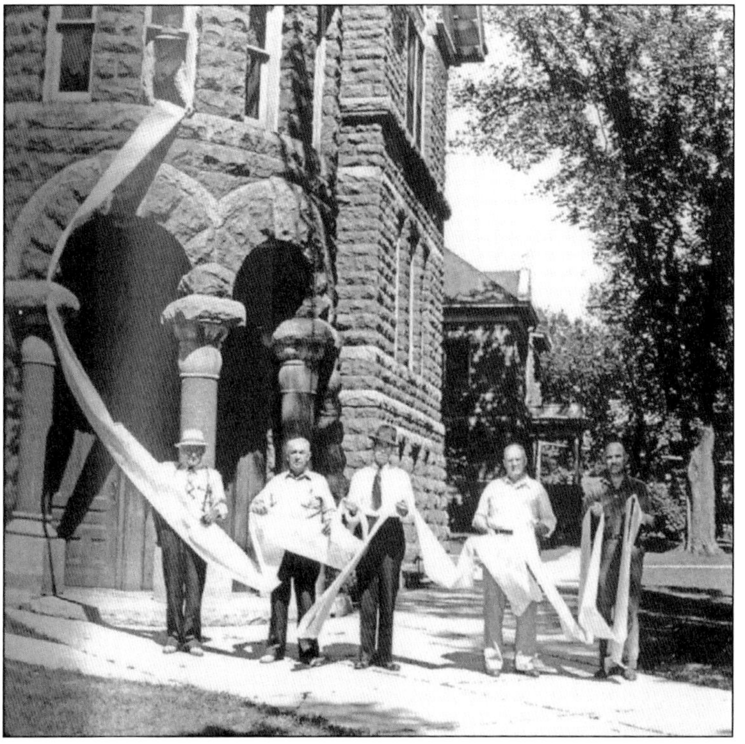

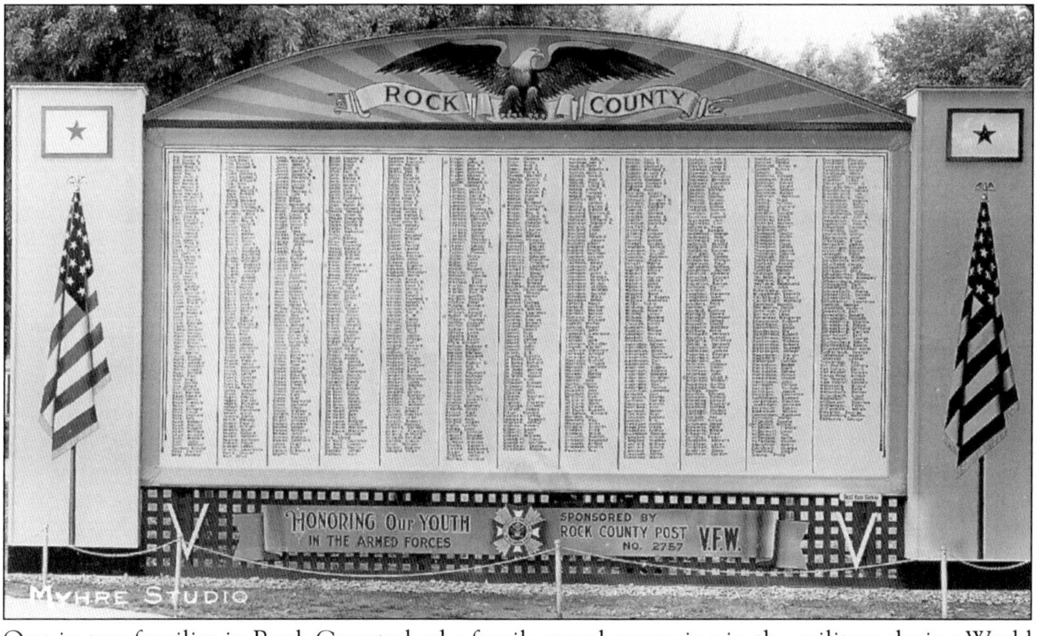

One in two families in Rock County had a family member serving in the military during World War II. Hundreds of families had a blue star in their window, meaning a family member was serving, and too many had a gold star, meaning a family member passed away while serving the United States. Everyone shared pride in what family, friends, or neighbors sacrificed for the war. This sign was built and stood one block north of Main Street on Cedar Street in Luverne for many years. It was commissioned by Rock County VFW Post No. 2757.

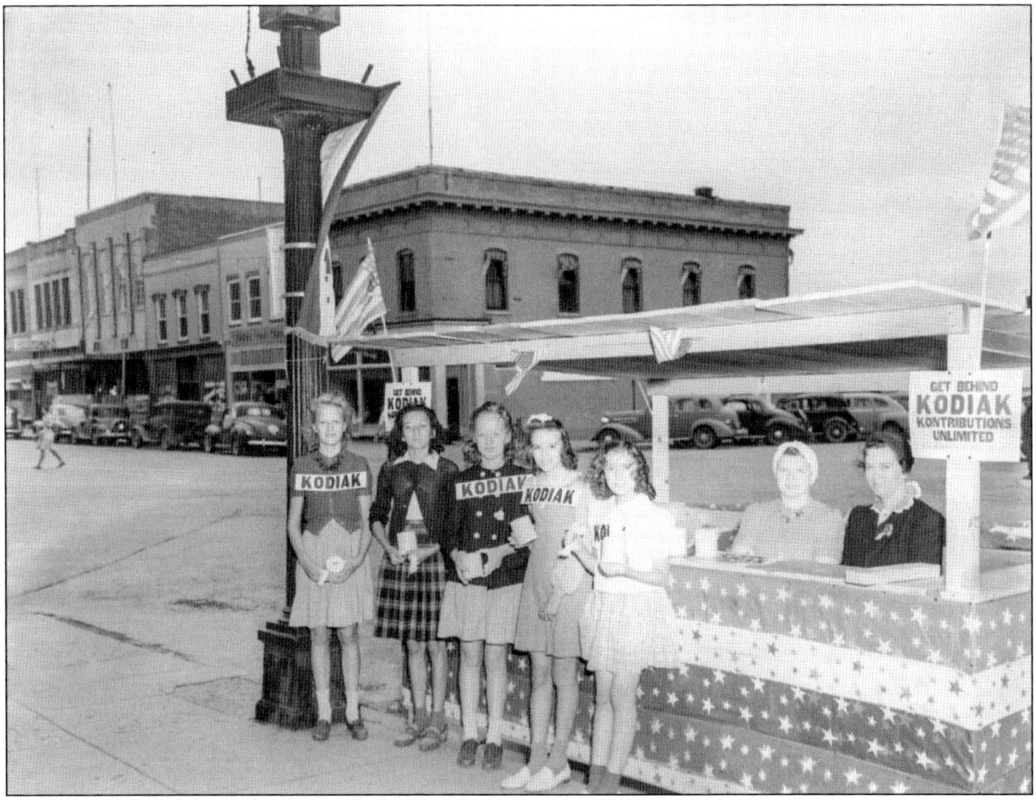

Throughout World War II, there were local fundraising events to support local troops. Pictured are supporters raising money for items to be sent to servicemen in Alaska.

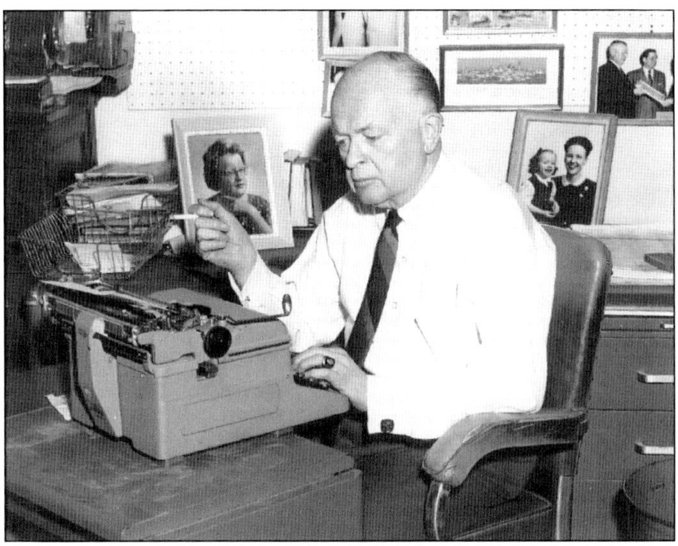

Through the smiles and the tears of World War II, *Rock County Star Herald* editor and publisher Al McIntosh kept readers up to date about it. His columns, "More or Less Personal Chaff," brought the stories home. In doing research for his 2007 miniseries *The War*, Ken Burns described McIntosh's columns as the "greatest literary find of the century." McIntosh's work was used extensively in the miniseries to interpret the lives and feelings of the people right here in Rock County.

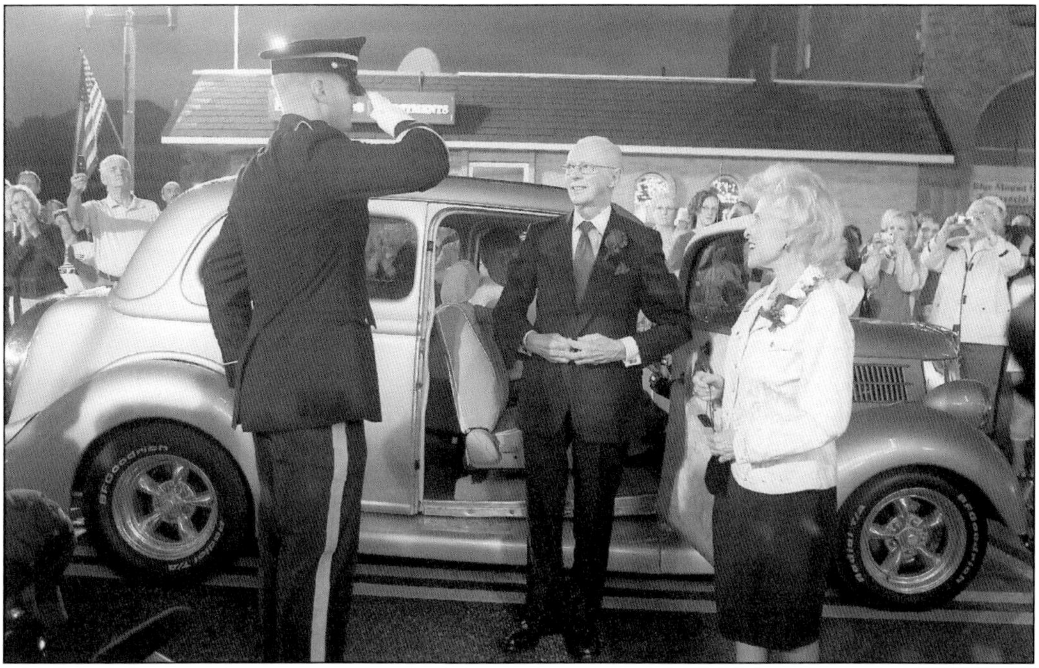

World War II pilot and hero Quentin Aanenson and his wife, Jackie Greer Aanenson, are pictured here at the world premiere of Burns's *The War.* Aanenson documented his war experience in a self-produced, two-part documentary, *The Fighter Pilot's Story.* Aanenson received worldwide acclaim for the precise and detailed biography of his life as a P-37 pilot in Great Britain and France during the war.

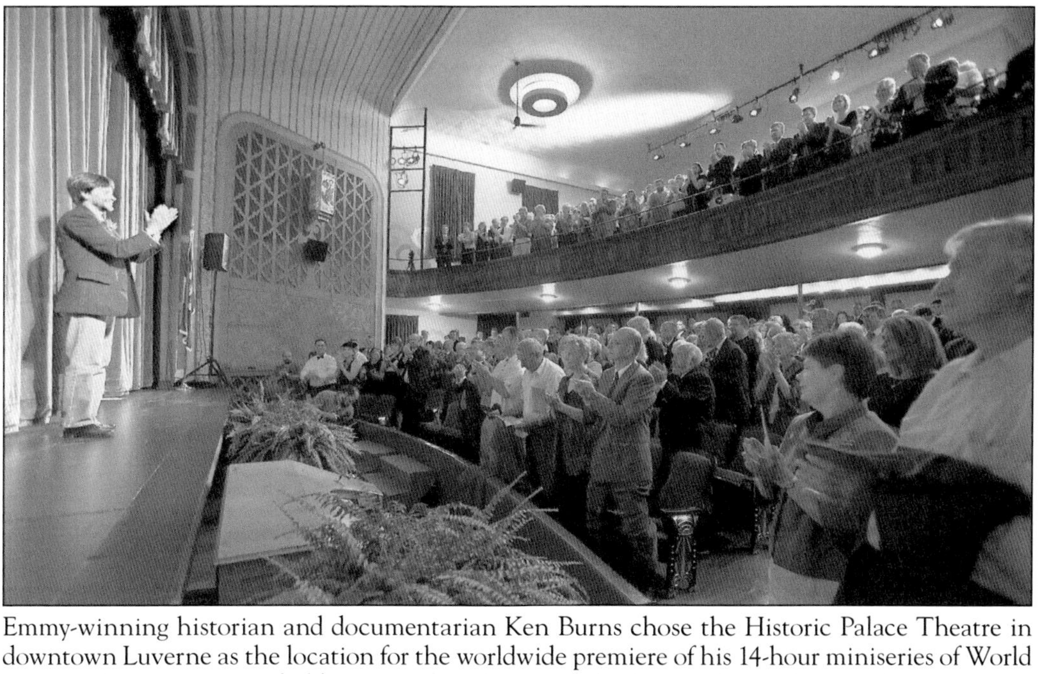

Emmy-winning historian and documentarian Ken Burns chose the Historic Palace Theatre in downtown Luverne as the location for the worldwide premiere of his 14-hour miniseries of World War II. The premiere was held on Saturday afternoon, the first weekend of September 2007, with Burns as keynote presenter.

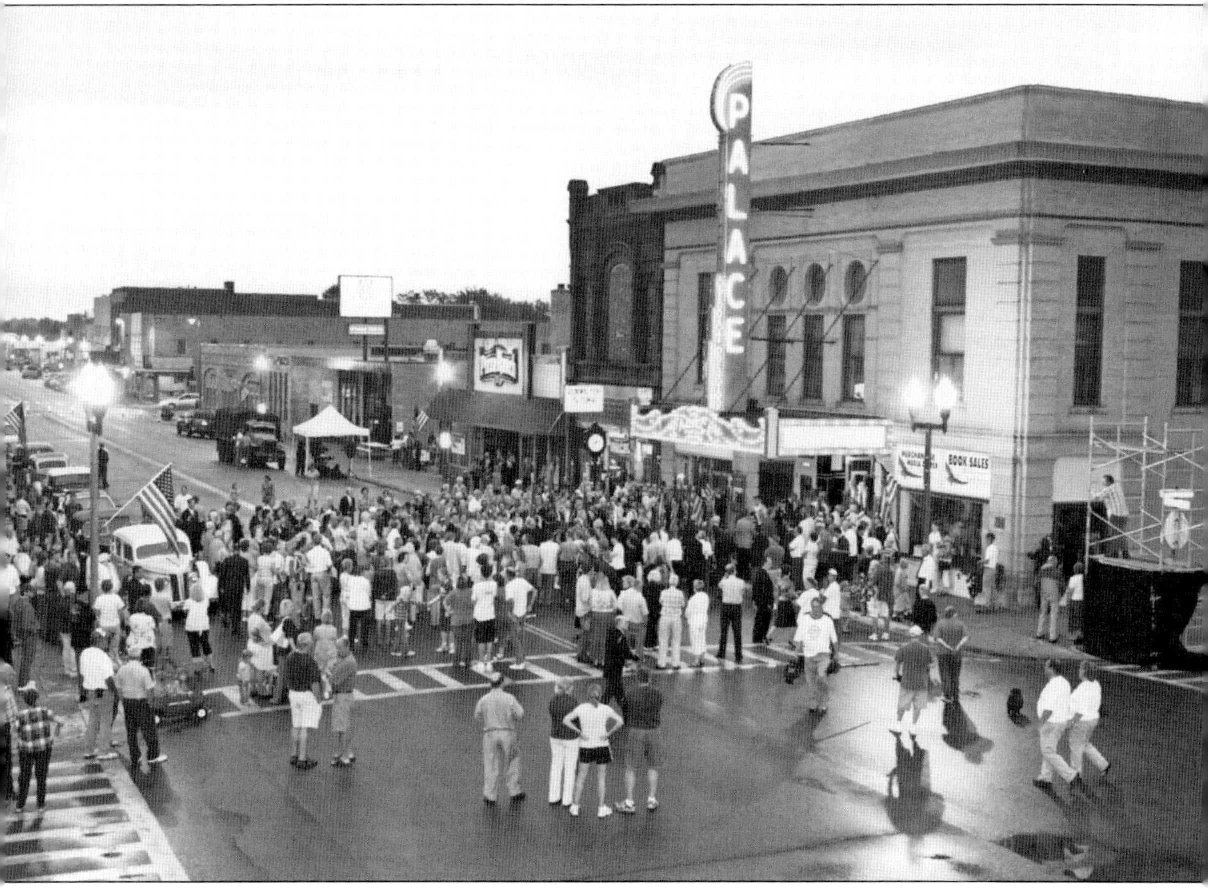

The Historic Palace Theatre held more than 400 people from all over the country when it hosted the world premiere of *The War*. Dignitaries, including many World War II veterans, were the first to witness the personal and private stories that Burns shared through his film.

Many people looking at this book are interested in the townships and where families resided in those townships. The following pages show a map of the entire county, dating back to 1935, followed by maps of each township and the residents at that time. This map shows the 12 townships that make up Rock County, which is bordered on the west by the state of South Dakota and on the south by the state of Iowa.

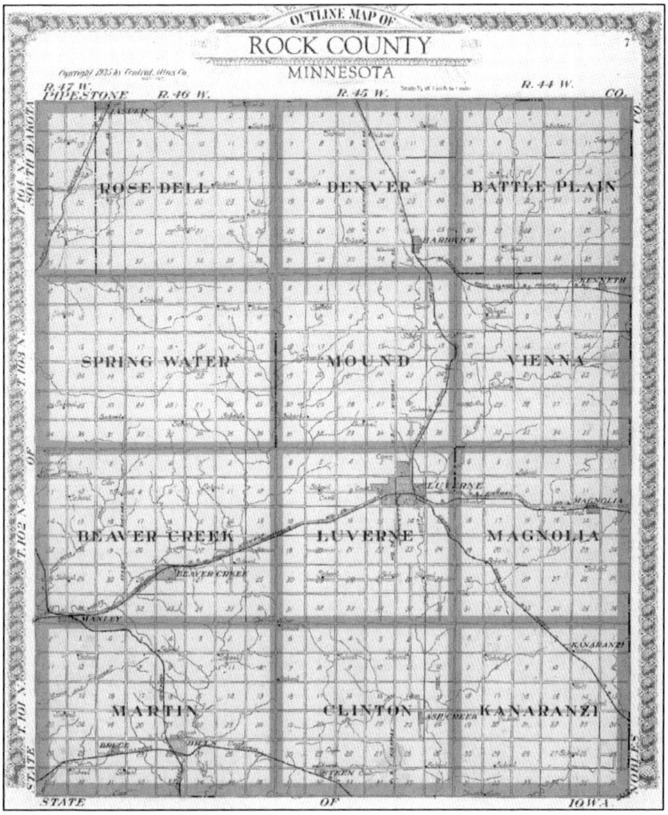

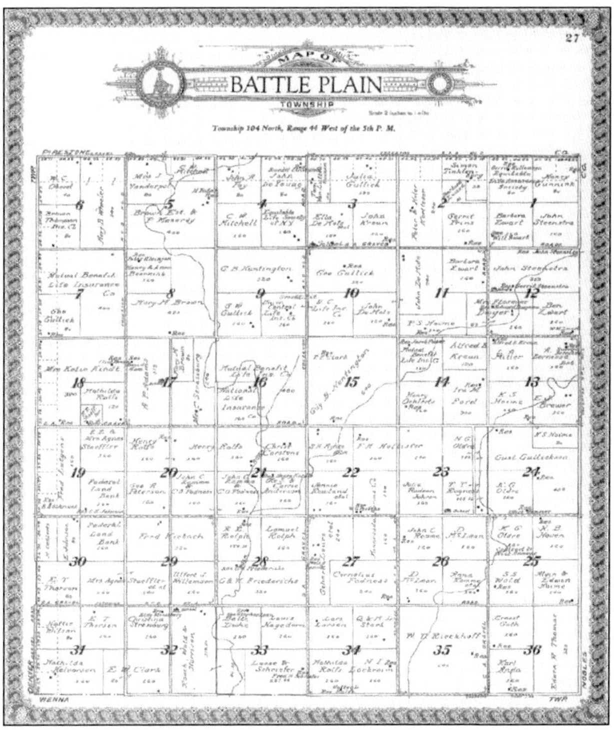

Formed on July 16, 1870, Battle Plain Township was originally called Riverside, but the name was taken elsewhere in the state, so it was changed to Battle Plain in honor of a great Indian battle said to have been fought there.

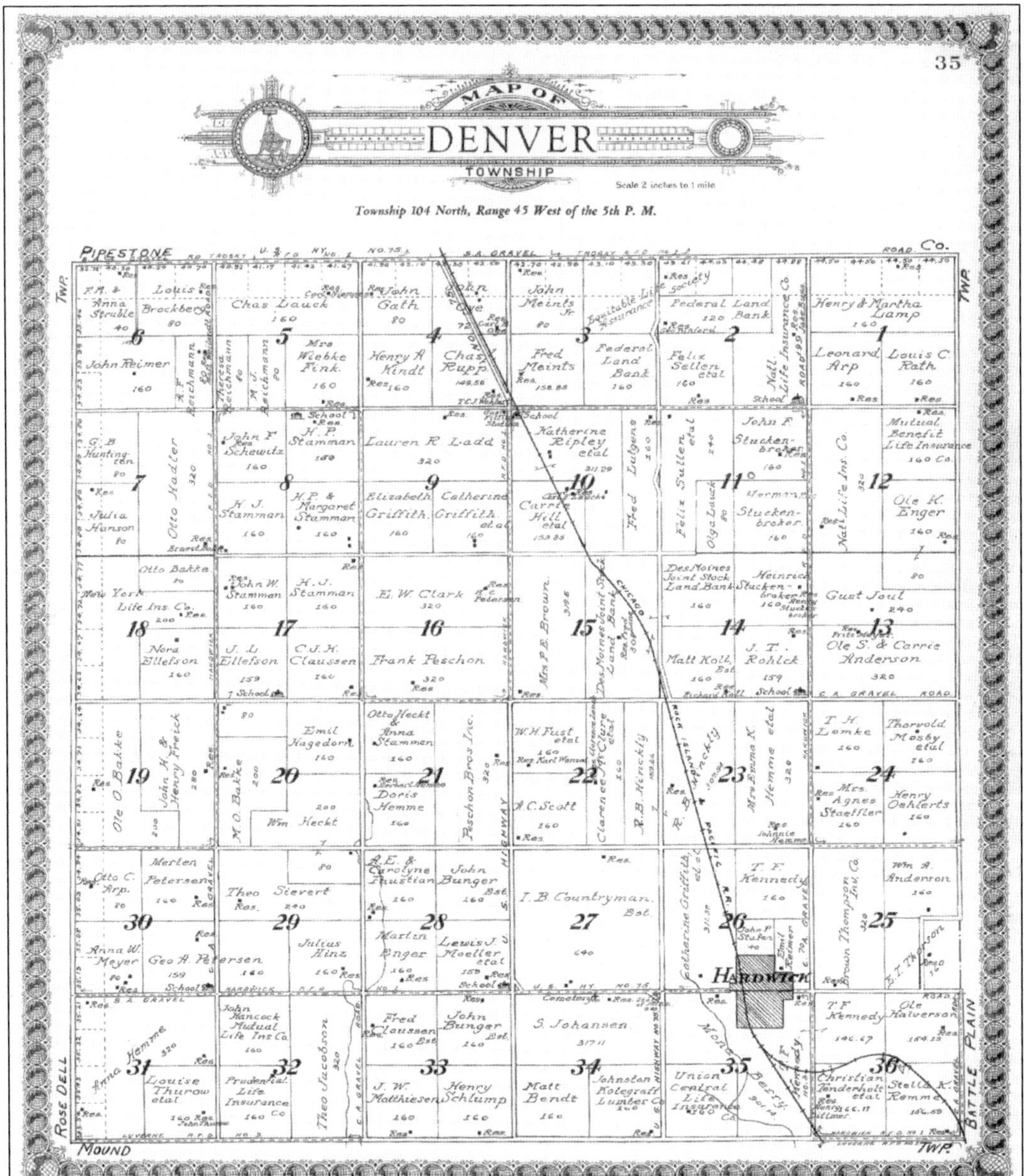

Denver Township was originally a part of Gregory Township, but on July 22, 1870, commissioners did away with the remainder of Gregory Township and renamed it Dover; however, there were too many Dovers in the state, so the name was changed on January 8, 1880, to Denver.

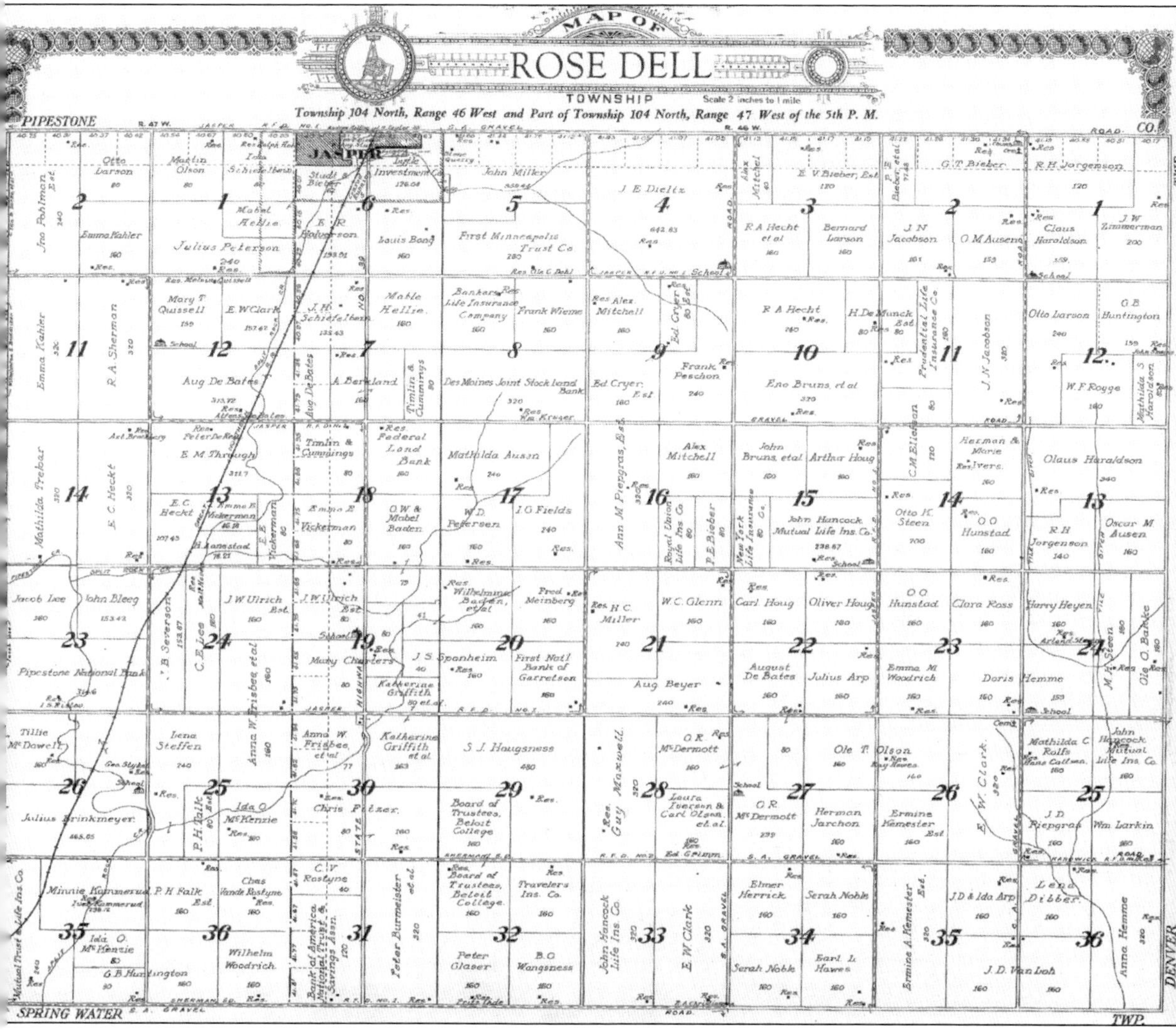

W.T. Vickerman, whose residence was close to the gorge, named Rose Dell Township after a rocky gorge filled with wild roses. The township was founded on August 17, 1877.

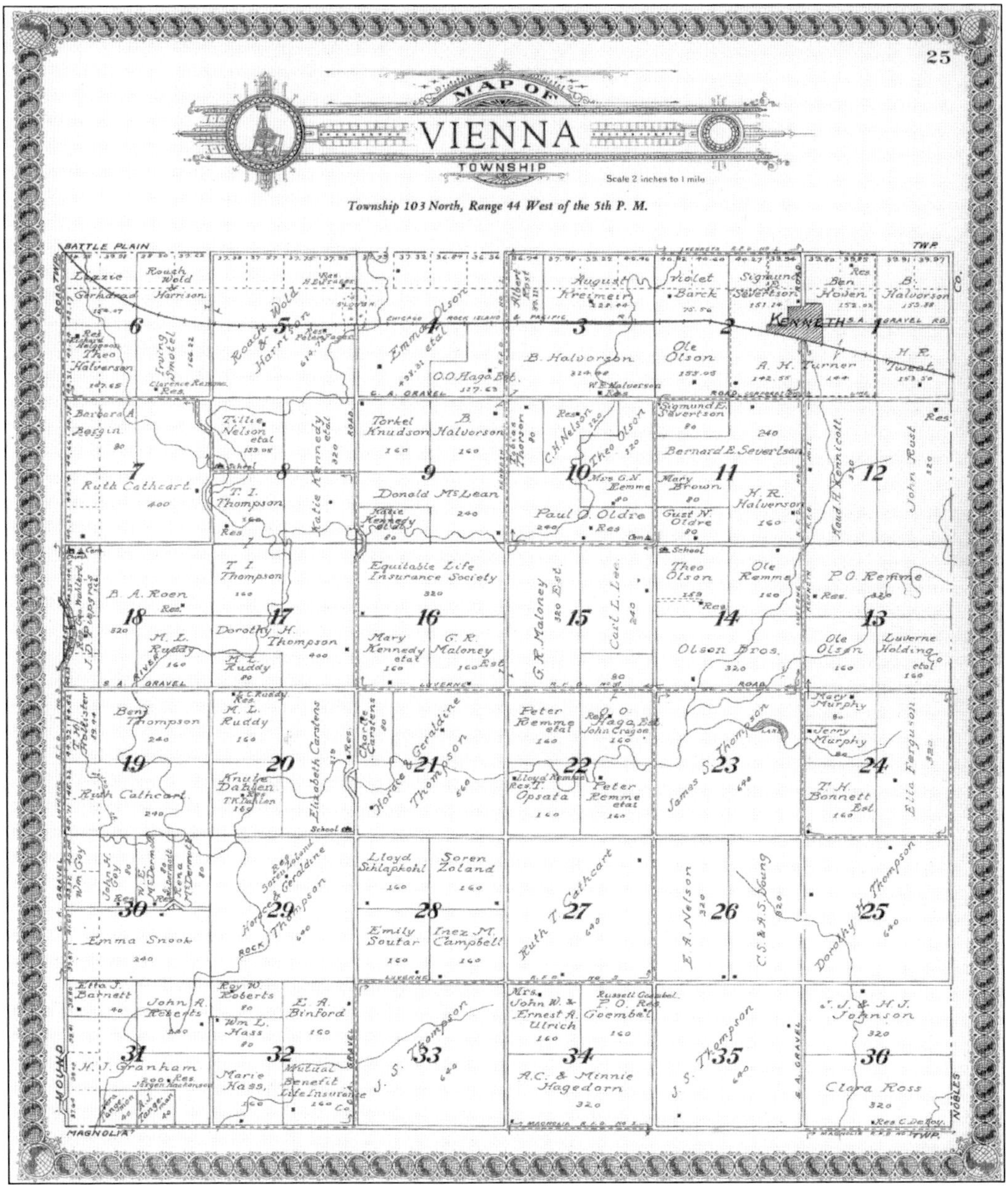

Vienna Township withdrew from Gregory Township, and on February 10, 1874, D.A. Hart, who headed the petition for organization, named it Vienna.

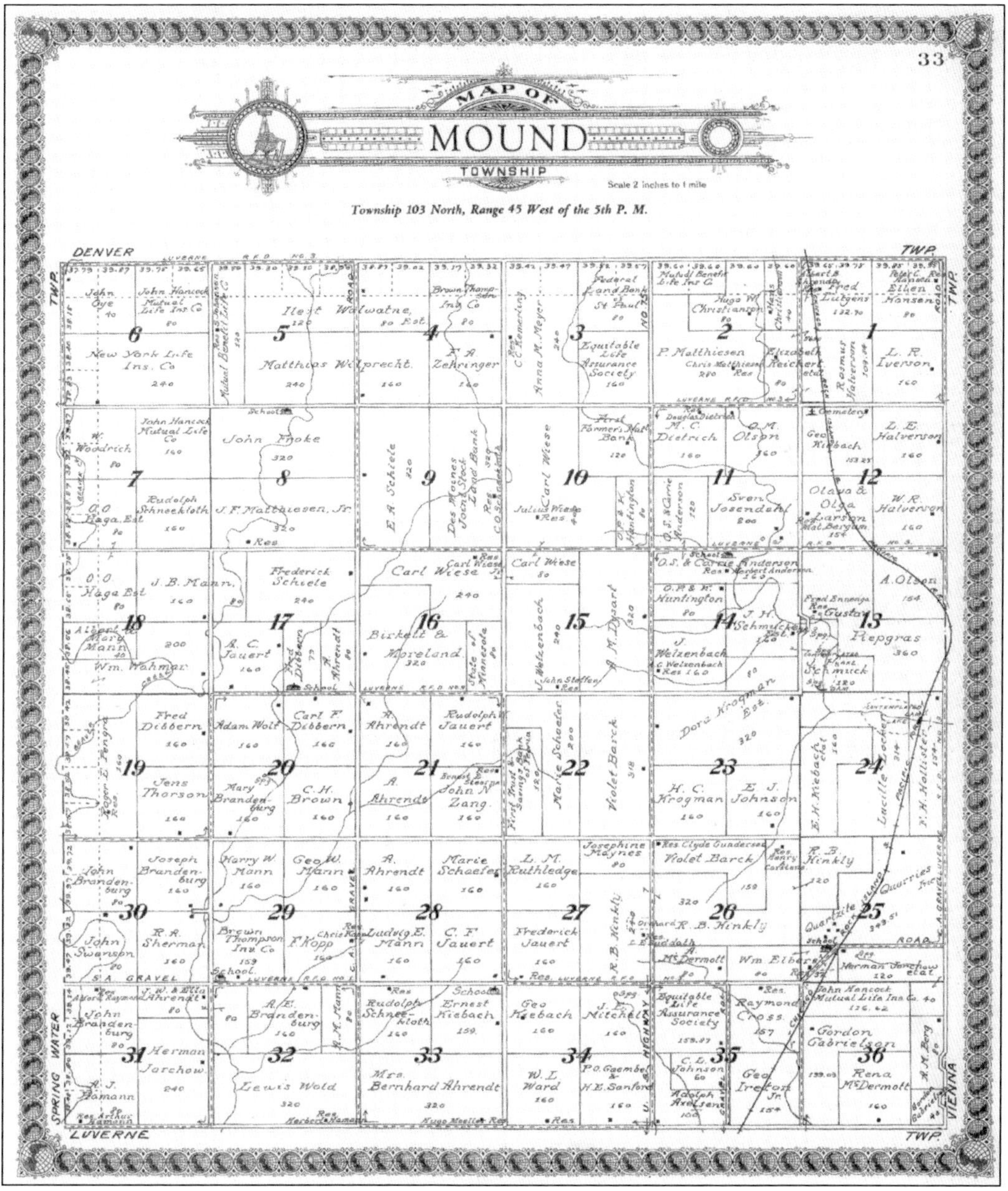

Mound Township also detached itself from Gregory Township, and on April 1, 1874, it was named after the vast pile of granite that was found in the area.

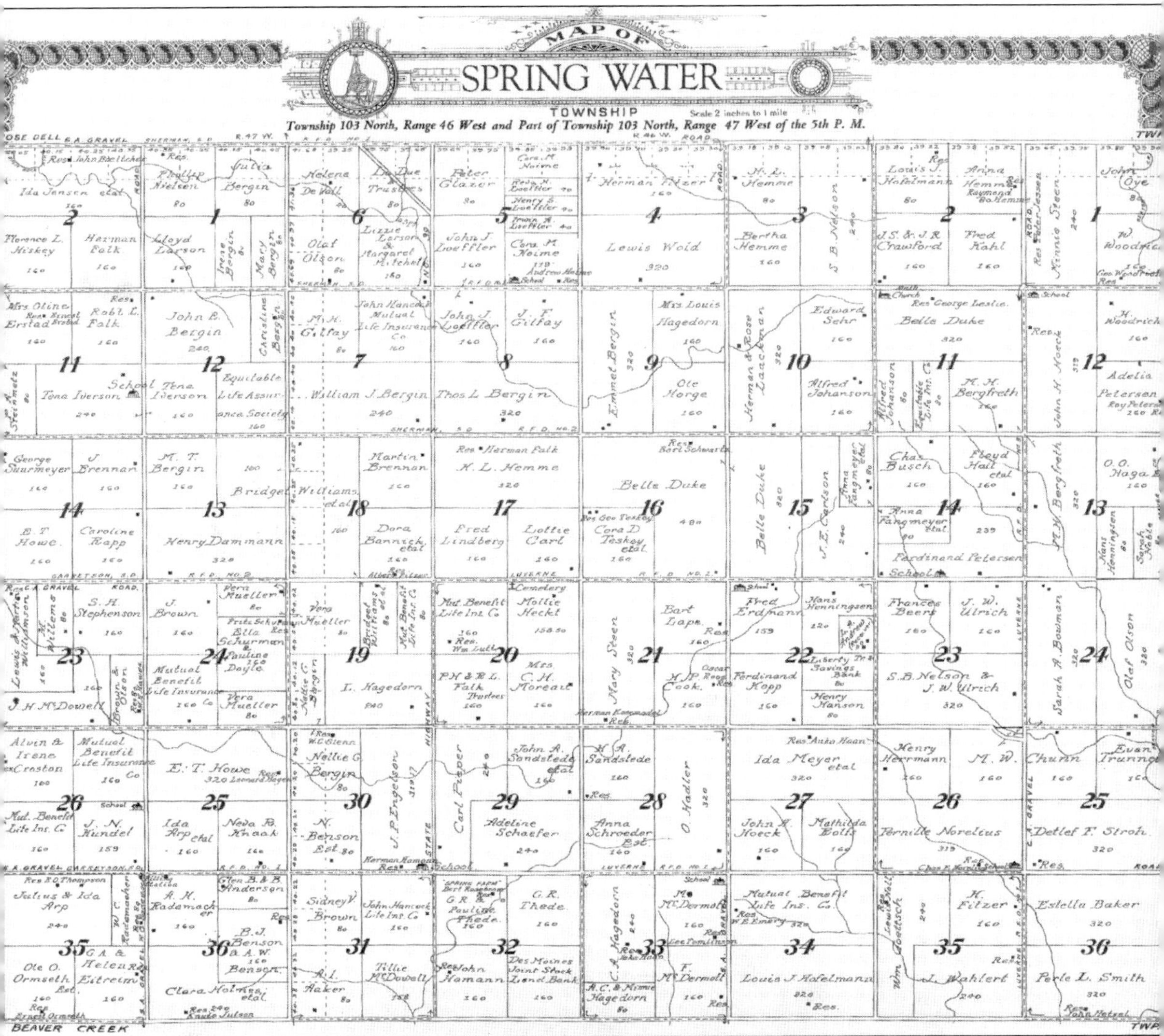

Spring Water Township was formed on May 5, 1874, and was named by a citizen who emigrated from Springwater, New York, who also found a large spring in the area.

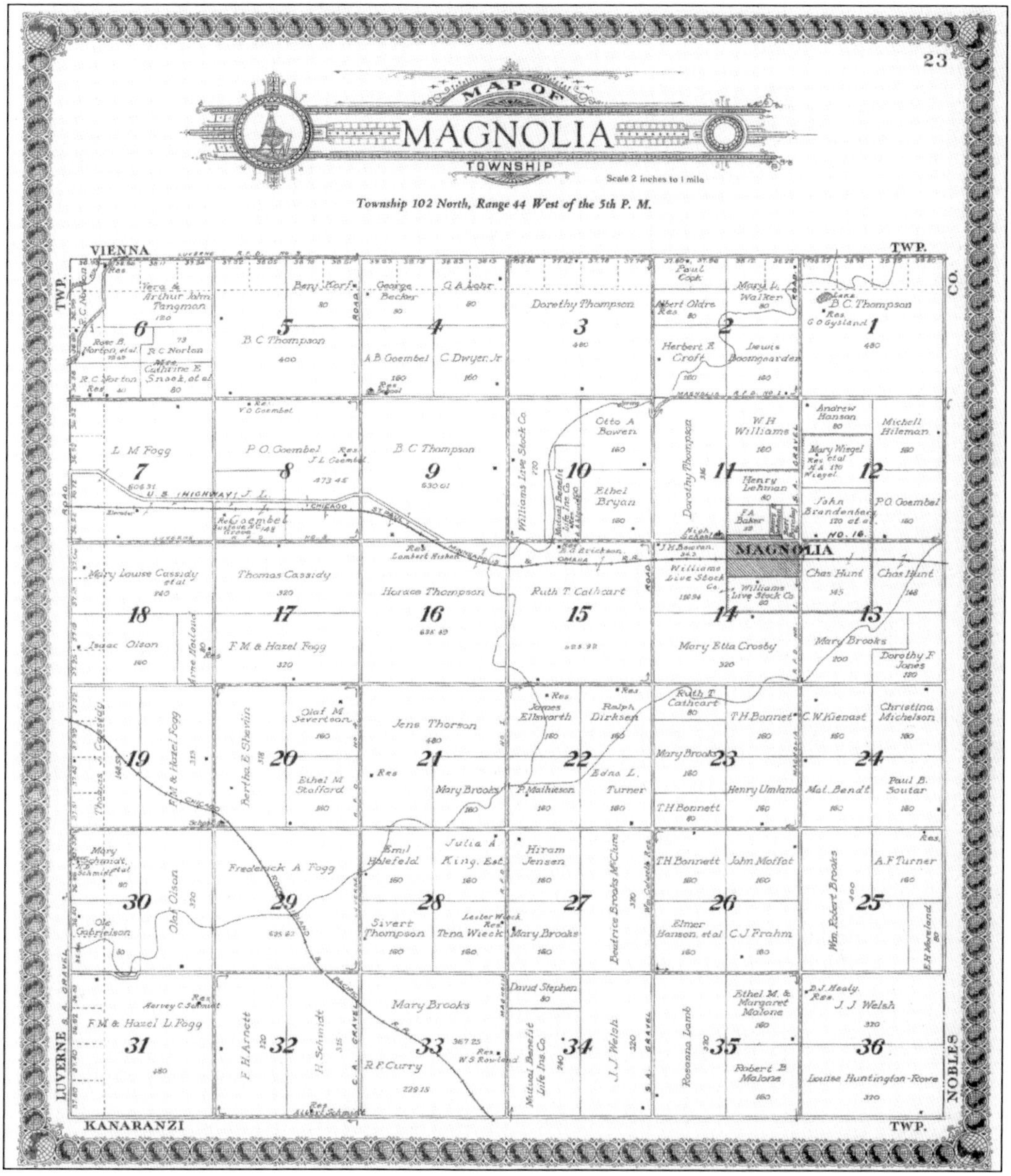

Magnolia Township was petitioned to be removed from Luverne Township on November 27, 1872. Philo Hawes suggested the name Magnolia, it having been the name of his former home in Rock County, Wisconsin.

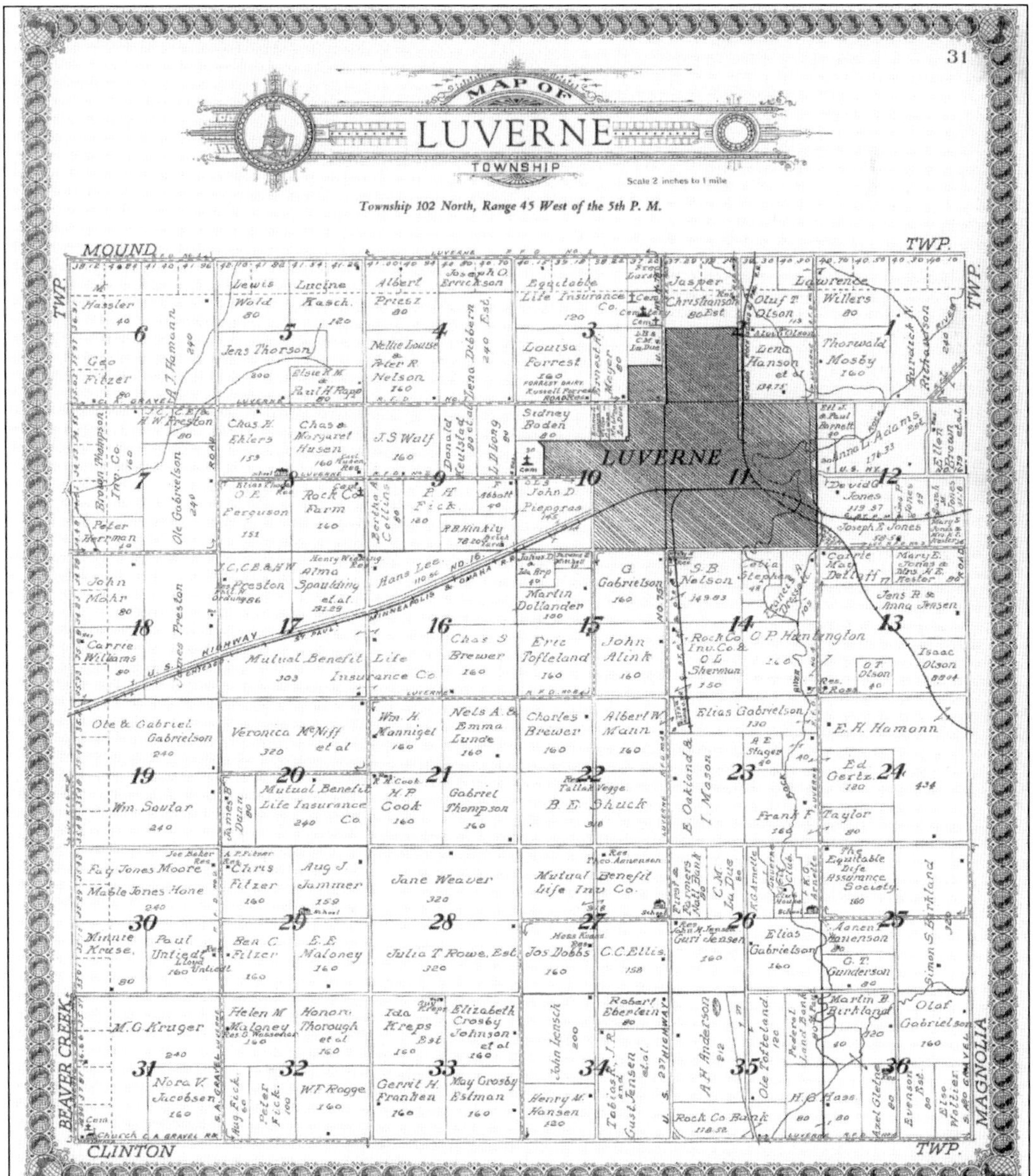

Luverne Township originally formed on February 15, 1871, and was named after the village and included the area of Magnolia, Vienna, Battle Plain, and Denver Townships.

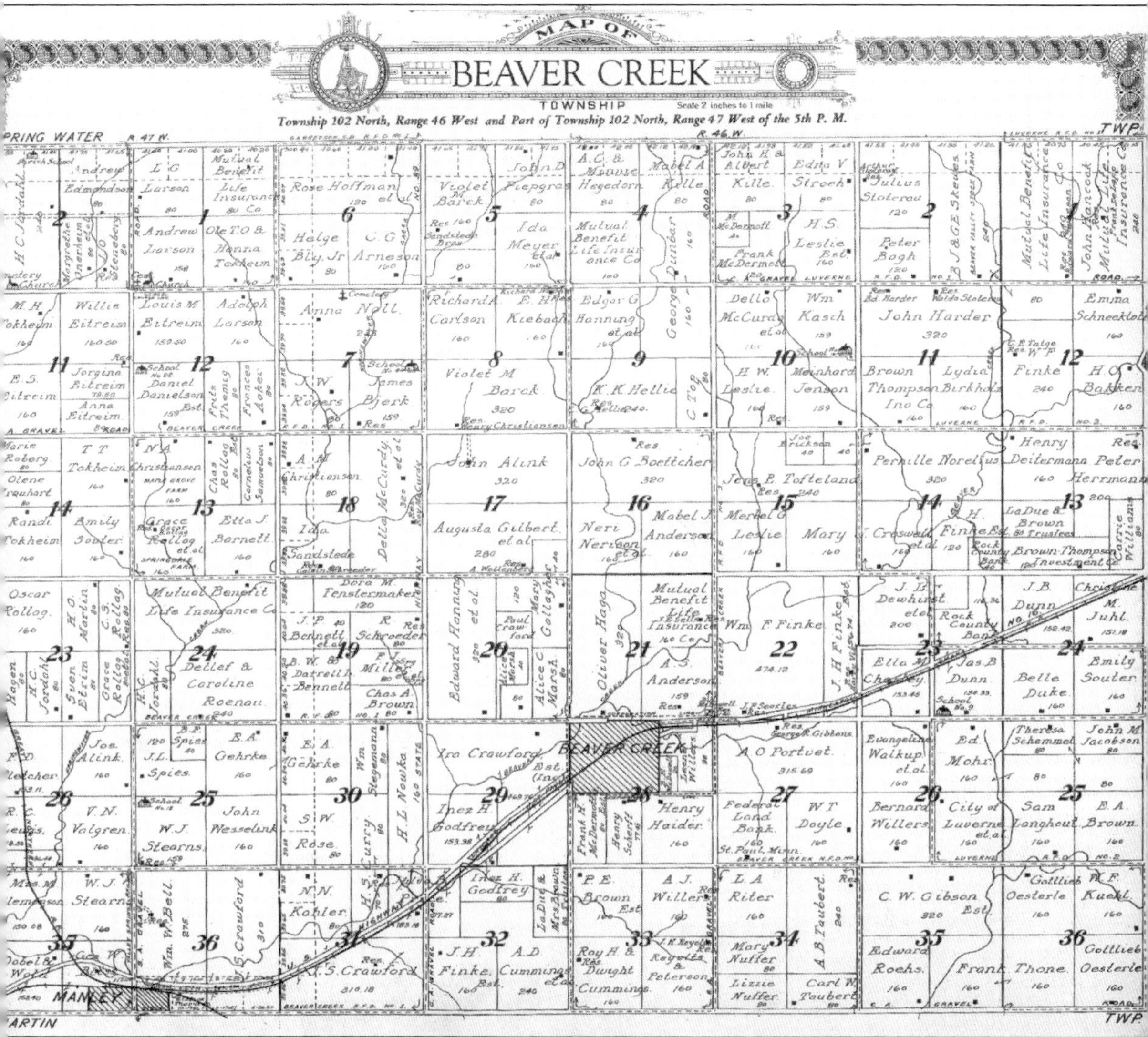

Beaver Creek Township formed on September 10, 1872, and was named for the stream that flowed through it.

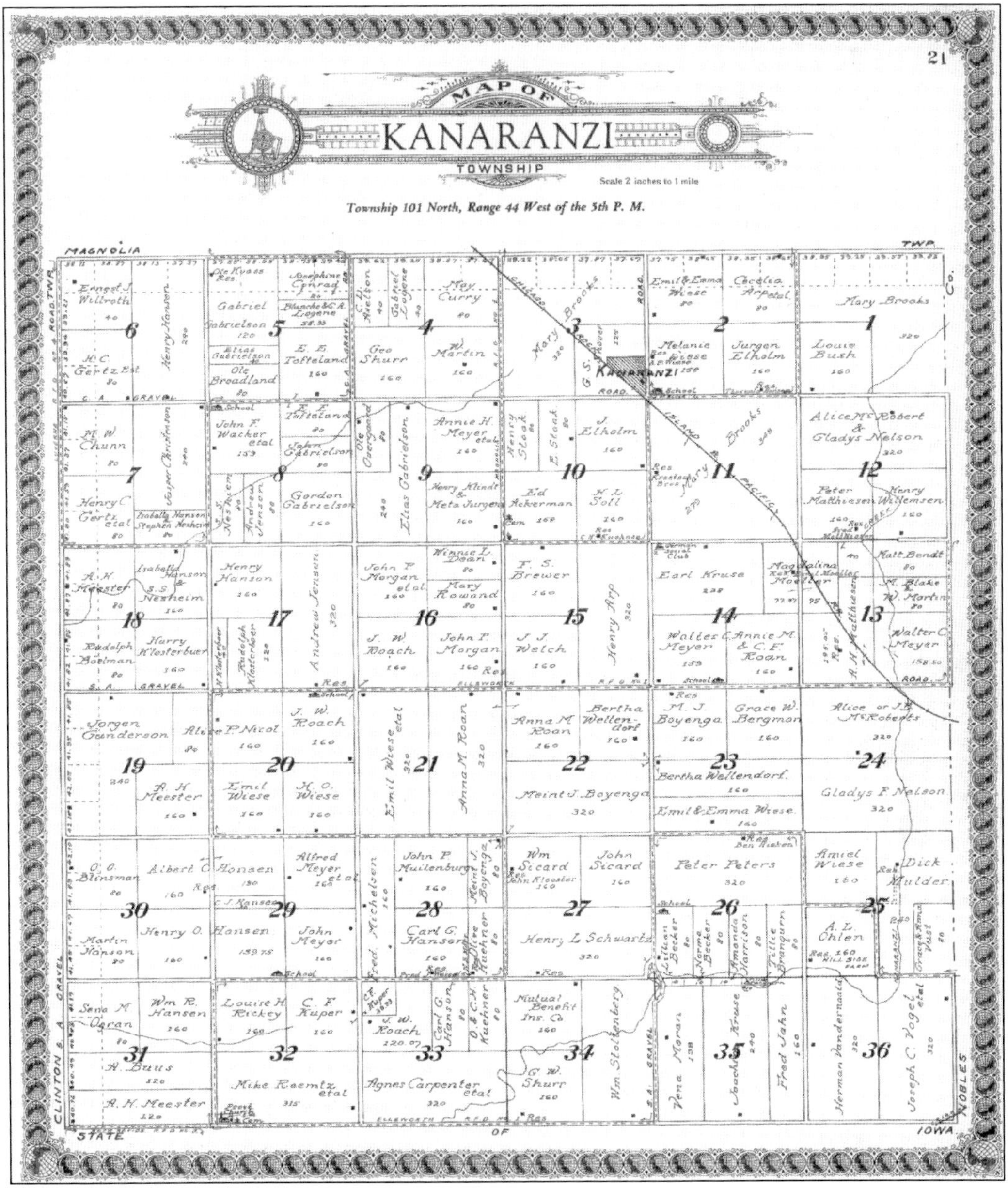

Kanaranzi Township's petition was approved on January 15, 1973. Its name was derived from a Native American name of the creek that ran through the township.

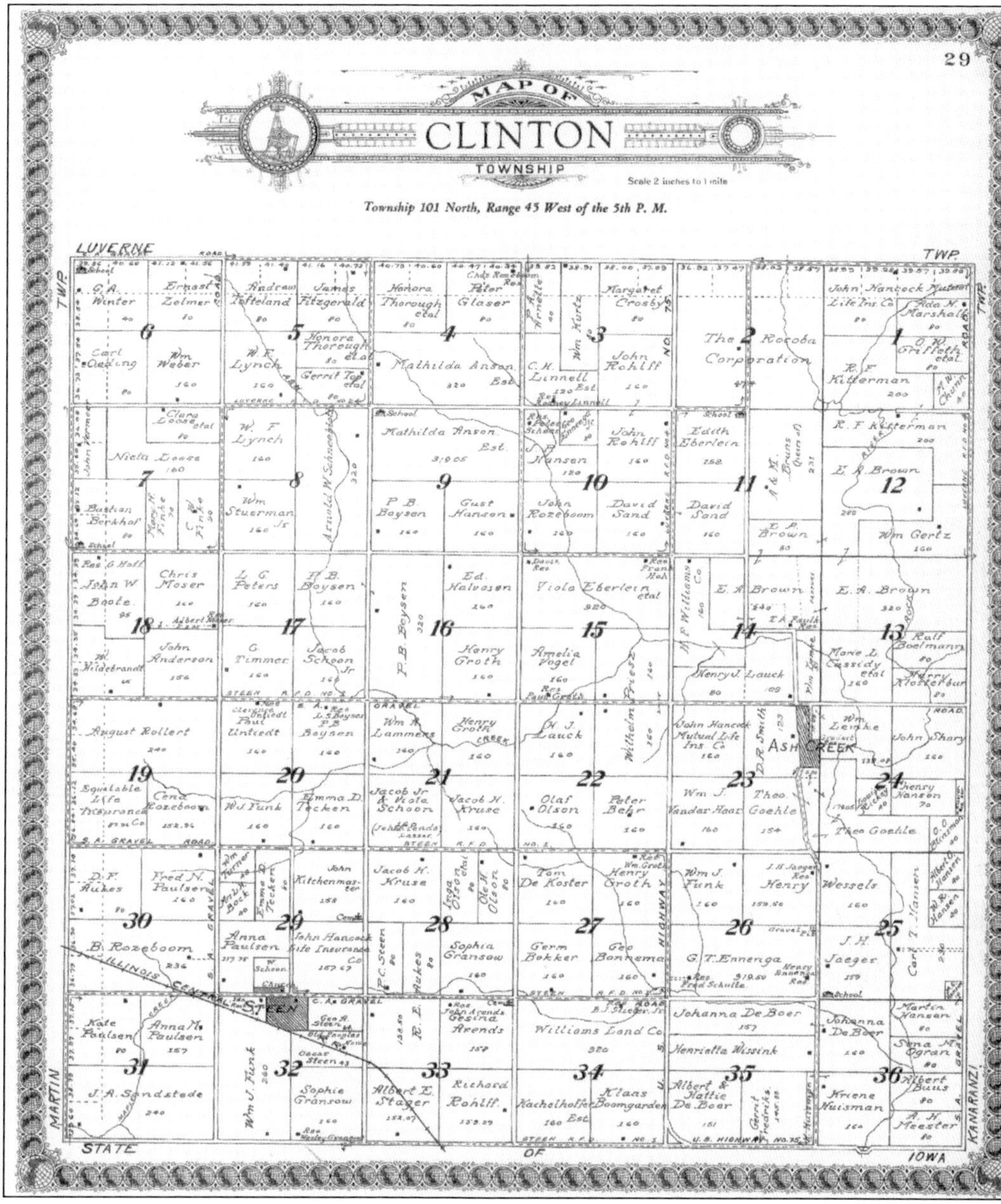

Clinton Township originally formed as part of Grant Township on February 18, 1871. Petitioners asked for a separate township, and on October 11, 1871, it was formed and named after the town of Clinton, New York, at the suggestion of one of the residents.

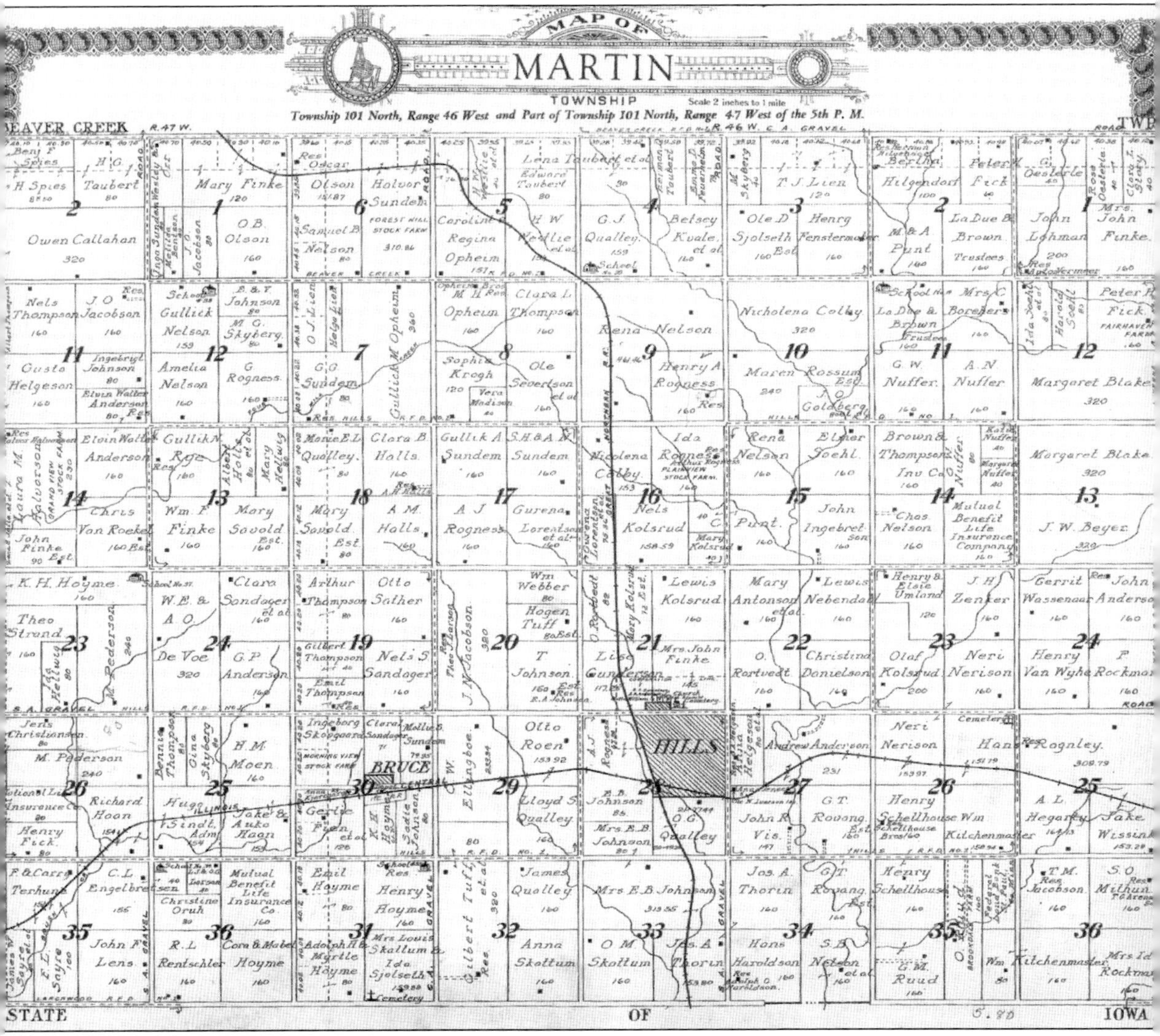

Martin Township was originally part of Clinton Township, and on January 15, 1873, it separated and was named in honor of John Martin, the first settler in the area.

About the Rock County Historical Society

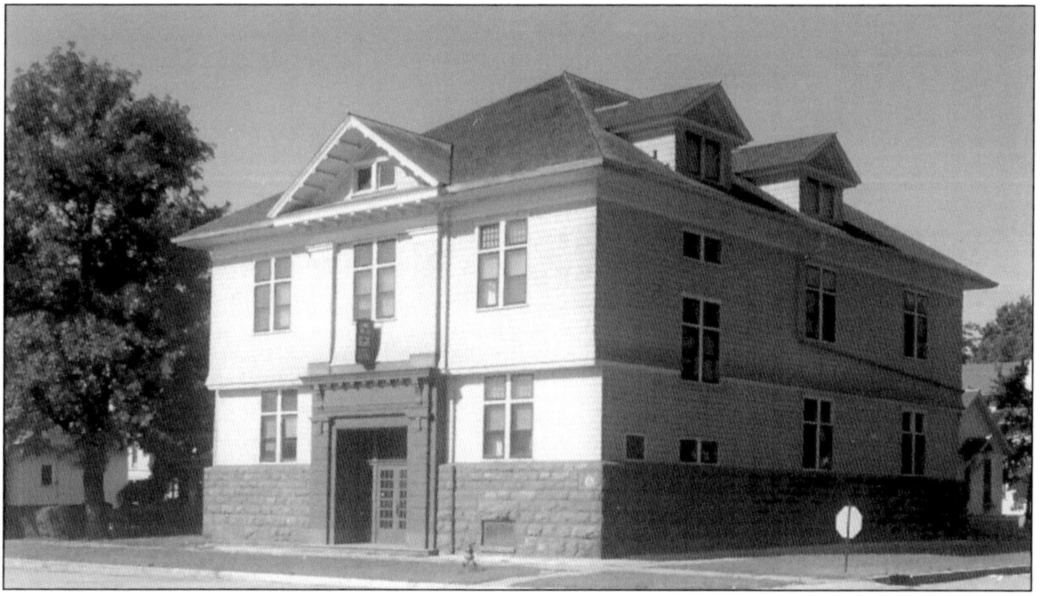

The Rock County Historical Society was originally formed in 1930 to collect artifacts and information on the history of Rock County. Having no place for the collection of historical artifacts, they were displayed in business windows. In 1959, the Hinkly House, built in 1892, was donated to the Rock County Historical Society. The Hinkly House has been restored to its former beauty and is open to the public. Other structures have become part of the society over the years. In 1996, it took over ownership of the Masonic temple to serve as the county museum. Four buildings were constructed at the Rock County fairgrounds that include the Fitzer Barn (agricultural artifacts), the one-room school, the summer kitchen, and the Ordung Building (agricultural, business, and miscellaneous items). Triannual meetings are held each year to keep members informed of progress. Members are proud of the society's founders and those who continue to capture the history of Rock County.